GREAT RAILWAY STATIONS
OF BRITAIN

An LMS Jubilee starts a train from St Pancras. (*British Rail*)

Other books by Gordon Biddle

Canals of North West England, 2 vols with Charles Hadfield, 1970, (David & Charles)
Victorian Stations, 1973, (David & Charles)
The British Railway Station – Railway History in Pictures Series with
                                      Jeoffry Spence, 1977, (David & Charles)
Pennine Waterway, 1977
Lancashire Waterways, 1980
Railway Stations in the North West, 1981
The Railway Heritage of Britain – with O. S. Nock and other authors, 1983

GORDON BIDDLE

GREAT RAILWAY STATIONS OF BRITAIN

Their Architecture, Growth
and Development

DAVID & CHARLES
Newton Abbot   London   North Pomfret (Vt)

IMPORTANT NOTE ON DRAWINGS The drawings have been specially drawn by Peter Fells to illustrate features and layouts as clearly as possible in diagrammatic form, and therefore are not to scale. Layouts show only main running lines and important associated features. Platforms are shown hatched, blocked areas represent station buildings, and broken lines indicate the extent of overall roofs. S B means signal box.

British Library Cataloguing in Publication Data

Biddle, Gordon
    Great railway stations of Britain:
    their architecture, growth and development.
    1. Railroads – Great Britain –
    Stations – History 2. Architecture –
    Great Britain – History
    I. Title
    725′.31′0941   NA6315.G7

    ISBN 0-7153-8263-2

Typeset by Typesetters (Birmingham) Ltd,
Smethwick, West Midlands
and printed in Great Britain
by Butler & Tanner Limited, Frome and London
for David & Charles Publishers plc
Brunel House Newton Abbot Devon

Published in the United States of America
by David & Charles Inc
North Pomfret Vermont 05053 USA

Contents

To Dorothy
For patience, help and understanding

Preface

In preparing this book I quickly concluded that there is no real measure of greatness; so much depends on individual opinions, tastes and prejudices, and in no activities do these vary so much as the practice of the visual arts and the application of technology. Because railway stations combine both in such a wide variety of ways, the difficulties multiply. Indeed, when one considers that there are those who would not have one brick of St Pancras disturbed yet would shed no tears for the loss of King's Cross, or some who welcomed the clean directness of the new Euston because they cursed the labyrinths of the old, then any attempt at a definition would be hazardous indeed.

Size is no yardstick either: by no stretch of the imagination could Clapham Junction be called 'great', for all its seventeen platforms. Function is a better one, bringing in smaller but important traffic centres like Inverness and Stafford, and so are appearance and structure, which mean we cannot ignore Monkwearmouth and Leith, while Shrewsbury qualifies on all three counts. But ultimately the choice is personal and I hope it will be considered representative.

Big railway stations were institutions. Some still are, others have declined and are now rather sad, and a number have completely disappeared. They all had an atmosphere that is as elusive of definition as greatness, except to say that it was, and still is, unique – quite different from an airport, for instance, even though a modern large station may look like one. It is all to do with sight, sound and smell, at one time registering steam, smoke, sunlight and gloom, constant movement and bustle. The same senses still come into play but in a different way, and of course there is still the overriding sense of going somewhere that only train travel can give, to which the station is the essential prelude.

My *Victorian Stations*, published in 1973, concentrated on the small and medium ones, referring to the larger places mainly in context. This book is not intended as an exact counterpart and in any case continues up to the present day, although it will, hopefully, help to complete the picture. In endeavouring to show how, why and where our large stations were built and to relate something of their continuing function, I have concentrated on the main stream of developments, including those major railway hotels that were part of a station or close to them. To go into every detail would need a book several times larger than this, although the chronology at the end will help to fill any gaps in the text. I have restricted source references to lesser-known or what I believe to be first-time quotations, and a full bibliography is included. In the case of London stations I have deliberately used a broad brush because their story is comprehensively recounted by Alan A. Jackson in his *London Termini*, revised and republished in 1985.

Part of the pleasure of what the late Canon Roger Lloyd called 'station sauntering' lies in their variety and individuality, even at their worst or most confusing. More than just recording events, I hope I may also be able to give some idea of what our large stations were like when the railways were at their peak, while for those who share my fascination for the Victorian palaces of travel there may be some pleasurable memories as well.

1

Impressions

On my study wall hangs a copy of Terence Cuneo's painting of an old London & North Western Prince of Wales class locomotive *Queen of the Belgians* standing in Birmingham New Street station in the 1930s, with a new maroon LMS Jubilee at the next platform. Several Prince of Wales engines were around the Midlands at that time, but *Queen of the Belgians* lasted longer than the rest and reached British Railways' ownership before she was scrapped. New Street has a special place for me because it is the first large station I remember – or perhaps I should say 'had', because some years ago it was completely transformed. Not that it was much of a place originally, but to even a four year old it had character, and one experienced a sense of excitement in coming out of the tunnels straight into the lofty cavern of its huge roof. As we walked along the platform and up the stairs on to the footbridge, I always looked for the signals hung beneath it and the man on the open staging above, in the hope that he might pull a lever and I could see an arm drop. There was no sense of remote control about that signal box.

It was not a pleasant station, with smoke continuously drifting out of the tunnels at each end, from which at intervals came a sound like a hunting horn cutting through the hiss of steam and the grinding of petrol tractors hauling trains of trolleys laden with mail bags up the steep ramps from the subways. They were indeed horns, blown by shunters to inform drivers of engines in the tunnels that the points were set for them to emerge. The other Birmingham station, Snow Hill, offered a complete contrast. Although much smaller, it was cleaner, brighter and far more spacious – as well it should have been for it was only twenty years old; there the engines were green, had a curious brass thing like an upturned bucket instead of a dome and pulled chocolate-and-cream coaches. It was my first sight of the Great Western. Snow Hill was different in other ways, too; the roof was open down the middle and goods trains pounded through, taking a run at the bank up to Hockley. This somehow seemed inferior. New Street may have been dirty but it never descended to goods trains.

A holiday on the south coast brought a first visit to Euston with its overpoweringly low roof, quite different from the lofty arch I was used to (it was not until later that I realised that the New Street I knew was only half of the station), and the cheap indignity of a wooden platform on the departure side. A year or two later, on a school outing, there was great excitement at seeing the blue-and-white streamlined 'Coronation Scot' backing into that same platform, which made it seem dingier than ever. Later still I came to appreciate the historic atmosphere of Euston's nooks and corners, for all their inconvenience, and instead of diving into the Underground I made my way outside to look at the Doric Arch.

Victoria – now that really was different. It was nowhere near as cluttered as it is now, there was very little steam and the overriding impression was of green electric trains emitting the throbbing beat of air-brake compressors. The same phenomenon hit me in a different form at the end of the war on my first visit to Liverpool Street when I saw engines that puffed while they stood still, an introduction to the pant of the Westinghouse brake pump that I encountered shortly afterwards on the Continent. Liverpool Street on that occasion did not impress me. I was herded into a train late on a gloomy winter's afternoon and sat squashed with eleven others in Air Force blue in the oldest coach I had ever seen. It did not even have full-height partitions between the compartments. We were *en route* to a station called Blake Hall somewhere in the wilds of Essex, and thence we knew not where. Liverpool Street was as dark and dirty as the ancient-looking engine that pulled our train, which gave a poor impression of the Great Eastern. It took an occasion with more time and leisure for me to appreciate that fantastic roof.

Liverpool Lime Street was captivating. It was a sunny day several years later and the slow, graceful curves of the roof arches seemed to be the perfect complement to the curve of the platforms as the light slanted through against the dark, mysterious background of the deep rock cutting beyond. I began to appreciate the visual quality that stations in such locations can have; I saw it again, differently, at Central, and at its best at Glasgow Queen Street. A long time afterwards I discovered the station paintings of Monet and Morbelli, and saw what they saw.

Serving His Majesty brought compensations in wider rail travel. My first railway station bath was at Bristol Temple Meads where, after several weeks' travelling, I luxuriated gratefully in a surprisingly modern underground bathroom disturbed only by trains rumbling overhead. Later I got to know the station better, including its peculiar smell. All large railway stations had smells, usually a compound of steam, smoke, hot oil, gas and, near the luggage lift, dirty water that oozed out of a hydraulic cylinder with a distinctive sighing sound. Michael Bonavia in *The Four Great Railways* writes of spilt milk, stale fish and horse manure blended in as well, with milk and straw predominating at Paddington and South Yorkshire coal at King's Cross. But Bristol's smell was unique, like a peculiar kind of gas, but more likely caused by a local bone works that manufactured glue.

Service life introduced me to stations at night and, if one had the energy, opportunity to observe the railway at work when passengers were few. I thought Crewe was singularly unimpressive for so famous a station, but it was incredibly busy with mail and parcels. It also had the best NAAFI canteen on any station where I was forced to wait at night. There were bearded heads on the moulded keystones over the doors and windows of the two older platform buildings, looking not too unlike Francis William Webb, the martinet Chief Mechanical Engineer who once ruled over Crewe Works and most of the town; later I found them elsewhere and realised that, true to Crewe fashion, they were mass-produced by a builders' supplier. Manchester London Road in the small hours, on the other hand, was an experience definitely to be missed.

The night-time environment of a station was caught by a writer on The Romance of Modern London published in the *English Illustrated Magazine* in 1893, who saw in the great London termini, dimly visible in a fog, something of the spirit of the temples of ancient Egypt: 'Go at night to St. Pancras . . . at an hour when no trains are leaving. Walk along No 3 platform as far as the first seat and then look back. If you are fortunate enough to catch . . . a hidden engine belching out clouds of steam that mingle with the fog overhead, it does not need a very powerful imagination to fancy you are in some great temple. The white clouds come from the altar fire; above it, half lost in vapour, is the great clock, its huge round dial like the face of a monstrous idol before which burn in solemn stillness the hanging lamps, silver and violet and rose.' There were many stations like that.

Although the fog and the steam have long gone and there is now a splendid new clock, St Pancras and other stations with high roofs retain their majesty. As a frequent traveller through St Pancras in the 1960s I got to know it very well. There was still steam, though rapidly reducing, and the sight and sound of a train being given a hearty push out of the station somehow seemed oddly appropriate to its architecture, a perfect demonstration of the twin analogies between steam locomotives and organs, and large stations and Gothic cathedrals. There was even an appropriate preacher in the fruity, well-modulated tones of the station announcer. I usually arrived when the destinations of the 'Thames-Clyde Express' were being announced, the string of familiar north-country stations inducing a surge of nostalgia in an exile: Leeds, Skipton, Hellifield, Settle, Appleby, Carlisle. And then for the Edinburgh portion a vision of the Borders: Hawick (he got the pronunciation right, too), St Boswells, Melrose, Galashiels, Edinburgh. The 'Thames-Clyde' was then the only titled train left from St Pancras so the bishop attended as well, in the shape of the station-master, a tall, impressive figure in tail-coated and silk-hatted vestments.

By contrast the station announcements at London Bridge in the rush hour could have been in a foreign language. On occasions I had to go to North Kent and quickly found that at London Bridge it was necessary not simply to ascertain the platform number from the departure sheets, which were arranged on hinged boards in book fashion, but the reporting number as well, and then watch out for it on the front of arriving trains that came thick and fast at that time of day. The gabbled unintelligible announcements, like the trains, were virtually continuous. In both directions I was travelling against the flow and marvelled at the purposeful manner in which commuters found their way in and out of that bewildering station, unlike the confusion of Victoria where it seemed that even the most regular passengers always wore an air of relief at being able to find the right train.

A career involving travel created opportunities to observe stations at close quarters and relate them to transport history and nineteenth-century architecture. Before the war and up to the 1960s, it was fashionable to sneer at the Victorians, particularly their architecture, until writers like Henry-Russell Hitchcock, Peter Ferriday and Robert Furneaux Jordan brought it into perspective and the Victorian Society started to gain influence. Awareness of stations as an important part of that view took longer, and in the 1950s was hardly recognised until Christian Barman wrote his *Introduction to Railway Architecture*.

The 1950s also recall some of the things that still reflected pre-war standards before modernisation and rationalisation set in, details now almost forgotten: racks of roof boards, wheeled water tanks with hoses for replenishing restaurant cars, pigeon baskets, milk churns, model ships in glass cases advertising services to the Isle of Man, models of the *Rocket* operated by a penny-in-the-slot for railway charities, a full-size, chromium-plated motor car engine in a display case at Coventry, barrows with rugs and pillows for overnight passengers at Manchester London Road; just a few of the features now gone from the station scene. Boys with baskets selling chocolate did not reappear, but some of the pre-war platform refreshment trolleys came back and of course one could still dine, as opposed to merely eat, on stations. Good meals were available in palatial dining-rooms like Paddington, where one was served by waiters, Newcastle and Edinburgh Princes Street, and at Leicester London Road in 1961 I ate lunch seated in a chair that had GCR in brass letters let into the back, presumably transported by some means from Leicester Central, using cutlery bearing two different sets of pre-nationalisation initials and three pre-grouping, including those of the Great North of Scotland Railway.

Changes at first were slow, although I felt a profound sense of shock at Birmingham New Street in 1949 to find the roof being dismantled and replaced by 'austerity' awnings without even the decency of valancing to cover the exposed ends of the girders. Sir Stafford Cripps seemed to have got at the signals, too, which had stubby little upper quadrant arms instead of the massive lower quadrants of the London & North Western. After Beeching, changes were rapid and I had some closures to beat. As it was, by the time I was able to spend some time at Glasgow St Enoch there were cars parked under its roof instead of trains and I missed seeing Middlesbrough's roof at first hand.

It was not an entirely negative period. Someone with vision discovered the original colour scheme and applied it to the Great Hall at Euston, at the same time removing the dreadful pre-war enquiry office that had ruined it, and the fact that ten years afterwards it was all pulled down does not detract from the concept. Later the roofs of Paddington and St Pancras were repainted in attractive colours that showed them off, and at York there was the happy thought of picking out some of the North Eastern Railway coats-of-arms in the roof spandrels in their correct heraldic colours. During the last fifteen years the realisation that the railways possess a large heritage of worthy and important buildings has slowly been gaining momentum, propelled partly by the somewhat arbitrary statutory listing process and partly by more enlightened attitudes inside and outside the industry. Not all railway structures are worth keeping by any means; some are past it anyway, and without a use restoration and preservation are purposeless. There have been set-backs, too, some avoidable had there been more imaginative planning and design, others inevitable in the climate of the times. The gains and losses are noted in Chapter 12. But, given the finance, overall the scene is now brighter than it has ever been since the 1930s, and the formation in 1985 of the independent Railway Heritage Trust is one of its most positive aspects. There has been an enormous improvement in new work as well.

I hope it may not seem pious to quote again that anonymous writer of 1893 when he said 'the great railway stations of London deserve to be visited every whit as much as St. Paul's Cathedral, the Abbey or the Tower, and they are as worthy a memento of the nineteenth century as those buildings are of the days that are gone'.

Not London, but Britain.

2
The Historical Background

The Victorians were proud of their great railway stations. They saw them as symbols of the new age of power and speed that would create universal prosperity and were fond of comparing them with medieval abbeys and cathedrals, as well they might for nothing on the same scale has been achieved since. Indeed, one has to go back to the roads of the Romans to find evidence of construction and engineering work carried out with single-minded energy on such a systematic scale as that of the railway builders. There the comparison ends, for the primary railway system of this country was created virtually from scratch in little over fifteen years, eclipsing the work of the engineers' immediate predecessors, the canal builders, whose initial network of under 2,000 miles took sixty years to complete, and their natural successors, the motorway builders who after twenty-seven years are not only still building but are having to rebuild some of the old.

The big stations built to serve the rapidly expanding railways were not all cathedral-like; too many simply grew from small beginnings by having bits added on as one expedient was followed by another, complete reconstruction not being tackled until the end of the century or later. But those that from the outset were built with foresight on a grand scale exhibited a quality of engineering daring and ingenuity that well deserved the analogy. The great vaults of St Pancras and the western train shed at Liverpool Street could justifiably stand comparison with Gothic abbeys, or the rounded arches and transepts of Paddington with a Roman basilica. The big difference lay in the purpose: one was to earn immortality, the other to earn a dividend.

The idea of the wheeled vehicle being guided along a fixed track progresses intermittently through history from the ancient civilisations of Babylon, Greece and Rome through central European mining practice of the late fifteenth century to the primitive wooden waggonways or tramroads of seventeenth- and eighteenth-century Britain that connected mines with navigable water. They were the direct forerunner of the railway that was heralded in 1825 by the opening of the Stockton & Darlington Railway, for which George Stephenson and his son Robert built steam locomotives and a track that were sufficiently reliable to operate a public service on a regular basis. Although the Stockton & Darlington was neither the first steam railway nor the first public one, it earned its place in history as the first combination of both. But its greatest significance in marking the beginning of the railway age lay in ending the monopoly of the horse.

Carrying passengers and some of the goods traffic was at first the responsibility of contractors who ran horse-drawn carriages and wagons on the railway, mixed in with the Stockton & Darlington company's own locomotive-hauled goods trains to which the former had to give way. The contractors paid tolls in the same way as stage-coach and canal-boat proprietors. It was 1833 before the railway took the passenger traffic into its own hands, by which time the potential of railways was widely recognised.

A number of other lines in the North East and elsewhere had followed the Stockton & Darlington, but the opening of the Liverpool & Manchester Railway in 1830 marked the completion of the first main line in the modern sense, with double track on which goods and passenger trains alike were provided by the company and hauled by their own engines. Unlike the Stockton & Darlington, the line was laid out for speed, again by Stephenson, which meant that it needed all the heavy engineering work of the modern railway – embankments, bridges, viaducts, cuttings and tunnels – so that from the outset 30mph was commonplace, an unprecedented speed described as akin to flying.

Longer trunk lines quickly followed. First was the Grand Junction Railway, opened throughout in 1837 from Birmingham to join the Liverpool & Manchester north of Warrington, followed in the next year by the final section of the London & Birmingham Railway. With the Grand Junction it formed a continuous route from London to Manchester and Liverpool, closely followed by the London & Southampton in 1840 and the Great Western from London to Bristol in 1841, while many more lines were under construction or were being actively promoted.

Although Britain's railway system tended to grow piecemeal, there were some who from the beginning foresaw a national network. The London & Birmingham and the Grand Junction were only the start of a great trunk line from London to Glasgow, Edinburgh and Aberdeen, most of which now forms British Rail's West Coast main line, originally planned by the big financial backers of the Grand Junction aided by their engineer, Joseph Locke, who built the greater part of it. Similarly the Great Western expanded into the West Country, South Wales and the West Midlands by overtly or covertly supporting other lines, the continuity of the broad gauge being guaranteed by having I. K. Brunel as engineer for most of them and by eventually absorbing them into its own system.

Corporate expansion was accompanied by the pursuit of personal power. George Hudson, nicknamed the 'Railway King', built a railway empire by financial chicanery which eventually caused his downfall, but for all that he saw the need for larger groupings. His ruthless policy of amalgamation ensured that by 1849 he controlled more than a quarter of the 5,000 miles of railway then constructed. He has been called the first railway tycoon, and despite his misdeeds the lines he initiated were mostly of sound construction with well-built, attractive stations, well above the average and in some cases very good indeed.

After the first flush of promotion, a tighter economy slowed things down for a few years. Recovery brought a rush to promote new lines and Hudson's period of power included the Railway Mania of 1844–8 when Parliament passed no fewer than some 600 railway Acts. Many were for purely speculative lines which were never built, or were never intended to be built, but when it was all over the railway map of 1852 contained most of the main lines which exist today.

The first passenger-carrying lines in north-east England took a somewhat casual attitude to their travelling customers. Passengers were, after all, only a sideline, so it is not surprising that the early stations were makeshift affairs. Until 1836 the Stockton & Darlington's passengers had to make do with a wooden coach shed without platforms at Stockton, and a converted goods shed at Darlington until 1842. Other railways in the area were as bad if not worse, and their patrons probably expected nothing better, being accustomed to waiting by the roadside for the local carrier's cart or at a posting inn if they were travelling further afield. But on the Liverpool & Manchester things were different. Proper terminals were built from the beginning, although several years passed before all the intermediate stopping places had stations.

There were several reasons for the erection of substantial buildings. Under the stage-coach system, inns served as stopping places where horses could be changed, tickets purchased and refreshments provided, while the canal companies generally only provided the 'track' for packet boats operated by private carriers who issued tickets from their offices at the wharves. The railways, on the other hand, provided both track and trains, so there was a need for ticket offices, somewhere for passengers to wait, and accommodation for staff and administration. Furthermore, terminal stations were also regarded as places where carriages could be stored and serviced, hence the provision of overall roofs. Lastly, as time went on it was realised that railway stations were dangerous places. Locomotives were moving about and at the larger ones there was a good deal of carriage shunting. Even though much of it was by hand (they were four-wheeled and quite light), the public could not be allowed to wander about at will as they tended to do on earlier lines. So after the first phase of construction the purpose-built terminus was designed to enable greater control to be exercised.

The first terminal stations were adequate enough for a few years, but as traffic developed they had to be enlarged or replaced, sometimes on a different, more convenient site. Not many of the early companies foresaw just how quickly rail travel would catch on and their stations become outgrown, although a few did erect temporary termini, albeit for other reasons, which gave them time to appreciate what was happening and then build permanent establishments with an eye to the future.

Following Hudson's example the established railways exercised a policy of consolidation by amalgamation and by 1862 most of the major companies that existed up to 1923 had been formed. There were still a lot of small ones and many lines had yet to be built, but most were eventually acquired or operated by their larger brethren. A second, smaller boom occurred in 1864, culminating in the financial crash of 1866. This second mania period resulted in most of the rest of the railway map being completed by infilling lines and extensions into remoter areas like northern Scotland and mid-Wales.

Then in the 1870s British industry entered a period of complacency in which the railways shared. They were essential to the economy and, despite economic depressions between 1873 and 1896, real incomes grew and more people travelled, so that passenger services reached their peak during the period up to 1914. The railways were a major power in the land, collectively the largest employer of labour, and with a total capital in 1870 of £530 millions they were the equivalent of the industrial giants of our own time. Indeed, the London & North Western Railway asserted that it was the largest joint-stock company in the world. Yet profits failed to rise in line with revenue, partly because of rising costs including wages, partly due to government regulation, and, not least, as a result of intense rivalry and competition. Each major company was jealously intent on safeguarding what it considered its rightful territory against invaders, and conducted its organisation on an appropriate scale. W. M. Acworth, writing tongue-in-cheek about the London & North Western Railway in *The Railways of England* in 1889, put it like this:

> The North Western territory extends from London in the south to Carlisle in the north, and from Cambridge in the east to Swansea and Holyhead in the west. The seat of the government is at present in London, but the capital is Crewe, a town of 35,000 inhabitants consisting entirely of the *employees* of the government and their families. The total number of the civil service does not fall far short of 60,000. The president is Sir Richard Moon, while his Prime Minister, who is known by the title of General Manager, is George Findlay . . .
>
> It will be, we are persuaded, in some such words as these, that, once the conservative mind of the British schoolmaster has awakened to the fact that the counties and Lord Lieutenants are anachronisms and that the United Kingdom has been divided and given to the great railway companies, the Board School pupil of the future will be taught his geography.

Faced with a poor return on capital, the railways saw no pressing need for improvements, considering that economy was paramount, until a combination of bursting capacity, competition and, not least, intense public criticism, started another and final period of construction. Many of the new lines were cross-country routes or branches, although there were some new main lines as well, like the Midland Railway's Settle & Carlisle line and the final links in its independent route to Manchester. The London & South Western attained its goal at Plymouth, while the Great Western embarked on a programme of new lines to shorten its principal routes that went on well into the twentieth century. Among new companies the Barry Railway and the Hull & Barnsley were the most important. The former was unusual in being a success. The latter, like most of the other lines built during the railways' final fling, was a financial failure. Competition reached its height with the Great Central, the last main line to London, which was opened in 1899 and never paid an ordinary dividend.

One of the results of this fierce competition was that very few towns of any importance were served by only one railway company. Hence the large number of towns with two or more stations. An exception was the north east of England where the North Eastern Railway had a rare monopoly, and there were odd pockets like Coventry where only Midland Railway goods trains from Nuneaton managed to pierce the monopoly of the London & North Western. Brighton station in the south and Inverness in northern Scotland were two more, where admittedly coaches from railways other than the owners' were seen, but only on through trains from up country which in this sense were not competitive.

The first two decades of trunk railway construction have been called the heroic era, when everything was done on a grand scale to emphasise the new industry's confidence in the future. While undoubtedly the object was display, in the main it was done with the good taste that the period still preserved and thereby gave the country monumentally classical stations like Euston, Huddersfield, Monkwearmouth and Newcastle, or the Tudor baronial magnificence of Bristol. Similar themes were used when embellishing tunnel mouths and sometimes viaducts, although usually engineers wisely left the grace of their great arcades to speak for themselves. The same taste was displayed in small country stations which were deliberately designed to fit easily into the local landscape or even to enhance it.

From the 1860s onward this enlightened attitude changed, partly reflecting the general debasement of Victorian taste and partly because the railways were now big business in which the strong competitive element compelled economy if dividends were to be maintained. Standardised equipment was developed, including buildings and their components, so that distinctive company styles appeared which no longer owed any allegiance to their surroundings. These new values also were part of a general trend in building, aided by the railways themselves in their ability to provide cheap and speedy transport of materials so that no longer was there reliance on the local product. However, when competition or local pressures forced a railway company to tackle outgrown or outmoded city stations, financial restraints could be overcome. Many important new stations were built, and old ones rebuilt, from the mid-1870s onwards. It was a period of great municipal and commercial building activity with which some railways felt obliged to keep up, while others were forced to do so by external influences. It was an era of bold, often brash, ostentation.

The railways' period of power and monopoly ended with World War I. Larger industrial combines were emerging and road motor transport rapidly became a major competitor. Under the 1921 Transport Act, 120 companies were grouped into four main line railways on 1 January 1923: the Great Western (which of course already existed but was greatly enlarged), the London, Midland & Scottish, the London & North Eastern and the Southern. Only a few minor lines escaped. The effect of enormous wartime traffic loads and reduced maintenance, followed by the financial problems of the 1920s, gave little opportunity for much improvement in stations, and it was not until the 1930s that much was done. The Southern was in the forefront, in connection with its substantial electrification schemes, but work on large stations was generally what today we would call 'cosmetic' and they continued to be essentially Victorian in character. Isolated exceptions were the Great Western's replacement of its remaining old wooden stations, like Leamington Spa, Newton Abbot and Swansea and a start on Plymouth North Road, while modern frontage blocks appeared at Newport and, in 1925, at Aberystwyth. The LMS and LNER combined their Wellington and New stations at Leeds to form City station but the platforms remained unchanged. The government loan schemes gave new opportunities, but the 1939–45 war interrupted them before much of the planned station work could be started.

Enforced neglect during World War II left the nationalised British Railways with a dreadful legacy of run-down equipment, and as priority had to be given to rolling stock more years passed before significant modernisation of stations could commence. Plymouth and Coventry were completely rebuilt in 1962, but otherwise attention was paid to smaller places and, from the mid-1960s, to realising the potential of site values by replacing under-used old frontage buildings with modern office blocks, often in conjunction with property developers, like Hull, Manchester Piccadilly and Holborn Viaduct, leaving their interiors little changed.

Numerous policy changes, largely because of repeated political intervention, did not help either, while rationalisation and the Beeching reshaping of 1961–5 brought closures. Cities with two or more stations had their services concentrated so that no large city outside London now has more than two principal stations and many manage much more efficiently with one. It did mean, however, the loss of some notable buildings and train sheds like Glasgow St Enoch, Nottingham Victoria and Birmingham Snow Hill, while Euston, Birmingham New Street and Leeds were completely rebuilt. Indeed, in many quarters scant regard was paid to historic buildings – the demolition of the Euston arch being the prime example – until the early 1970s when a growing appreciation of Victorian architecture and artefacts brought pressure on the Department of the Environment for greater safeguards by listing more of them as Buildings of Historic or Architectural Importance. This induced deeper consideration by British Rail who realised that often a policy of conservation could not only win friends and attract customers, but in some cases could be cheaper than pulling down and rebuilding. The result has seen excellent, and some quite extensive, restoration schemes, although not all have been without their battles and the conservationists by no means have had it all their own way.

New work has had a mixed reception. It would have been difficult to rebuild London Bridge station without improving it, but at Victoria, where for years the frontage and concourse have been a jumble, the new office block taking a slice out of the middle of the train shed simply takes maximum site utilisation a stage further and places the platforms in the equivalent of a tunnel. Important historic elements are to be retained in the redevelopment of Fenchurch Street and Liverpool Street; it remains to be seen how the new will measure up against the old.

3
The Choice of Sites

In the Victorian city one of the most important buildings was the railway station. During the 1840s and '50s it would almost certainly be the newest secular building, possibly the most imposing, and sometimes exercised a direct influence on mid- and late nineteenth-century city centre development, depending on its location. It could become the core of a new commercial area of a city, yet equally it could attract development that was the exact opposite and become surrounded by a seedy district of mean streets and small businesses. Some stations remained where they were first built, right outside the centre, thereby condemning the inhabitants and the railway to perpetual inconvenience. How did these different circumstances come about?

Throughout the railway age a number of influences were at work, varying in degree with time and place. Geography played an important part, as did local commercial, civic and social pressures; access and, later on, relationship with the existing railway network also affected events; but the two dominant factors were finance, particularly the cost of land, and the politics of railway competition.

The first railway termini built in the 1830s were located outside or on the edges of the towns they served. The Liverpool & Manchester Railway of 1830 approached Liverpool from the east on high ground, requiring the excavation of a deep rock cutting at Olive Mount followed by a long tunnel from Edge Hill down to the docks at Wapping. The passenger terminus was located in Crown Street on the outer fringe of the city where the land started to fall steeply to the centre. It required a second shorter tunnel from Edge Hill. The line was therefore largely unseen where it penetrated the urban area. Trains through both tunnels were worked by rope haulage and stationary engines.

At the Manchester end of the line George Stephenson planned to build a station in Quay Street, close to the wharves of the Mersey & Irwell Navigation and well located to serve the centre of the town, the warehouse area, the river and Salford. To reach it the line would have to cross newly developed land and there was strong opposition from landowners and navigation interests, resulting in defeat of the parliamentary bill of 1825. The company was more successful in the following year with a revised bill containing provisions for a less controversial terminus proposed by the engineer Charles Vignoles,

London & Birmingham coat of arms over the entrance doorway
at Birmingham Curzon Street in 1984 (*Author*)

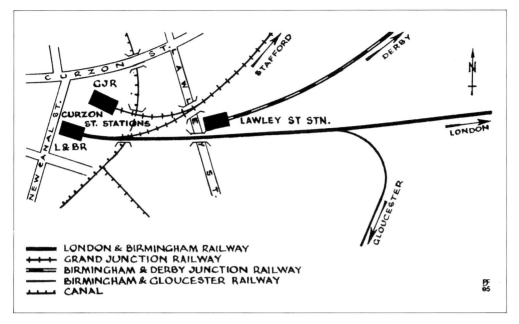

Fig 1. Birmingham stations in 1841

gained by a more northerly route to a station on the Salford side of the Irwell in New Bailey Street. But the board still wanted to terminate in Manchester and Vignoles' plan represented little more than a means to ease the bill through Parliament, for in 1827 it was revealed that land had been purchased in Manchester and negotiations for more were under way. Eventually a large enough site was acquired, and in 1829 the company obtained a further Act authorising it to cross the Irwell and built a station in Liverpool Road, Manchester. The site was further out than Quay Street but was close to the important Castlefield canal and warehousing complex.

The first lines to Birmingham, on the other hand, made no attempt to reach the town centre. For its northern terminus the London & Birmingham Railway selected a site in Curzon Street on the edge of the urban area. The line approached from the south east and ended at the foot of the hill on which Birmingham stood (Fig 1). The Grand Junction Railway, approaching from the north west, went to the expense of making a broad sweep around the town, first to a temporary terminus at Vauxhall and then to its own station alongside the London & Birmingham's, in order to facilitate the exchange of through traffic that was envisaged from the outset. A third railway, the Birmingham & Gloucester, entered from the south west and made a similar swing round into the L&B station, while a fourth, the Birmingham & Derby Junction Railway, made a more direct approach from the east to a separate station in Lawley Street nearby. So in the four years 1838–42 four railways reached Birmingham to use three adjacent termini on the edge of the town, forming an unusually close and, at that time, convenient interchange which avoided heavy and expensive engineering works to gain the town centre.

The Great Western's Bristol terminus at Temple Meads was half a mile or more from the city's commercial centre and the docks (and still is), on a piece of marshy ground between the Avon and the Floating Harbour. The Avon had to be bridged, but the expense of another bridge and acquiring heavily built-up land was avoided.

Because the London & Southampton Railway was closely associated with the building of Southampton docks it was able in 1835–6 to purchase land outside the town wall cheaply with the help of the corporation, although the price was higher when more was required three years later.

Brighton station, completed by the London & Brighton Railway in 1840, was built at the town's northern edge on an awkward hillside site overlooking the town about half a mile from the sea. Because of the slope, a level area had to be expensively excavated, although it would have been difficult to proceed further. No less than four routes were considered, although only two were serious contenders. George Stephenson chose a longer but easier 'natural' route terminating near Brunswick Square in a fashionable area close to the Hove boundary, and not surprisingly opposed by the residents. The natural site would have been the Steine, at the foot of a valley leading to the sea front, but that would have spoiled the essential character of the resort, not to mention the Royal Pavilion. John Rennie's more direct line was authorised, including its hillside station, less convenient but safely out of the way behind the town. Since that time the town has grown towards and past the station: Queens Road was built specifically to give better access, and with corresponding movement of the commercial area over the years the station has become much more central than it was.

The needs of the first junction stations were quite different. Their main purpose was to act as interchange points where routes crossed or diverged, for which reason local traffic was largely, but not always, incidental. Normanton was an important interchange station from 1840, taking its name from a small village whose rise was entirely attributable to the railway. Although it declined in importance somewhat after 1850, it was not until the present century that a reversal of the same influence paradoxically put Normanton back to almost the same relative obscurity, in railway terms at least, from which it started. Swindon took its name from the small town near the railway. It had little traffic potential but was the most convenient point for the junction with the line to Cheltenham and, later, South Wales and for the Great Western's locomotive works. Crewe could provide even less traffic; it was built virtually on a green field site in the middle of nowhere. The Grand Junction Railway selected it for a first-class station because it was on the turnpike road four miles from Nantwich and six from Sandbach, where coaches from Macclesfield and Whitchurch and an omnibus from Nantwich could meet trains. That was in 1837. When the Chester and Manchester lines were opened in 1840 and 1842 respectively, Crewe became an important railway junction. Removal of the Grand Junction's locomotive works from Edge Hill in 1843 firmly established Crewe as a railway town.

These instances and others like them show strong geographical influences at work, although the deciding factor was always financial. Land beyond the town's limits was cheaper than developed land within the urban area and also avoided the costs of demolition and, where it could not be ignored, resettlement. In *The Impact of Railways on Victorian Cities*, John R. Kellett has exhaustively examined the land cost factor in routing railways through London and four of the largest provincial towns. Railway companies in Britain were individually incorporated by Act of Parliament which gave public and legislature the opportunity to examine in detail their aims and objects, impose restrictions and grant special powers. Corporate status gave the railways certain privileges not available to other businesses – at least until legislation in 1844 and 1856, consolidated in the Companies Act of 1862, started the growth of public companies. Not least among the railways' privileges was the power to compulsorily purchase land for construction, although of course the price still had to be negotiated and, if agreement with the owner could not be reached, a jury could be summoned to arbitrate. Large plots in many cities were part of landed estates while others might have a number of small owners. Railways could find it cheaper to plan their lines through the latter areas because small owners were less skilled in bargaining and could be easily overridden, but not always. Equally it might be cheaper in the long run to survey a route through the land of two or three large owners, perhaps paying more but saving on negotiating time and legal expenses.

Inexperience in estimating costs and anticipated revenue could affect the location and structure of a station. The first railways had no precedents on which to base land prices and took some time to accumulate experience. Estimates of revenue were usually based on existing road, canal and river traffic which the railway hoped to attract to itself, but it was all very hit and miss. Many landowners, too, not only had the haziest idea of the value of their property but considered the railways fair game. Kellett cites the Glasgow Asylum authorities who demanded £44,000 for land over the Edinburgh & Glasgow Railway's tunnel to Queen Street station and settled for £873. But in general, railway land prices in cities rose rapidly so that, in combination with over-cautious expectations of revenue, early railways were under capitalised and had to cut back when it came to providing terminals. Lack of finance and anxiety to have its line open as quickly as possible in order to earn revenue prompted many a railway to start life with a temporary terminus, some of which might last far longer than was intended or convenient. Even the Great Western, which I. K. Brunel built on the grand scale, including the Bristol terminus, made do with a temporary one in London for its opening in 1838 and went on doing so for sixteen years. In his biography of Brunel, L. T. C. Rolt suggests that the great engineer must have been considerably irked by the poor shop window his railway presented to London at the wooden terminus in Bishops Road. Glasgow Queen Street, opened in 1842, very centrally situated though it was, quickly became far too small and both difficult and expensive to enlarge, defects it has retained to this day.

Occasionally an existing building might be converted for use as a station, although such instances were rare and generally confined to smaller ones. One exception was the Eastern Union Railway's terminus at Norwich Victoria. In 1849 the railway bought the Victoria pleasure gardens and converted the exhibition hall and circus into an unusual circular booking hall and entrance.

Because travel was so enormously speeded up by railways, the distance from a town centre to the station at first seemed immaterial. The rail journey was so fast compared with stage-coaches and canal boats that the 10 to 15 minutes spent in getting to and from the station did not matter. It was more important that two railways forming a through route should have their stations close together. Sometimes this happened, but more often it did not, leaving legacies of inconveniently separated termini which, in the case of London, Glasgow and Manchester, have resisted even British Rail's efforts at rationalisation.

We have seen how the first stations at Birmingham were built close together; the same happened in Edinburgh where the North British, Edinburgh & Glasgow and Edinburgh Leith & Granton railways' stations were cheek by jowl, and the Great Western and Bristol & Exeter stations in Bristol. Close proximity of stations did not always spell harmonious relationships between their owners, though. Pursuit of inter-company politics rarely stopped short of inconveniencing passengers and frequently blocked the establishment of a common station. The case of the Preston stations in the early 1840s is a prime example worth examining in some detail (Fig 2).

Preston's strategic location at the head of the Ribble estuary between the coastal plains and the hills of north Lancashire, coupled with its importance as a regional centre and manufacturing town, made it a natural focal point for railways. This was particularly true of the main line up the western side of England from London to Scotland, which at that time was seen as the ultimate objective, even though a number of years were to pass before the companies making it up came into unified ownership. When the North Union Railway reached Preston from the south in 1838, the Lancaster & Preston Junction Railway to Lancaster and the Preston & Wyre Railway to Fleetwood were already under construction. The NU station was in Fishergate while the other two railways proposed to terminate at separate but

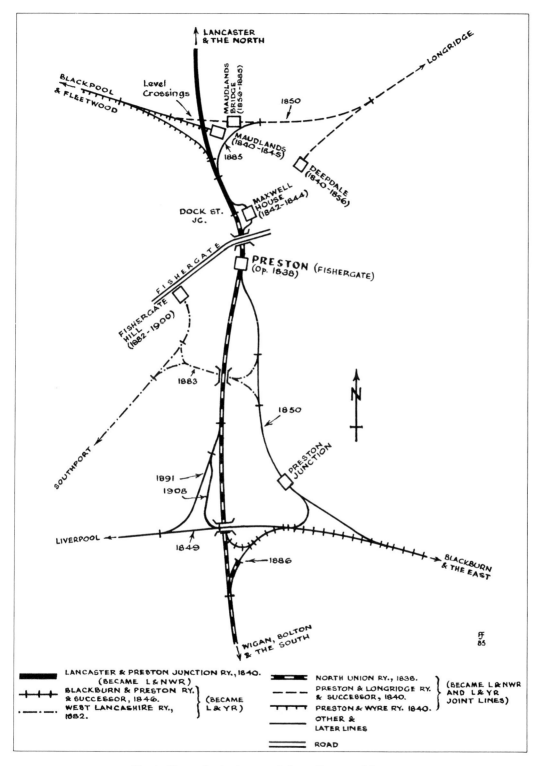

LANCASTER & THE NORTH

LONGRIDGE

BLACKPOOL & FLEETWOOD

Level Crossings

MAUDLANDS BRIDGE (1850-1885)

1850

MAUDLANDS (1840-1845)

1885

DEEPDALE (1840-1856)

MAXWELL HOUSE (1842-1844)

DOCK ST. JC.

FISHERGATE

PRESTON (Op. 1838) (FISHERGATE)

FISHERGATE HILL (1882-1900)

1883

N

1850

PRESTON JUNCTION

SOUTHPORT

1891

1908

LIVERPOOL

1849

1886

BLACKBURN & THE EAST

WIGAN, BOLTON & THE SOUTH

FF 85

LANCASTER & PRESTON JUNCTION RY., 1840.
(BECAME L & NWR)
BLACKBURN & PRESTON RY. & SUCCESSOR, 1846. } (BECAME L & Y R)
WEST LANCASHIRE RY., 1882.

NORTH UNION RY., 1838.
PRESTON & LONGRIDGE RY. & SUCCESSOR, 1840.   } (BECAME L & NWR AND L & YR JOINT LINES)
PRESTON & WYRE RY. 1840.
OTHER & LATER LINES
ROAD

Fig 2. Chronological map of the railways of Preston

reasonably adjacent points some 200yd north, on the understanding that the NU would build a connecting line. When it came to it, however, the NU refused unless the L&PJ contributed to the cost. If a through service was to be provided, the Lancaster company had no option and the connection was duly built for the openings in 1840. It also began a bitter feud.

Two years later a third railway on the scene was nearing completion, the Bolton & Preston, which would secure a much shorter route from Manchester than that of the North Union which naturally did not welcome the newcomer, much less the rapport it had established with the Lancaster & Preston. So the L&PJ was summarily informed that it could only continue to use the NU station on payment of a toll, which the L&PJ not unreasonably refused to do as it had already paid part of the cost of the line between the two stations. Fortunately the Bolton & Preston was able hastily to finish its own station at Maxwell House near the L&PJ's Dock Street terminus (which does not appear to have been a proper station at all), so that the Lancaster company could use that instead.

Although the two companies continued to exchange through carriages, the North Union withdrew through fares and imposed a toll of 6d per passenger over the offending 200yd. Many refused to pay, got out and walked while the carriages were being transferred, only to find that by the time they had rebooked as well their train had gone. So after the opening of the Bolton & Preston line in 1843, the town found itself with three main stations, all fairly close together. Maxwell House was used for through services between Manchester and the north, which worked tolerably well, while the North Union station was intended for through services from the south under an arrangement that did not work at all. The third, the Preston & Wyre's station at Maudlands, was used for the trains to Fleetwood, some of which also ran from Fishergate station where the P&W seemed to have a slightly better relationship with the NU. Eventually pressure from the Board of Trade, which was concerned for passengers' safety, together with a series of amalgamations, brought about the common use of the NU station. It was also used by the East Lancashire Railway, opened from Blackburn in 1846 and from Liverpool in 1849.

A fourth railway with its own station was the Preston & Longridge, a short local line opened in 1840 to a station in Deepdale Street and operated for its first eight years by horses. In 1850 it was connected to the Preston & Wyre and six years later a station called Maudlands Bridge was opened nearer the centre of the town, although it was not until 1885 that Longridge trains were able to run into the main station at Fishergate. By 1866 all the lines into Preston had become part of the London & North Western or the Lancashire & Yorkshire Railways, some of them jointly, and Fishergate was operated as a joint station. Through sheer lack of space it continued to be inadequate for well over twenty years, as will be shown in Chapter 10.

The events at Preston well illustrate the intense independence of small local railways at that time. From the outset the route northward was seen as part of a grand scheme for a west coast main line to Scotland, yet the fierce parochialism of two short links in the chain created insufferable chaos at an important station which was only resolved by successive amalgamations.

The final twist in this tangled story took place in 1882 when the West Lancashire Railway was opened from Southport to a separate station at the foot of Fishergate Hill, about ¼ mile from the main station. The next year a connection was opened to the East Lancashire line, by now part of the Lancashire & Yorkshire Railway, and Fishergate Hill was closed to passengers in 1900 when all services were at last concentrated at one station. The fact that both stations were in Fishergate did nothing to help the unknowing passenger, even though only the West Lancashire officially used that name, while the presence of a third station called Preston Junction, two miles out of Preston on the Blackburn line, compounded the confusion.

If the fun and games at Preston seem barely credible, they were nothing to the state of affairs that lasted for over thirteen years at Aberdeen. In 1850 the route to the far north of Scotland lay through the city, reached by a chain of railways from the English border in which the final link was the Aberdeen Railway that stopped short at Ferryhill just outside the town. The line onward to Inverness was the responsibility of the Great North of Scotland Railway which, since 1846, had been prevented from building anything at all by a combination of boardroom quarrels and an inability to raise money, aggravated by the financial crisis of 1847. At length in 1854 the company managed to open part of its line from Kittybrewster, on the north side of Aberdeen, but Inverness was only reached in 1858 by using the line of another company.

The original intention was to build a joint Aberdeen terminus in Market Street. The need for Great North trains to reverse in and out was not felt to be an encumbrance, but in 1852 a cheaper site for a through station was found in Guild Street. However, as neither company could agree on sharing the cost, each set about building its own terminus. In 1854 the Aberdeen Railway opened an extension from Ferryhill to a small two-platform station near the harbour lower down Guild Street, and the Great North followed suit in 1855 when it started running goods trains over its extension to Waterloo Quay, followed by passenger trains the following year. Waterloo was even less convenient for the town, situated on a cramped site at the bottom of a steep descent from Kittybrewster, nearly ½ mile from Guild Street, and having only three short platforms. By constructing lines along the quay, over which the harbour trustees allowed only horse-drawn wagons, goods traffic was exchanged after a fashion, but as wagons had to be either individually manoeuvred on turnplates or back shunted it was doubly slow and tedious.

Passengers and mails were transferred by horse omnibus and a post-office van for which adequate time was allowed in the timetable provided that trains arrived on time, which was infrequent. Trains from the south were invariably late, the worst offender being the morning mail from Perth which was usually delayed by late-running connections from England. Under the Post Office contract the Great North was obliged to wait for it, so to get trains away as quickly as possible the Waterloo station gates were closed at the advertised departure time and opened again only for the mail van. As the Inverness mail was the last through train of the day from Aberdeen, passengers missing it could travel no further than Keith and the more knowing ones preferred to spend the night in Aberdeen. There were stories of the omnibus racing along the quayside trying to reach Waterloo before the gates were shut, only to find them deliberately closed in the passengers' faces even though the Inverness train was still in the station loading mail.

Repeated public agitation in Aberdeen and further afield for a proper connecting line had little effect while the railways were trying to out-manoeuvre each other, and it took the promotion of a direct Perth–Inverness line over the Grampians in 1861 to make them realise that something had to be done. Even then there were several more years of argument over the route before the Great North finally capitulated to public pressure for a line down the Denburn Valley to a new joint station which was opened in 1867, by which time the direct line from Perth to Inverness had been open for over four years.

Why did these conditions last so long? The Great North's main aim was to end its physical isolation, while the Aberdeen Railway saw its future more as a route to the south than as a link in a line to the north, a comparatively remote area that would generate far less traffic. As a route to Inverness it was very circuitous anyway, and it was doubtless recognised that it would be only a matter of time before Inverness interests obtained the direct line they wanted. So probably in the Aberdeen Railway's view there was no desperate political or financial advantage in having a common station, while the difficult geographical approach from the other side of the city presented expensive engineering problems with which the Great North was loth to grapple alone.

Farcical though such circumstances may have been, they certainly were not funny for the passengers and contrasted strongly with the American concept of the single 'Union' station owned by a separate company which accepted all comers on payment, or the single *Hauptbahnhof* in Germany. We shall see later how individuals' plans for single 'General' stations in London and Glasgow in the mid-century received scant support from the government or the railways, a fate that befell an earlier scheme at Newcastle-on-Tyne.

Richard Grainger, who with John Dobson carried out the enlightened redevelopment of Newcastle in 1835–9, put forward in 1836 a plan for a general station to serve the five railways at that time proposed to enter the city, including a bridge over the river. In a way it was a forerunner of the Union station concept, as Grainger proposed to build the station and the bridge himself and either let or sell them to the railways when they arrived. The station would not have been central, however, and as a compromise he proposed a tunnel and incline to the site of the Newcastle & Carlisle Railway's station at The Spital which had been authorised but not yet built. The general station would have been just east of what became Forth goods yard, thus partly defeating the object of concentrating all the railways at one place. We shall see later how Newcastle's eventual station, which really was central, came about in quite different circumstances.

In Britain the joint station actually owned by two or more railways was the nearest equivalent to the Union station. The earliest plan to share a station was the Great Western's proposal to use the London & Birmingham's Euston terminus, for which land was allocated, but the Great Western abandoned the idea when negotiations became difficult, probably after it chose the broad gauge, and went to Paddington instead. The first purpose-built joint station was Derby where Francis Thompson's Tri-junct station for the North Midland, Midland Counties and Birmingham & Derby Junction railways was completed in 1840. As a joint station it lasted only until 1844 when the three companies amalgamated to form the Midland Railway.

Physical confrontations between disputing railways in the 1840s and '50s were not uncommon. Railway history is enlivened by 'battles' at places where competing lines met, when trains would be obstructed or rails removed and armies of navvies lined up. At Wolverhampton in 1851 one engine even butted another, to the cheers of the watching crowd. Such events at Havant, Nottingham, Clifton near Manchester and other junctions between rival lines might have been great fun for the onlookers and future railway historians, but not for the unfortunate passengers who were the victims of inter-company ferocity that, in the short term, exceeded even the goings on at Preston and Aberdeen.

It might be thought that the idea of a station jointly owned by two or more railways, in addition to saving the expense of separate establishments, would also help to promote friendly relations, but at Chester and Manchester this was far from the case. Chester General station in 1849 was jointly owned by a group of companies: the London & North Western, Chester & Holyhead, Birkenhead and Shrewsbury & Chester railways. The LNWR was the most powerful and had considerable influence over the next two, a dominance it sought to extend to the Shrewsbury & Chester and its partner, the Shrewsbury & Birmingham Railway. These two together represented a possible future threat to the LNWR's monopoly by letting the rival Great Western into the area from Birmingham, thus putting it within striking distance of Liverpool. So the two Shrewsbury companies had to be subdued.

Let E. T. MacDermot, historian of the Great Western, tell the story of the battle of Chester:

> There [Chester], the Joint Committee, on which the North Western with its subject the Chester & Holyhead, and its terrorised ally, the Birkenhead, had a large majority, refused to allow passengers to be booked to Wolverhampton and beyond via Shrewsbury, and, on the Shrewsbury Company persisting, had their booking clerk dragged out of his office and his tickets thrown after him. The Birkenhead Company having declined to convey third class passengers by more than two trains, one very early in the morning and the other late at night, the Shrewsbury & Chester established a service of omnibuses to and from Birkenhead. These were excluded from the station by barricades of wood and chains across the approaches. Their time bills and notices also were torn down. All this in a station of which the Shrewsbury Company were part owners was, of course, quite illegal, and they had no difficulty in speedily obtaining an injunction to stop it . . .

The LNWR's high handedness was all to no avail because in the end the Great Western succeeded in acquiring the Shrewsbury companies, thereby becoming joint owner of the stations at Shrewsbury and Chester and, moreover, the Birkenhead Railway later on, thus not only gaining the coveted route to Liverpool but to Warrington and Manchester as well. Out of pique the LNWR found itself another site in Chester at which it announced it would build its own separate station, but no more was heard of it.[1]

The North Western was also a partner in London Road station, Manchester, with the Manchester Sheffield & Lincolnshire Railway, where each had separate offices, staffs and waiting rooms. In 1854 the MSLR agreed that as an economy the North Western should act for both companies. At that time the North Western headed a cartel which, among other things, operated an aggressive policy against the Great Northern Railway. When this was publicly exposed in 1857, the MSL promptly changed sides and allowed the Great Northern to run a London–Manchester service over its line from Retford into London Road station on similar timings to the North Western's service from Euston. It happened that the staffing agreement expired at the same time, and when MSL booking clerks tried to repossess their office the North Western threw them out, nailed it up and painted out the nameboard. Passengers were refused bookings to King's Cross, those arriving from London by MSL trains were intimidated and even taken into custody – quite illegally – and MSL trains were physically prevented from departing, while both sides slashed their fares. It took parliamentary assent to the new alliance in the following year to make the LNWR desist and agree to a settlement.

It is now time to pay some attention to London where the situation was completely different. The capital is the only city where some attempt was made to control the ingress of railways. Four lines entering London from the north and west between 1838 and 1868 stopped short at the New Road, as

Euston Road and Marylebone Road were then known. They were the London & Birmingham at Euston, the Great Western at Paddington, the Great Northern at King's Cross and the Midland at St Pancras. Right at the end of the century the Great Central did the same at Marylebone.

Kellett shows how the land to the north of the New Road contained inferior property – in Paddington's case it was virtually open – and so could be bought relatively cheaply with few conditions attached. The expensive Crown lands and the Portman estate around Regents Park were avoided. South of the New Road, however, the picture was one of much higher class development which would have made purchase excessively expensive and restrictive. From the south the Thames was a natural barrier which no railway crossed until the opening of Victoria in 1860. In the east the City would have no truck with railways in the physical sense, making a further barrier which only the London & Blackwall managed to penetrate at Fenchurch Street – and then only a matter of a few hundred yards after fierce resistance – until Broad Street was opened in 1865 and Liverpool Street ten years later; both, again, were allowed only a short distance inside the hallowed square mile.

Other reasons lay in the 1846 report of the Royal Commission on Railway Termini, which was accepted by the government. The commission advised against railways entering that area of central London enclosed by Marylebone and Euston roads, City Road, Finsbury Square, Bishopsgate Street, London Bridge, Borough High Street, Vauxhall Bridge, Grosvenor Gardens and Park Lane; what Professor Jack Simmons has called the London Quadrilateral. Limited penetration might be allowed south of the river, where land was cheap, no great damage would be done and there was a need for better communications from the adjoining parts of Surrey and Kent where the population was thicker than north of the capital. Waterloo station on the south bank was accepted because it had been sanctioned by Parliament the previous year, but that was all. The suggestion of a central station serving all the northern lines was dismissed in favour of a ring line to connect them.

The proliferation of termini in London was, and is, unique. No other city in the world has so many; currently there are fifteen. Unimpeded competition in Britain ensured that provision of a single central station rarely happened anywhere, except (and unusually) in Stoke-on-Trent and Middlesbrough where there was no competition, Aberdeen (eventually, as has already been noted), and Bristol, Hull and Newcastle where other termini were very small and unimportant. London's stations were spread out, too. As the crow flies it is the best part of 4 miles from Paddington to London Bridge and more than 3½ from Victoria to Liverpool Street. If Piccadilly Circus is regarded as the centre of the metropolis, only Charing Cross station can be called anything like central. Furthermore, only one line actually crossed central London, following the somewhat tortuous Snow Hill route by using part of what is now London Transport's Circle Line to connect Paddington, St Pancras (indirectly) and King's Cross with Ludgate Hill and Blackfriars (then called St Pauls), where it crossed the river to join the southern lines. It was sanctioned by Parliament to cut across the 'Quadrilateral' – the only one – and was completed in 1866 following the opening of the first part of the Circle Line in 1863, which itself did not complete the full circuit until 1884.

It was not that the need for a central station went unrecognised. In the mania period of the mid-1840s a number of proposals were made, including one for a station on the Embankment which would be served by a line between Paddington and Fenchurch Street. The commissioners' main arguments against a central station were the traffic congestion it would generate in its vicinity, the high cost and disturbance to property. They felt that the number of passengers crossing London was too small to warrant the upheaval, quite failing to foresee how quickly London would develop as a focal point for railways.

During the next twenty years, parliamentary select committees expressed similar opinions, resulting in the position we see today, and it was not until 1858 when the Act for Victoria was secured that railways from the south started to seek footholds on the north bank of the Thames, yet not seriously denting the Royal Commission's precepts. Victoria, Charing Cross and Cannon Street are all termini on or close to the ends of bridges over the river, all built in the 1860s. In the City, Blackfriars, opened at the end of the widened Blackfriars railway bridge in 1886, and Holborn Viaduct, opened in 1874 to relieve Ludgate Hill, are close to its boundaries and quite small.

Two men, Thomas Page, an engineer concerned with a Thames Embankment scheme and Charles Pearson, solicitor to the City Corporation, gave evidence to the commissioners for a central terminus. Pearson returned to the fray in 1850 with a scheme for an underground line to a large central station at Holborn. It failed to attract sufficient financial support to satisfy Parliament which instead authorised another scheme for what became the Metropolitan Railway between Paddington and Farringdon.

Some of the other schemes are of more than passing interest. In 1853 Henderson, of Fox Henderson & Co which had erected the Crystal Palace, proposed an iron station on piles in the middle of the Thames which might at least have solved the problem of land. [2] Then in 1863 Col Yolland, a Board of Trade inspector of railways, advocated a junction of the London & North Western, Midland and Great Northern railways with the southern lines at Charing Cross. The Midland and the GNR were strongly in favour; indeed the Great Northern suggested two terminals, one on the south bank and one on the north to which the northern and southern companies could respectively run, but nothing came of it. In 1881 a civil engineer, Russell Aitken, proposed a central terminus for the southern lines gained from the London Chatham & Dover and London & South Western railways at a point where they crossed at Vauxhall, by which other lines could be reached. A new railway would cross the Thames on a skew bridge whence Aitken planned to take it along the Embankment to Westminster, where it passed between the Houses of Parliament and the Abbey, and then through a tunnel to a grand 'Albert Terminus' in Northumberland Avenue where a link would also be made with the Inner Circle.[3] Considering the likely uproar over the Westminster section, it is not surprising that no more was heard of that scheme either.

Kellett concludes that high land values, competition and government disfavour combined to create a central prohibited area which the railways could not penetrate. It was a pity, and by the time the 1905 Royal Commission on London Traffic had recognised the problem it was too late to remedy.

A Royal Commission also reported on the advantages or otherwise of a central station in Glasgow, the only other city where railways received government attention. Like the London commission it reported in 1846, but here was completely ineffective. It did nothing positive to encourage a scheme like G. W. Muir's for a central station in Trongate, which he tried to revive again in 1864, nor did the commissioners in any way restrain the competing schemes of the railways, which simply ignored the report. Glasgow at that time had four stations. Bridge Street, south of the Clyde, was a joint station run by two railways that by 1850 were part of the competing Caledonian and Glasgow & South Western respectively; further out was Southside station, another terminus used by the Glasgow Barrhead and Neilston Direct Railway, a protégé of the Caledonian and for a short time used by the latter for their English services. North of the river, Queen Street, terminus of the Edinburgh & Glasgow Railway, was in the city proper, while Glebe Street, or Townhead as it was otherwise known, further to the north, was little more than a mineral yard to which the Caledonian ran its Edinburgh trains, and at first its English services before transferring them to Southside. Totally inadequate, Glebe Street was replaced by the Caledonian's more central Buchanan Street station in 1849, which then became its main terminus from the south.

For some years schemes for better located stations were scuttled by lack of willingness by the competing railways to settle differences, helped first by the Admiralty and then by the Clyde Trustees who imposed severe restrictions on the height and dimensions of proposed bridges across the Clyde. Then in 1864 the City of Glasgow Union Railway was promoted by the Edinburgh & Glasgow (shortly to be snapped up by the Caledonian's deadly rival the North British Railway) and the Glasgow & South Western. The new company was authorised to build a 'General Terminus' in St Enoch Square and connecting lines. After it had taken five years to bridge the Clyde at great cost, the central land ownership pattern was found to be so complicated and uncertain that it was decided to avoid further delay by building a temporary terminus in Dunlop Street while things were sorted out. It was opened in 1870. Initially the Caledonian had expressed interest as well, but the Midland Railway, which was allied with the North British and GSW, would have none of it and by 1873 had enough power behind the throne virtually to veto a second Caledonian approach. The Caledonian's English ally was the London & North Western, with which the Midland was aiming to compete for the Scottish traffic. Consequently the Caledonian was forced to build its own Central station in 1879, after further delaying tactics by the Clyde Trustees. They were rather more amenable over the bridge further upstream leading to St Enoch station, which was opened in 1876 and was taken over by the Glasgow & South Western solely in 1883. As a result of this long drawn out competitive chess match, Glasgow suffered from inadequate stations for over thirty years and never achieved a cross-city main line.

The four main line termini with which Glasgow ended up were at the most half a mile apart, and three were very central (an advantage shared only by Birmingham) whereas in Manchester it is nearly a mile through the streets from Piccadilly to Victoria and was almost as far to Central. Manchester's ring of stations was like Glasgow's. As a writer put it in 1887, 'Manchester, after the bad example of the capital, has adopted the singularly inconvenient system of practically disconnected railway communications'.[4]

After the Liverpool & Manchester Railway entered the city from the west in 1830 to terminate at Liverpool Road, the Manchester, Bolton & Bury Railway in 1838 approached from the north to a station in New Bailey Street, just across the river in Salford, closely followed in 1839 by the Manchester & Leeds Railway from the east to Oldham Road station. The early pattern was completed by the opening of the joint London Road station in 1842 by the Manchester & Birmingham Railway, approaching from the south, and the Sheffield, Ashton & Manchester which joined it from the east a short distance out. All four stations were widely spaced, Liverpool Road and Oldham Road being at opposite extremities of the town.

A plan to link them was published in 1839 and in the same year the Manchester & Leeds proposed a central station at Hunts Bank reached by new lines from Oldham Road and Liverpool Road, and by a tunnel from the projected London Road station where vehicles would be transferred by a lift. Not surprisingly the tunnel and lift idea was not supported, but the M&L opened its Hunts Bank station — called Victoria — in 1844 and, after initial hesitation, the Liverpool & Manchester completed its link, mainly on a viaduct, five months later. A connection with London Road by a roundabout route mainly intended for goods trains was made in 1848, while the Liverpool line was connected to London Road in the following year. But these connections did nothing to provide inter-station services, while Salford remained a terminus for some East Lancashire trains right up to 1966.

The opening of Central station in 1877 was purely a competitive measure providing a third choice of route to Liverpool and London. At both Manchester and Glasgow the number of termini has now been reduced to two, but this still acts as a hindrance to through traffic.

In Europe the central station could form the focal point of town planning, like the Gare de l'Est in Paris, Amsterdam, Geneva, Ghent; or carefully designed to fill a street vista or the side of a square such as Turin's Porta Nuova station of 1866, the first Rome Terminus of 1874 and, nearer our own time, the overpoweringly monumental complex of Milan Central, designed in 1913 but not completed until 1930. Indeed, in most large continental cities the station was deliberately fronted by a square to set it off. The first Euston station was like that. When it was finished in 1838, it fronted the large open space of Euston Square which ideally set off the view of Philip Hardwick's great Doric Arch and four flanking lodges from the Euston Road, but then the London & Birmingham Railway spoilt it all by building a pair of hotels in front. The arch and two lodges were still visible between them but the overall effect was ruined and, in 1881, completely obliterated when the hotels were joined by a connecting block.

In only two British towns can the station be said to be part of a deliberate scheme of development. Winton Square, Stoke-on-Trent, was wholly the creation of the North Staffordshire Railway. The station containing the railway headquarters occupies one side facing the company's North Staffordshire Hotel. The other two sides are occupied by matching houses built for senior railway employees, all in a rich neo-Jacobean style of architecture. As a piece of railway town planning it is unique. At Huddersfield a planned environment happened more by accident than design. The giant classical station was built on the only suitable site on the railway's route through the town, between a viaduct and a tunnel, where its imposing columns close the vista up Northumberland Street and form one side of the irregularly shaped St George's Square. Although built later, the opposing buildings are mainly by the same architects and form a complementary group.

The attitudes of local authorities and the general public towards the siting and appearance of stations varied. The Midland Counties Railway's proposals for its Derby terminus included a site in the town centre, while the North Midland and Birmingham & Derby Junction railways wanted to make an end-on junction station by Nottingham Road. It was the local corporation that insisted on the more sensible idea of a joint station for all three, although its choice of site was less so, on flat land subject to flooding a good mile from the town. However, after much argument the municipality finally got its way by undertaking to improve road access. The university's opposition to Cambridge station which successfully kept it 1½ miles away from the centre of the city, where it remains, is well known, but criticisms generally were

directed against stations that were too far away or were inadequate, and it
could sometimes take a long time to wear the companies down. One of the
earliest examples is Liverpool, where public complaints about the inaccessi-
bility of Crown Street were reinforced by the cost to the railway company of
running free coaches from the centre, so that in 1836, barely six years after its
opening, the Liverpool & Manchester built a new station in Lime Street.
What was more, the city's Common Council let itself be persuaded to
contribute £2,000 towards a suitable façade in keeping with the new central
square being planned to contain St George's Hall. Civic generosity of this
kind was rare. When the Lancashire & Yorkshire and East Lancashire
railways extended from their Great Howard Street terminus to a new joint
station in Tithebarn Street in 1850 the changed times and the Liverpool
locale dictated no such encouragement.

The cost of reaching more central sites was high. The estimate of £100,000
for the cutting and tunnel from Edge Hill to Lime Street, including the
station, was well exceeded, while the line into Tithebarn Street was partly on
an expensive viaduct. Likewise the viaduct across Salford to Manchester
Victoria, over a mile long, entailed considerable cost. Expensive tunnelling
was required at both ends of Birmingham New Street station, and Snow Hill
in the same city needed at one end a tunnel and at the other a viaduct and
another tunnel. Steeply graded tunnels were necessary to reach stations in
deep valleys, like Queen Street and Buchanan Street in Glasgow and
Exchange station at Bradford, in order to gain the desired central locations.

If the 1862 scheme for a new central station in Bristol at Queen Square,
with an extension to Clifton, had gained full civic support, it might have
materialised and would have had a far more convenient location than
Temple Meads but, as with two other similar schemes, the cost of crossing
streets and the harbour would have been high and its future usefulness on a
terminal line instead of as a through station questionable. The idea was
revived in 1902 when a Bill was promoted for a new line to London
independent of the Great Western, from a central station in Colston Street via
Bath and across Salisbury Plain to join the London & South Western near
Basingstoke and thence to Waterloo. A branch was proposed to Avonmouth.
There was considerable influential local support, including this time the
Corporation, but naturally the GWR opposed it and the Bill was rejected by a
Commons committee.

The benefits of a new central site reached by a tunnel soon brought
operating problems. They created bottlenecks as traffic increased, only eased
by building duplicate tunnels or, at Lime Street and Bradford, opening them
out into cuttings so that widening could take place. At Birmingham Snow
Hill the tunnel was actually lengthened at one end by building over the line,
where smoke-logged shunting operations took place. Queen Street tunnel in
Glasgow is still a bottleneck, aggravated by the 1 in 42 gradient which was

The drama of Liverpool Lime Street: light and shade at the platform ends set against the blackness of the rock cutting beyond, in 1954 (*Author*)

operated until 1908 by a stationary engine and rope at Cowlairs.

For the first seven years trains leaving Euston were hauled up Camden Bank by cable, and until 1870 the tunnel leading from Liverpool Lime Street was operated in the same way. After cable working generally was superseded by locomotive haulage, banking engines were needed to give the heavier trains a push, often done by the engine that earlier had brought the train into the station. Such sights and sounds were familiar at these stations and others like St Pancras and the eastern exit from Manchester Victoria. They were very spectacular in the days of steam, but not much fun for the rear enginemen when the gradient was in a tunnel, and expensive for the companies.

Approaches on viaducts were equally constricting, like those east and west across Leeds to the New station and across Salford to Manchester Victoria, which were built with sharp curves to avoid property and thus endowed with permanent speed restrictions which still hamper arriving and departing trains. The Salford viaduct contrasts with the straight, fast main line approach to Piccadilly station in the same city.

The demolitions involved in building a central station could have beneficial side effects in terms of slum clearance, although to the railway companies the only advantage was the acquisition of cheap property while to the unfortunate inhabitants they were a disaster. The clearance of a notorious slum area to build New Street station was considered to be a public service which prompted further schemes in Birmingham. To make way for St Pancras seven streets of people were evicted, none of whom received compensation, and similar instances occurred elsewhere throughout the century until the Great Central was built at its end, when the company was required to rehouse dispossessed inhabitants where it cut through the middle of Nottingham and parts of north-west London.

Today any development scheme, whether it be a new road or a shopping centre, that is likely to disturb an historic site, an architecturally important building or something considered to be of public value, immediately and quite rightly arouses protests from conservation groups and environmentalists. In the years of railway development there was surprisingly little opposition to what latterly has been called railway vandalism. Wordsworth and Ruskin inveighed against railways through their favourite stretches of countryside while A. W. N. Pugin castigated their architectural styling, but generally the only meaningful protests came from those with vested property interests and a few purely local groups of public-spirited citizens. Indeed, the instances where there was public reaction are the more interesting for their comparative rarity.

One of the worst acts of railway vandalism that went apparently unhindered was the destruction of the partly ruined Berwick Castle to make way for the railway, leaving only a fragment and using some of the stone to build a mock-Gothic station. Today we would consider it adding insult to injury. Much the same happened to the remains of St Pancras Priory at Lewes. The city of York in 1838–9 desired a convenient station so much that it seems to have positively welcomed one inside the medieval walls that required an arch cutting through the fabric, subject only to the York & North Midland and Great North of England railways making some repairs and an access road. It is interesting, too, that the station covered the known sites of three Roman baths, which today would arouse demands for at least exploratory excavations before work commenced. Of course, the chairman of the York & North Midland, George Hudson, was a city councillor, was soon to be called the 'Railway King' and, by the time the station was opened, was Lord Mayor. Furthermore, as a loyal son of the city he was successfully promoting York as a major railway centre.

Hudson was also prominently involved in the location of Newcastle Central station. In his capacity as chairman of the Newcastle & Darlington Junction Railway and the projected Newcastle & Berwick he met the Town Improvement Committee in 1844 when, in exchange for their support for the Newcastle & Berwick Bill in Parliament, he undertook to guarantee a high-level bridge across the Tyne that would carry a road as well as the railway, thus providing a long-wanted improvement in communications with Gateshead. Part of the deal included land for Newcastle station and its approach lines, involving demolition of much of what remained of the medieval city and displacement of some 800 families. A long section of the city wall and two towers disappeared under the west end of the station, along with a number of town houses, part of a public open space called the Forth, the Royal Free Grammar School which included the church of the ancient St Mary's Hospital, and the site of the White Friars' Convent. Worse still, the lines from the bridge cut right across the castle bailey, completely severing Henry II's Black Gate from the keep. Yet no one seems to have complained.

At Carlisle the railway passed alongside the castle and city walls, and the neo-Tudor station fitted in quite well. It was apparently one of the few towns where amicable discussions were held by all the parties – two railway companies, the city council and representatives of the inhabitants – leading to agreement on a level site in Court Square where there was sufficient space. Although clearance was necessary, the demolished buildings were of low value. Chester station was well away from the historic core of the city, although the line to North Wales pierced a corner of the walls. However, the story was quite different at Shrewsbury where the four railways serving the town wanted separate stations but were required by Parliament to contribute equally to one general station controlled by a joint committee. The town was divided between two sites, neither suitable to the railways which for once united in favour of a location alongside the castle in the neck of a loop of the Severn, the only place where the river would not separate the station from the town. The railways won and today the station completely ruins the aspect of the castle and the view up the river at what has been called England's finest Tudor town.

If there seemed to be little concern about railways in historic English towns, the same cannot be said about at least two of Scotland's ancient cities. The city and Royal Burgh of Perth soundly rejected the Board of Trade adjudicators' recommendation that the proposed general station should be placed on the South Inch. Four railways were authorised to converge on Perth in 1845, from the south, the north, across Fife from Edinburgh and from Dundee in the east. A general station was to be built on a site determined by the Board of Trade which appointed Captains Coddington and Cleather to report. The South and North Inches were stretches of riverside parkland granted by charter to the city in perpetuity, and the captains contended that a station of 'highly ornamental character' such as they contemplated, suitably screened by trees, would not detract from the public's amenities but actually improve the city's appearance. The burghers would have none of this; the South Inch provided a magnificent setting and must remain a public open space. The railways appear to have kept out of it, except the Perth & Dundee which was required by the Admiralty to provide a minimum clearance under its bridge across the Tay, which would mean an uncomfortably steep gradient from a station on the Inch. Under the Act, the adjudicators in any case had to satisfy all four railways, which quickly decided on a site further west between the infirmary and the prison. To reach it, the Dundee & Perth had to obtain a further Act to vary its line through Perth, involving crossing seven streets and ending at an awkward trailing junction south of the station, dictating reversals in and out. But the South Inch remained inviolate.

For over half a century Edinburgh witnessed sporadic infighting between citizens concerned to protect Princes Street Gardens and railway companies wanting more space. The Edinburgh & Glasgow Railway's terminus at Haymarket was opened in 1842. The North British Railway brought in the East Coast route from England in 1846, approaching from the opposite direction to a terminus (the future Waverley station) by the North Bridge. The only possible route for a connecting line was through the narrow valley between the Old and New Towns occupied by the gardens and overlooked by the castle. Six weeks later, the Edinburgh & Glasgow opened an extension through a tunnel and the gardens to join the North British at an end-on station, providing through running but only at the price of four years' dispute with the Proprietors of Princes Street, and their supporters.

After much acrimony during which, among other things, the railway offered to roof the line over, they obtained authorisation, provided it was in a deep cutting with near vertical retaining walls to keep it as narrow as possible, and shielded by a high embankment and parapet screened by trees and shrubs. When the North British later wanted to remove the fifteenth-century Trinity College Chapel to enlarge its yards at Waverley, legislation obliged it to re-erect the building elsewhere. Rather than wait while Edinburgh argued over a suitable site, the company successfully applied for the requirement to be waived in return for a payment of £18,000 to the town council. The NBR knew the nature of its opponents; disputes over the new location dragged on for thirty years before the church was eventually rebuilt, by which time many of the stones had been stolen.[5]

At least the Edinburgh stations were all together at a location that could not have been more central, for the third, known as Canal Street, stood at right angles to the other two at the end of a steeply graded cable-worked tunnel running under the New Town. Built by the Edinburgh Leith & Granton Railway (later the Edinburgh Perth and Dundee), the station was opened in 1847. The company was incorporated into the North British in 1862 which closed Canal Street station in 1868.

Further trouble over the combined Waverley station arose each time the North British wanted to enlarge it or improve the western approaches, but it became so notoriously inadequate far beyond the confines of Edinburgh that complete rebuilding was the only answer – and to make it workable meant quadrupling the line through the gardens. The public that had been so loud in their condemnation of Waverley station now proceeded to put obstacles in the way. Eventually extra land in the gardens was conceded but under the law of servitudes, the Scottish equivalent of 'ancient lights' in England, the height of the new station was restricted to 42ft – at the old one it had been 30ft – which is why the roof is comparatively low. It was opened in 1900. It cannot be said that the railway through Edinburgh is unseen, but now that the smoke and steam have gone it is relatively unobtrusive.

A much worse fate nearly befell Leeds in the 1860s. Its three stations were all termini: Wellington and Central were fairly close but cramped; Marsh Lane was a small station, some distance away on the eastern fringe and mainly used for local traffic. Like Manchester and Glasgow, the city acted as a barrier to through communications, which the North Eastern Railway proposed to remedy by building a new line from Marsh Lane right across the centre of the city to a station close to the infirmary. There was public outcry: Leeds was proud of its street improvements, new buildings and, above all, its magnificent Town Hall completed only a few years before. A committee formed to fight the scheme put forward alternatives, the North Eastern withdrew and produced a new plan for a through station alongside Wellington which won general acceptance, and Leeds New station was opened jointly with the London & North Western in 1869. Both ends were approached by viaducts and embankments, the North Eastern's from Marsh Lane still slicing across the edge of the city, cutting off the old part and the parish church from the shopping and commercial centre but causing less visual and physical damage than the earlier scheme.

The construction of the Great Central Railway across Leicester in 1896–8 aroused similar public excitement at the prospect of demolishing the remains of the medieval castle and the Roman Jewry Wall. The council won a fight to retain a section of Roman pavement over which the railway had to build a viewing room under the station platform.

Transformation of complaints into opposition when it came to agreeing a plan for improvements was not confined to Edinburgh and Leeds. As part of its campaign to promote itself as a resort, Bournemouth had for some years agitated for a central station in place of two small ones on opposite sides of the town. Eventually the London & South Western Railway produced a plan for a connecting line with a station close to the centre, having 'the appearance rather of a winter garden than a railway station' with a 200ft ornamental frontage space. But the Improvement Commissioners and townspeople had second thoughts, decided not to risk the company's enticements and turned it down. The railway was built further north and a new East station opened in 1885, renamed Central but not really central at all.

Sheffield had a long-standing dispute with the Midland Railway, going back to North Midland days of 1840 when George Stephenson had insisted on bypassing the town in favour of an easier and more lucrative route to the east. As a result, where north–south communications were concerned, Sheffield had to suffer being at the end of a branch line from Rotherham for thirty years, and the Midland's name became a dirty word. The council appointed a special committee to discuss a new line through the city, without result, and in 1864 a locally promoted scheme was put in front of Parliament only to be defeated in favour of one of the Midland's own. Sheffield's location in a deep hollow ensured that any line from the south would be difficult and expensive. It was 1870 before the new line from Chesterfield was opened, with a through station in Pond Street, at a cost of well over £1 million. The years of animosity soured Sheffield's relations with the Midland for a long time afterwards. Criticisms of the enlargement and new frontage completed in 1904, making Sheffield station the biggest provincial one on the Midland, were prompted as much by old-established habit as by intrinsic faults.

The Midland was also cast as villain in Nottingham, where the dingy, outgrown station attracted public condemnation for many a year, particularly after the town was put on the company's new main line from London to the north in 1880. It was 1904 before a new station was completed.

Efforts to obtain a more central station in Plymouth were bound up with a desire to break the monopoly of the Great Western, to which end local interests supported the rival London & South Western Railway's steady progression through North Devon and into North Cornwall. The Great Western's terminus at Millbay dated from 1849 and was down near their docks. In 1876 the South Western managed to get into Plymouth over the Great Western's branch from Launceston, which it joined at Lydford, and continued over the Great Western to reach its own new terminus in Devonport. A new joint through station at North Road was opened in the following year, but that, too, was hardly more central than Millbay. In 1883 two bills were promoted for independent lines down the Tamar valley to enter Plymouth from the west, one of which included a new central station near Tavistock Road. With South Western backing it was successful, and in 1890 gave that company a true main line into Plymouth via Devonport where the terminus was altered into a through station. South Western trains from Waterloo went on using North Road, but entered it in the opposite direction to GWR trains from Paddington, a curious feature of the two routes which also occurred where they crossed at St David's station in Exeter. During the hard bargaining that accompanied the political manoeuvring between the companies, the Tavistock Road station scheme disappeared. The Chamber of Commerce had been applying strong pressure for a station in east Plymouth and the South Western opened its own Friary terminus there in 1891. So in the event Plymouth never had its central station.

When railway promotional competition entered its final phase towards the end of the last century, the best routes and sites had already been taken. Expansionist companies like the Midland and the Great Central had to undertake highly expensive engineering works, and we have seen what it cost the Midland to force a direct line through Sheffield, while the Great Central added to its self-inflicted penury by building across the heart of Nottingham and Leicester and through north-west London in order to secure competitive station sites. One of the most ambitious programmes was intended to be the final refinement of the Midland Railway's new trunk route from London to Scotland, completed by the opening throughout of the Kettering–Nottingham line in 1880. In 1898 the company gained authorisation for a new main line from Royston, midway between Sheffield and Leeds, through Dewsbury to Bradford where it would join the existing line out to the north. It involved a two mile tunnel among other heavy construction works, but would have shortened the distance and would certainly have put Bradford on the railway map – at the expense of Leeds. Because Bradford's two stations were in effect at the ends of branch lines, albeit important ones, the city had always suffered from lack of through services. Facing each other less than ¼ mile apart, the termini formed the supremely ludicrous example of ill-conceived duplication and there had been several unsuccessful proposals for a link going as far back as 1846. However, having reached Dewsbury and built a branch to Huddersfield, the plan got no further. It reappeared in a modified scheme in 1911, using part of the Lancashire & Yorkshire's line and involving construction of a viaduct across the centre of Bradford with a new high-level station. Bradford Corporation supported it with an offer of £8,000 a year off the rates for twenty years, but then World War I broke out and, despite successive assurances right up to the 1940s that it would still be built, the line never materialised. It was the last of the grand gestures but, had it been completed, would surely have been the greatest railway white elephant.

4

Gateways

To consider the first purpose-built terminals we have to go back to the opening of the Liverpool & Manchester Railway in 1830. The stations at Liverpool and Manchester were unpretentious, although Crown Street at Liverpool had a certain plain Georgian dignity. The two-storey building was long and narrow with a prominent cornice hiding a low-pitched roof. The entrance appears to have been in the end wall facing Liverpool, sheltered by a wooden porch. A wall and gates separated the forecourt from the street. Facing the rails a flat canopy was supported on columns close to the edge of a very low, narrow platform which seems to have been of little help in boarding trains as it stopped well short of the track. The canopy in turn supported a wooden roof over the lines (Fig 3).

At the Manchester end of the line, the station in Liverpool Road had less appeal. As the railway terminated on arches and the station was entered from the street below, there was little scope for architectural treatment other than surface embellishment which was applied sparingly. The stuccoed front was heavily rusticated on the ground floor, and ashlar stone was used for the door casings and deep, flat lintels. The first- and second-class entrances had paired incised pilasters on either side, repeated on the tripartite window above the first class, in front of which an elegant stone plinth carried a sundial. The roof was concealed by a stone parapet. Upstairs at rail level passengers appear to have boarded their trains in the open. A shed with one open side was built further up Liverpool Road in 1831, beyond the passenger building, for storing coaches.

Liverpool in the 1830s was expanding fast. The city had wealth and culture, and its thriving seaport trade ensured that throughout most of the nineteenth century it could pour money into rebuilding the centre, with new streets and buildings which, to a considerable extent, reflected a good taste not found in comparable cities elsewhere. After London, the corporation of Liverpool was the richest in England; hence its willingness to part with £2,000 towards the façade of the Liverpool & Manchester's new station in Lime Street. It was important that it should be good enough to face the new concert hall being planned, and £2,000 was nothing against the £400,000 that St George's Hall eventually cost.

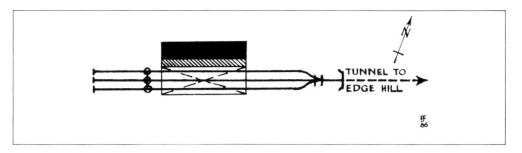

Fig 3. The earliest type of terminal: Liverpool Crown Street, 1830

Lime Street would be, in the words of the directors, 'the great public entrance into Liverpool', and its classical stone façade was both handsome and practical. Along the screen wall, Corinthian columns supported a heavy entablature, broken by four equidistant Roman arches surmounted by high, corniced parapets, one containing the city's coat of arms. Two of the arches led into open courtyards on each side of the train shed and the other two into offices of which the screen formed the front, lit by series of windows between the columns. It was completed in 1837, nearly a year after the station was brought into use, and effectively masked the adjoining train shed and station buildings at the rear.

Six Liverpool architects seem to have been concerned with the Liverpool & Manchester in its early years. The city's rapid growth and prosperity attracted able men, and the corporation itself retained its own surveyor and architect. At the time the Liverpool & Manchester was being built, John Foster Jr held the post. He had a large practice, had been engineer to several dock schemes and was responsible for a number of new public buildings. On the death of his father in 1824, he succeeded him as surveyor and architect to the corporation, and in turn was succeeded in 1835 by Joseph Franklin who also was responsible for much public work in the city. John Cunningham was a third prominent local architect who did work for the railway, and the other three were Daniel Stewart, Thomas Haig and Arthur Holme.

Carol L. V. Meeks in *The Railway Station* suggests that Foster may have been responsible for Crown Street. The railway company appointed him Principal Engineer on the Wapping Tunnel contract under George Stephenson in 1827, but possibly because of disagreement he relinquished it after a couple of months. He designed the Edge Hill engine house exteriors and the famous Moorish Arch, and some two months after the opening he and Daniel Stewart provided drawings for Crown Street's overall roof. Hitchcock suggests George Stephenson as the more likely designer of Crown Street, but in the light of Stephenson's usual practice of leaving that kind of work to someone else, it seems improbable.

In Manchester, Haig and Franklin designed a number of warehouses, followed in 1835–7 by the new arrival station (see Chapter 6). They also designed the second Edge Hill station, opened in 1835. It bears a striking resemblance to the office block at Lime Street which can be seen on a contemporary engraving through an arch in the screen wall. Foster designed the screen, while Cunningham is credited with the station offices and, with Holme, the overall roof, in both cases subject to Foster's approval. There are similarities in the deeply incised rustication at Liverpool Road and Edge Hill, although the buildings were built in different styles and materials, while there is a similarity in outline between Edge Hill and the Lime Street offices, if nothing more. So the identity of the architects of Liverpool Road and Crown Street is obscure. Liverpool Road could have been by Haig with or without Franklin (or vice versa), possibly by Cunningham, or by Foster. Haig does not seem to have been associated with railway work at the Liverpool end, but Crown Street could have been done by either of the other three. What does seem probable from the evidence is that Foster had overall responsibility for all the architectural work.[1]

The whole purpose of the Lime Street façade was to create a symbolic gateway to the railway, using the Roman triumphal arch as its theme. It was quite deliberately expressed in the classical terms of the Renaissance because contemporary thought still saw in the buildings of ancient Greece and Rome the representation of great and noble concepts, which was exactly how the railways were presented. Hard-headed though they were, many of the men reshaping the country were also incurable romantics in the spirit of their times, and there was no denying that the railways were achievements without previous parallel. They eclipsed everything that had gone before and completely revolutionised society. It was therefore considered entirely fitting that railway buildings should become the symbols of the new age.

The idea of the triumphal classical gateway was expressed at its most magnificent at Euston. The directors of the London & Birmingham Railway saw it as the beginning of 'the Grand Avenue for travelling between the midland and northern parts of the kingdom . . . well adapted for the national character of the undertaking', which is how they put it to their shareholders. This notion of the whole nation's involvement was widely shared. Napoleon had been defeated and Britain's rapidly spreading influence was confirming her status as leader of the world. Why, then, should it not be said that, in the words of John Britton in 1839, 'the Railway is a great national undertaking and . . . the national character is, in some respects, involved in the execution of the whole'?[2]

The Doric Arch or propylaeum, to use its correct name, marked not only a new form of transport far speedier than anything previously dreamed of and the gateway to the north where so much of the country's wealth was being created; it also symbolised man's conquest of nature in building the massive earthworks, tunnels and viaducts to take the railway. People flocked to see it. 'When Euston was first built, it was regarded not as a railway station but as a spectacle,' recalled an anonymous author in 1896.[3] In our own time Meeks,

Gateways 1: the Doric Arch at Euston in the 1920s (*Author's Collection*)

writing in 1956, thought it thrilling, despite over a century's grime, mutilation and accretions, and Sir Albert Richardson in 1939 considered that the general effect, devised to harmonise with C. A. Busby's Euston Road terraces opposite, was superb.[4]

The theme of a monumental screen front had been developed by earlier architects. Robert Adam's Admiralty screen and Sir John Soane's treatment of the Bank of England were examples of a concept that was well understood. The Lime Street façade was its first application to a railway station; Euston was the most monumental, for which the architect, Philip Hardwick, chose Greek rather than Roman styling. Since the rebuilding of Covent Garden Theatre in 1809, Greek architecture had undergone something of a revival, its severe lines suggesting a dependable solidity mixed with discipline and economy, a concept ideally suited to the railway. The arch was the giant centre-piece of a long composition comprising distinct elements: the portico itself, 72ft high, with an attached lodge on each side, followed by two more beyond. The spaces between the lodges were filled with tall, ornamental iron gates and railings, forming a total screen 300ft long. The four great columns of the portico were hollow, 8ft 6in in diameter at the base and 44ft 2in high, surmounted by a deep entablature containing a cornice with projecting lions' heads along the sides, a true Doric frieze decorated with triglyphs, and a hollow pediment containing offices and store rooms lit by skylights. They were reached by a spiral staircase inside one of the columns.

Philip Hardwick was architect to the Duke of Wellington, and among his more important works were the Goldsmiths' Hall and, after Euston, the New Hall and Library at Lincoln's Inn, but it is for the Doric Arch that he is best remembered. He also designed the gates which were made by J. J. Bramah of lock fame. A hard sandstone was used for the masonry, brought by canal, river and sea from quarries at Bramley Fall near Leeds. The contractors were William, Thomas and Lewis Cubitt, and when William was embarking on King's Cross station in 1850–1 he remarked that 'a good station could be built at King's Cross for less than the cost of the ornamental archway at Euston Square'. The façade cost £35,000 and attracted other critics, among them John Ruskin and the fanatical Gothic revivalist A. W. N. Pugin, who called it 'Brobdignagian absurdity'.

Unlike Lime Street, the Euston screen was detached from the station itself, and the same principle was adopted at the northern terminus at Curzon Street, Birmingham, where Hardwick designed another grand entrance as a counterpart to Euston. The Curzon Street block had a more practical purpose in housing the railway's offices. It comprised a lofty three-storey building fronted by four impressive Ionic columns, 45ft tall, mounted in pairs on two rectangular plinths and supporting a plain entablature, dentilled cornice and a parapet concealing a low-pitched roof. In the centre a handsome doorway and fanlight surmounted by the railway company's coat of arms gave on to a spacious square hall running the height of the building and lit by a lantern light in the roof. Stairs and landings gave access to rooms on all four sides. The rear elevation was rather different, with square corner pilasters and two Ionic columns flanking a plain doorway in the centre. Hardwick's original design included a small archway or lodge attached to each side of the main building, flanked by iron gates and railings, but only one was built, (p 22).

Early in 1839, some nine months after the London & Birmingham's Curzon Street station was opened, the Grand Junction Railway extended its line from a temporary terminus at Vauxhall to a new station alongside. Again the screen technique was used, and Joseph Franklin from Liverpool was brought in to design it. The company was controlled by Liverpool financiers and Franklin's façade, though shorter and less elaborate, bore a striking resemblance to Foster's at Lime Street. Four large Roman-arched doorways were set in the stone wall, interspersed with pilasters and niches under a deep cornice and parapet. The lower portion was heavily rusticated, with plain ashlar above. Although not a patch on the London & Birmingham's entrance, it was a dignified composition.

In many ways the triumphal arches and porticoes erected by the early railways can be regarded as the final fling of eighteenth- and early nineteenth-century classicism before the full onslaught of Victorian Italian-

Mocatta's 1841 Palladian frontage at Brighton is almost hidden by the iron *porte-cochère* in front and overwhelmed by the train shed behind, both built in 1883. Photographed in 1968 (*Author*)

ate and Gothic. A much more modest but nonetheless handsome five-arched arcade was designed by Sir William Tite for the entrance to Nine Elms station, the metropolitan terminus of the London & Southampton Railway opened in 1838. The arches and columns were emphasised by rusticated wings, lodges and ornamental gateways on each side. At Southampton Tite designed a much grander entrance, again employing a five-bay arcade but this time surmounted by an elegant balustrade and clock, all part of a handsome three-storey block with prominently pedimented window hoods and a deep cornice. As R. A. Williams commented in his history of the London & South Western Railway, it was as though the station proclaimed that the railway was Southampton-born and London merely its outpost. It was opened in 1840.

David Mocatta expressed the same Palladian theme in a larger and more emphatic manner at the southern terminus of the London & Brighton Railway opened in the following year. His Brighton station had a projecting arcade of nine Roman arches across the front of a long two-storey block with attics at each end and a balustrade and central clock between them. The arcade was continued by balustraded wings forming a columned terrace extending around each end of the building. The columns were of hollow iron painted a stone colour to resemble blue lias, and the external stucco was

'neatly jointed to imitate stone'. Decoration of the clock mounting, by a
sculptor named Hemming, was specified as 'representing some emblem
suitable to the occasion or the arms of the company'.[5] Viewed from the town
below, it must have made an imposing sight and was well in keeping with
developing Brighton.

The nobility of Euston found a quick imitator in William Parsons' design
for the first Midland Counties Railway station in Campbell Street, Leicester.
Parsons, the Leicestershire county surveyor who later did more railway
work, used a five-bay portico with Tuscan columns as the centre-piece for
his two-storey station building which had small flanking lodges attached.
Although doubtless it owed some of its splendour to the fact that it housed
the company's headquarters, it was even so a remarkably handsome
compliment to Leicester, although later additions spoiled its symmetry. The
same railway's first station at Nottingham, a terminus opened in 1839, was
much smaller but still vaguely classical. A two-storey frontage block had side
pilasters, cornice and pediment. It lasted less than ten years, being replaced
by a through station in 1848 after the line was extended to Lincoln. This
second station was larger and had a 180ft long single-storey frontage,

Gateways 2: the Euston style at Leicester. The Doric portico and façade at Campbell Street station of the Midland Counties Railway shortly before demolition, c1890. The right-hand wing was a later addition (*Leicester Museum of Technology*)

classically inspired with a projecting five-bay colonnaded flat portico on Tuscan columns. In outline it was not dissimilar to Lincoln St Marks, opened in 1846, with detail differences but perhaps by the same designer.

One of the interesting things about early railway architecture is that so much of it, certainly in the provinces, was executed by relatively little-known local men. The great names do appear here and there – Hardwick and Tite we have already encountered, the latter being a particularly prolific railway architect – but in general the designers of stations were not well known outside their own districts, reflecting the local nature of the earlier lines. The designers of four important stations right at the end of the classical era certainly fall within that category.

James Collie was the designer of Glasgow's first purpose-built terminus, in Bridge Street, for the Glasgow & Paisley Joint Line Committee, opened in 1840 and completed in the following year. The façade featured a Doric portico *in antis* (that is, recessed into the main building), which had two storeys. The portico was some 65ft long, the four columns were 30ft high and the frieze was decorated with alternate triglyphs and wreaths. Glasgow would not gain a better station for thirty years.

In 1844 George Hudson purchased the Brandling Junction Railway in County Durham, running from Tyneside to Monkwearmouth on the north bank of the Wear opposite Sunderland. In the following year he was elected MP for Sunderland, to celebrate which he erected a new station designed by Thomas Moore of Bishopwearmouth. Of all the stations built on Hudson's lines, it was probably the finest in scale and execution, a great three-bay Ionic portico two storeys high flanked by lower wings curving back to colonnaded walls on either side. It seemed quite out of place in Monkwearmouth, even more so today, and ceased to be a terminus in 1879 when the line was extended across the river to Sunderland and its importance was much reduced. It was closed in 1967 and is now a railway museum.

It was not often that rival railways erected a great monument to celebrate

Gateways 3: the massive portico at Huddersfield in 1972, after cleaning (*Author*)

the ending of their differences, but that was the reason behind Huddersfield's immense and splendidly classical station, ranking with Euston and New-castle as the finest in the country and, as we have seen in Chapter 3, standing proudly at the head of a street vista that could hardly be bettered. A bitter quarrel between the Huddersfield & Manchester Railway & Canal Company and the Manchester & Leeds Railway was resolved by an agreement, part of which was that the two companies should jointly build the railway through Huddersfield, including the station. James Pigott Pritchett of York and his son, James Pigott Junior, carried out the ambitious design. Pritchett Senior was architect to Earl Fitzwilliam who laid the foundation stone of the immense five-bay Corinthian portico and centre block, 68ft high, the latter having giant pedimented end-gables matching the one on the portico itself. On each side a long, elegant colonnade reached out to a matching terminal pavilion, effectively screening the train shed, in length totalling 416ft – longer than Euston and almost as high. The station was opened in 1847 but not completed until 1850, by which time the owning companies had respectively become parts of the London & North Western and Lancashire & Yorkshire railways. Rather oddly, although the arms of the LYR appear on one pavilion, the other displays those of the earlier partner, the Huddersfield & Manchester.

Now that the Euston Arch has gone, only one other classical station ranks in size with Huddersfield, although not with the same degree of elegance. If the original Liverpool Lime Street façade formed the overture to British classical station symbolism, then Newcastle Central represented the final chorus. Building of the train sheds started in 1847 and took three years, but the frontage took much longer. The result was one of the most monumental of all our stations. The architect, John Dobson, was born not far away in North Shields and was a pupil of the neo-classical architect Sir Robert Smirke. He was also influenced by the work of Sir John Vanbrugh whose great house at nearby Seaton Delaval he restored after a fire in 1822. He went on to design many of Newcastle's finest buildings and streets in partnership with Richard Grainger in the 1830s, work that has been compared with that of John Nash in London.

The site for the station faced Neville Street which was widened for the purpose, and here Dobson designed an immense frontage 600ft long. Projecting from it were two 200ft long arcades 35ft deep, each of seven Roman arches, flanking a striking central feature, a large projecting seven-bay portico 200ft long and 70ft deep. The arches were separated by coupled Doric columns, and on the portico each pair bore a separate entablature supporting a seated figure. The arcade entablatures were plainer and continuous, and the undersides of the arches were decorated with square panels. In describing the principles inspiring his design, Dobson set out the guiding tenets that influenced Foster, Hardwick, the Pritchetts and others who adopted classical forms for their stations:

Gateways 4: Thomas Prosser's entrance to Newcastle Central in 1973, a modification of John Dobson's original design (*Author*)

> Railway buildings ought to do much for architecture, being quite a new class of structures erected for purposes unknown until the present age . . . they suggest or ought to suggest a character of their own and fresh combinations in designs; and being generally on an extensive scale, they offer opportunities that have hitherto been of rare occurrence. They are, moreover, especially public works – structures constantly seen by thousands and tens of thousands of persons, and might therefore do much towards improving the taste of the public. That they have done so, or have been calculated to do so, cannot, we fear, be asserted for them generally. In more than one instance, expression has been falsified or forfeited by the adoption of some style intended to be reminiscent of mediaevalism – of times whose spirit and whose institutions contrast very strongly with the present railway age, in which it is either our good luck or our misfortune to live . . . for what class of mediaeval structure are there that have aught in common with railway stations and termini?[6]

It was a counterblast to Pugin and the thrusting Gothicists (Chapter 5). The design won Dobson an award at the Paris Exhibition of 1858, and a water colour by him was exhibited in the Royal Academy in 1850. The station was described in *The Athenaeum*[7] as 'equal to Vanbrugh's grandest designs, and if executed will be the finest thing of its kind in Europe. Newcastle may be proud of its architect.' Alas, it was not to be executed as Dobson originally intended.

The station was being financed jointly by the York, Newcastle & Berwick and Newcastle & Carlisle railways. Prudham stone was used, and when the walls were about half way up the first company decided as an economy measure to move its offices there from York. It had been formed not long before by the merger of two smaller companies and was paying much the larger share of the cost. Dobson was asked to redesign and economise, which he did by replacing the proposed arcade with offices and reducing the amount of ornamental work on the portico. *The Civil Engineer & Architect's Journal* commented, somewhat tartly: 'The designs have been tampered with, and have suffered accordingly.'[8] When Queen Victoria came to open the station in 1850, the portico still had to be built, despite the expenditure of close on £100,000, and some ten years elapsed before Thomas Prosser finished it. The companies owning Newcastle Central became part of the North Eastern Railway in 1854 and Prosser was the new company's first architect. Although his portico was similar in dimensions and outline to the original design, it was plainer and heavier, lacking Dobson's delicate touch. Dobson, who for some time had suffered ill health, was intensely grieved but, despite his disappointment, Newcastle Central remains in the forefront of British railway architecture and his greatest memorial.

5

Matters of Style

Concurrently with the massive grandeur of eighteenth- and early nineteenth-century neo-classical architecture, there flourished a related but more humanistic school that produced buildings loosely called 'Italian' in style. It frequently incorporated classical elements but was essentially more domestic in character. Brick could be used where it was available, reserving stone for dressings and decoration, which reduced costs and thereby added to the appeal Italianate styling undoubtedly aroused in the designers of public buildings, particularly railway architects. There was the added advantage that the style could be used with equal effect in small buildings and large without losing that dignity considered essential by many of the early railways. Motifs from various styles other than Gothic were freely mixed, generally employing round-headed arches to produce a cheap yet impressive building, while arched or classical arcades lent themselves admirably to platform shelters and entrances. Italianate stations proliferated during the 1840s and up to about 1855 with innumerable variations, to such an extent that they were dubbed 'the English railway style'. The villa theme was particularly popular.

London's first terminus, the London & Greenwich Railway station at London Bridge, opened in 1836, was literally the end of the line, for nothing more was provided than iron gates at the end of the viaduct on which it ran all the way from Greenwich. Tickets were bought in the company's separate offices close by, a building of some merit to be considered in Chapter 9. A most impressive Corinthian arch was designed which might have been second to Euston had it been built,[1] but otherwise that was it until 1844 when, in partnership with a joint committee of the London & Croydon, London & Brighton and South Eastern Railways (which in the meantime had arrived on the same site), a new station was opened. Appropriately it was jointly designed, too: Henry Roberts acted for the joint committee and George Smith for the London & Greenwich. Smith was one of the City of London's district surveyors with a practice in the city; Roberts also had an office in London and is chiefly remembered for his later work in improving working-class housing.

The building they designed was enthusiastically welcomed by the *Illustrated London News* which described it as in the Italian palazzo style, 'the prevailing one in the company's buildings' (which company?), 'the choice having been determined by the convenience of the general arrangements, its cheapness, and the suitability of its picturesque decorations, to the bustling character of a railway line'. Italianate lent itself to assymetrical forms, demonstrated at London Bridge by placing a 71ft high clock tower in the form of a campanile at one end; 'a striking and appropriate feature', according to the *ILN*. Thomas notes the resemblance of the campanile to those at Osborne House, Queen Victoria's Isle of Wight residence built in 1845–51, which itself was derived from the work done for the Duke of Sutherland by Sir Charles Barry who did so much to promote Italian Renaissance styling. Unfortunately for London Bridge, only about half of the 128ft long building was completed, and that only lasted until 1850. Its successors will be discussed in Chapter 6.

Disagreement with the Greenwich company led the South Eastern and the London & Croydon to build a separate terminus in the Old Kent Road nearly a mile to the south. They called it Bricklayers Arms after a nearby inn, and optimistically advertised it as serving the West End. It only lasted as a passenger station from 1844 to 1852, although royal trains continued to use it for some years. The entrance was through a brick Italianate screen across the head of the station designed by Lewis Cubitt, and although contemporary engravings over-enhance the appearance it was quite notable, comprising a series of arches topped by an unusual pantiled cornice, with a mildly Baroque clock in the middle on which perched a fanciful little turret. It was in its description of the Bricklayers Arms screen wall that the *Illustrated London News* gave railway Italianate its appellation. Along the departure side, the station offices were fronted by a Doric colonnade.

The style had certainly caught on. George Townsend Andrews used it in a fairly severe and restricted manner in grey brick with stone trim at York's first station of 1841, where his original two-storey design for the Tanner Row

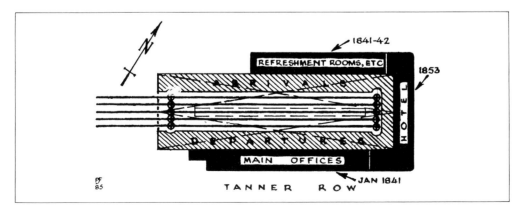

Fig 4. Development of G. T. Andrews's first York station, showing the original 1841 layout with later buildings. By 1853 platform extensions had been added and the train shed altered

elevation had a third storey added, probably shortly after 1860.[2] The ground-floor centre-piece comprised rusticated stone round-headed openings, enlivened by flanking series of Tuscan columns *in antis*. Ranged along the opposite arrival platform a shorter, plainer red-brick two-storey block was added a few months later, and then in 1851–3 a three-storey hotel was erected across the head of the station, very plain, almost Georgian in appearance (Fig 4). Andrews was one of a small number of architects which tended to specialise in railway work. A pupil of P. F. Robinson, who was noted for his country house and estate work, Andrews won a Society of Arts premium in 1824 and two years later set up in York where he quickly won the patronage of George Hudson. Ultimately it was his undoing, as after Hudson's fall in 1849 Andrews, too, encountered financial difficulties resulting from his railway investments and was forced to sell his art collection to pay off creditors. He died in 1855 at the age of fifty-one after a prolific career in Yorkshire and the North East which included office buildings, churches, hotels and many railway stations. He was Sheriff of York in 1846–7.

In 1844 Andrews' Gateshead terminus was opened for the Newcastle & Darlington Junction Railway, completing a through route from London to the Tyne. The main building had a long single-storey façade with a projecting Ionic colonnade, forming the centre-piece of a restrained Palladian composition which must have been well in keeping with Grainger and Dobson's work across the river in Newcastle. Like Andrews' York station, it was interesting for the manner in which he integrated the buildings and the train shed. Andrews was much more ambitious in his Hull Paragon station of 1848. Here he forcefully punctuated the long, gold-grey ashlar façade with two large Italianate blocks, one three-storeys high and fairly plain, the other lower but lavishly endowed with a projecting ground floor with coupled engaged Doric columns forming a colonnade beneath a terrace at first-floor level, overlooked by pedimented windows and pilasters and surrounded by an elegant balustrade. The colonnade was later infilled with windows. Between the two blocks he inserted a charmingly matching porch.

The Italian style particularly lent itself to stations in elevated locations where it could occupy a commanding position. London Bridge was like this, and similar advantage was taken of the site of Manchester London Road, opened in 1842, where an enormous rectangular doorway, almost the full height of the heavily rusticated building, with matching quoins and pantiled roof, made a powerful composition looking down the sloping approach. Inside the station immediately behind it there appear to have been some offices, the refreshment room and an engine stabling area, copying Brunel's idea at Bristol,[3] while the public entrance was through a colonnaded block down the side, like Bricklayers Arms.

Sancton Wood, architect to the Eastern Counties Railway and other lines in eastern England and in Ireland, took advantage of an elevated railway terminus at the second Bishopsgate station, London, of 1848–9, to put his new Italianate frontage block at the head of a pair of balustraded stairs leading up from the centre to doorways in the two corner blocks, set off by a semi-circular forecourt enclosed by a low wall. They gave an air of quiet distinction to what was otherwise a fairly dull building, and once more the public entrance and offices were at the side. The same effect was gained at the palazzo-styled Tithebarn Street station, Liverpool (later named Exchange), opened by the Lancashire & Yorkshire and East Lancashire railways in 1850. It was fronted by a balustraded terrace approached from below by a single staircase which left it looking unbalanced. The *Illustrated London News* said the building was 'second in architectural effect to none in Liverpool', a statement open to question, and the whole place was completed in six months, probably to designs by Sir John Hawkshaw, the L&Y company's engineer.

A few years earlier Sir William Tite had been active in the same city, designing the second Lime Street station entrance block. He retained Foster's earlier screen but built a new range of buildings alongside the station in Lord Nelson Street, completed in 1849; 270ft long, they incorporated the now familiar features of pedimented windows, dentilled cornice and rustication. Between the projecting end-blocks he inserted a long Doric colonnade of eighteen columns, supporting a balustraded cornice at first-floor level, thus creating a more effective entrance arcade than the customary canopy.

The Leeds & Bradford Railway's 1846 terminus at Bradford Market Street was much the best of the city's original stations. It had a modest Venetian front with a hooded clock in the centre of the parapet, contrasting with the Lancashire & Yorkshire's nearby Exchange station of 1850, a poor place which seems to have had no frontage at all, any more than its successor had. Bradford's third station, the 1855 Adolphus Street terminus of the Leeds, Bradford & Halifax Junction Railway, had by far the largest façade, a three-storey block in a weak Italianate style with a little central pediment.

What might be termed Glasgow's second proper station, Queen Street of 1842, was nothing compared with the Doric style of Bridge Street, yet the main entrance had certain pretensions and might even have been monumental had the Edinburgh & Glasgow Railway pursued its ideas for a grand archway in 1855–6. As it was, it built a short screen giving on to a small glass-roofed courtyard in front of the booking office, made up of three Roman arches flanked by two smaller ones set in rusticated ashlar stone, with a cornice and balustrade above. Had it not been for the unequal height of the arches on the steep slope of Dundas Street, they could have looked reasonably imposing. Glasgow lost another early opportunity for a handsome station when Tite's plans for a central Caledonian Railway station in Dunlop Street in 1848 fell foul of the Admiralty's requirement of a swing bridge across the Clyde, making the whole scheme too expensive. Tite produced an Italianate design with a handsome Roman classical colonnade and two porticoes which certainly would have put Bridge Street in the shade.

Further north, the second Dundee West station, built in 1862, had a two-storey Italianate centre-piece topped by a balustrade and a small central pediment underneath a Florentine clock turret. Roman arches and windows in the ground floor of the flanking offices and screen wall made it a straggling composition that lasted less than thirty years before being rebuilt (Chapter 9).

So far we have been concerned with terminals. Providing the necessary accommodation at a through station usually meant a long building flanking the platform, which introduced problems of composition. At Manchester Victoria (1844), the Manchester & Leeds Railway's designer overcame the difficulty by adding three projecting blocks, originally intended to be linked by colonnades but substituted by recessed canopies on bold brackets articulated with the fenestration behind. It was unusual and effective. The blocks were carefully detailed and the larger central one, which had a clock in the middle of the parapet, still survives with an upper storey added later. At Cambridge, opened in the same year, an outstanding degree of elegance was achieved by making the frontage an arcade of fifteen arches. The arms of the colleges are displayed in the spandrels, possibly a gesture by the Eastern Counties Railway to the university which had strongly opposed the railway. Although Sancton Wood was the company's architect, Francis Thompson appears to have been involved in the design.

Thompson had built the long façade to the Tri-junct station at Derby in 1840, totalling 1050ft and mostly comprising a 40ft high screen wall alongside the train shed. Such length combined with low height would have been monotonous were it not for the carefully spaced round-headed openings placed along it with different widths and treatment, and varied parapet heights broken by coats of arms and other motifs. As it was, the effect was of considerable elegance, culminating in the bold projection of the central two-storey entrance and office block that had a lofty two-stage arch surmounted by a deep parapet and large armorial bearings. The work was carried out in local red brick with stone dressings.

Francis Thompson was responsible for some of the most sensitive early railway station architecture, particularly his small stations on the North Midland and Chester & Holyhead railways. He was born in Woodbridge, Suffolk, and his father, grandfather, uncle and younger brother were all architects or architect builders. During his lifetime he made two journeys to the United States, but his work other than on railways – some of which still remains to be unravelled – is as yet undiscovered.[4]

When Thompson turned to design Chester General joint station in 1846–50 he used the same theme as at Derby. The façade screen was the same length and, like Derby, was symmetrical but much more intricately detailed in

The central portion of Francis Thompson's façade at Chester in 1983; this is less than half the total length (G. W. Buck)

Venetian mode. The brick is darker, and the central block has a flat canopy between two tall projecting blocks with corner towers. The arcaded walls stretching away on either side have lower complementary towers toward the ends, and pantiled roofs complete the effect, which compared with Derby was one of greater delicacy.

Although Italian and classical styles predominated during the first two decades of railway architecture, not all designers thought in terms of ancient Greece or Rome, or the Renaissance. The Gothic Revival was by now well under way, a movement that began in the mid-eighteenth century and strove for a 'romantic' effect. Its chief proponent was A. W. N. Pugin, an eccentric who put Gothic styling into a straitjacket of medieval purity that admitted no deviations. Pugin saw it in religious terms; any other style was pagan and he was the chief inspirer of Victorian Gothic churches, although his strict principles were frequently debased. Other architects enthusiastically seized on Gothic for buildings of all kinds and developed it in a way that horrified Pugin, by seeking inspiration from castles and Tudor manor houses as well as ecclesiastical architecture. Later on, under the influence of John Ruskin, the addition of naturalistic decorative treatment became popular, and in artistic circles a 'Battle of the Styles' between the advocates of Gothicism and classicism raged for years.

For his Great Western wayside stations between Paddington and Bristol, I. K. Brunel favoured attractive Tudor styling for one of the functional, basically standard designs which characterised the line. The principal stations, on the other hand, though varied, tended to be mediocre by comparison; only Bath and Bristol received special treatment. The line through Bath was prominent and great care was taken to ensure that as far as possible it fitted into the city. Cuttings, bridges and viaducts were given classical or Gothic forms and the station, opened in 1840, has an

Railway Tudor 1: Brunel's façade at Bristol Temple Meads, from an early engraving by S. C. Jones, showing the company's horse bus bringing passengers out from the city (*City of Bristol*)

asymmetrical main frontage on the town or up side of the line, which here is elevated. The building is curved at one end to accommodate the awkward curve of the viaduct, and has a fine range of radial fanlights over the ground-floor door openings. Above, mullioned windows, including an oriel over the main doorway, are surmounted by a parapet with three Dutch gables. The up-side entrance is quite plain, and naturally all is executed in Bath stone; an unexciting composition, and odd in expressing Tudor-Jacobean forms rather than Georgian or classical, as though Brunel considered Bath Abbey the more important influence, but nevertheless a station about which Bath could not complain.

Brunel's crenellated Elizabethan office block at Bristol Temple Meads, fronting on to Temple Gate, was the first attempt to express the grand station theme in the Gothic idiom. It is said that he was inspired by Thomas Rickman's New Court extension to St John's College, Cambridge, completed a decade earlier. Equally, his station could have been intended to complement Tudor Bristol, of which a certain amount survived, while Brunel, always the innovator and rarely a traditionalist, would undoubtedly wish to be at the forefront of anything new, which Gothic then was. As a grand gesture it did not equal Euston and the other classical stations that followed, but its turrets, battlements and flanking archways did form a satisfyingly appropriate prelude to Brunel's magnificent train shed behind and, indeed, the character of most of the line all the way to London. If Brunel was in fact trying to keep up with the times, it is ironic that Pugin, leading proponent of the Gothic Revival, mocked it as a 'mere caricature', scorning its 'mock-castellated work . . . shields without bearings, ugly mouldings, no-meaning projections and all sort of unaccountable breaks . . . a design at once costly and offensive and full of pretension'. Pugin, despite his fanatical belief in Gothic architecture, did not limit his strictures to the despised classical; that which served no function was equally inadmissible however it was clothed. At Temple Meads maybe he was right; Henry-Russell Hitchcock half suggests he was. Certainly Brunel was better at embellishing pure engineering forms than attempting architecture for the sake of it, but for all that his Bristol frontage is an important and fascinating example of the exuberance of the early railway builders and of Brunel in particular.

Britain had to wait eight years for its next large Gothic station which Sir William Tite essayed in grey sandstone at Carlisle for the Lancaster & Carlisle and Caledonian railways. Both lines were engineered by Joseph Locke, Thomas Brassey was the contractor and Tite attended to the architecture – a triumvirate responsible for a number of important railways at home and in France. Carlisle was opened in 1847 but not completed until the following

Railway Tudor 2: the centre-piece of William Tite's frontage at Carlisle, in 1979 (*Author*)

year. It stands close to the city walls opposite the Citadel – Sir Robert Smirke's assize courts built in 1810–11 – and the station's long, irregular Tudor façade keeps them good company. The detailing is finer and more elaborate than at Bristol, with more striking features, such as an octagonal lantern turret, a five-bay entrance arcade containing the royal arms and those of the owning companies and a line of octagonal crenellated shafts punctuating the parapet. To one side, masked by the later County Hotel, is an interesting bay window giving on to the former first-class refreshment room.

In the following year Perth General station was opened, in which the Caledonian was also a partner. Tite designed it with so many similarities to Carlisle that it seems that the two jobs were run completely in tandem. Perth is a little less elaborate with a slightly lower turret, and was Tite's third attempt. The earlier designs were considerably more ornate than Carlisle, with two different towers (one with tall corner turrets) but an almost identical arcade. Both were rejected, doubtless on grounds of cost as their elaborations would have been extremely expensive, which perhaps led Tite to produce a modified version of Carlisle in which the arcade was dropped in favour of an iron *porte-cochère*.

A local man, T. K. Penson of Oswestry, designed a very fine two-storey Tudor building in the collegiate manner for the joint station at Shrewsbury, opened in 1849, with twisted pepper-pot shafts rising above the parapet and a prominent clock tower containing a double oriel window. Everything is there, right down to the gargoyles, and when a further storey was needed in 1903 it was ingeniously added below in such a way that today we can

Railway Tudor 3: Tite's repeat performance at Perth, photographed before 1884 when the station was extended and the frontage hidden by new platforms. The building alongside the 'Dundee Dock' is on the far left and the original train shed can be seen on the right (*Perth & Kinross District Libraries*)

scarcely discern the difference. If anything, the extra height enhanced the building's appearance.

Tudor and Jacobean styling marked out all the earlier stations on the North Staffordshire Railway, including its headquarters at Stoke-on-Trent, opened in 1850, where the station frontage exhibits a splendid display of Jacobean motifs in dark red brick and stone. Beneath the central one of three Dutch gables, a large and elaborate bay window almost blocks a terrace formed by the top of an arcade of engaged Tuscan columns in which the Roman-arched openings have radial glazing. Intricately pierced parapets, elaborate mouldings and diaper brickwork lend a spirit of richness to the whole building which is complemented by the railway's North Stafford Hotel on the opposite side of the square. They were the work of Henry Hunt.

In complete contrast, the end of the railways' pioneering period saw the boldest stroke of station design then attempted and, in this country, not repeated since. The example of using a façade to express the profile of the train shed was set by the Gare de l'Est in Paris, built between 1847 and 1852, starting a fashion widely followed in France, Germany and the United States but completely foreign to British stylists, literally as well as figuratively. Only King's Cross and, to a lesser extent, Fenchurch Street, used the idea in this country. (Manchester Central and the small Dundee East cannot really be

George Berkeley's façade at Fenchurch Street in 1956, profiling the train shed roof behind (*Author*)

said to have proper façades – see Chapter 8.) Indeed the functional severity of King's Cross was criticised by contemporaries who regarded architecture in relation to stations as a means of disguise. Here, architecture was used to display function; there is no doubt that King's Cross is a railway station. The great yellow brick screen wall merely frames the glazed ends of the twin-arched train shed. Originally a pair of segmental-arched arcades filled the recesses formed by the three vertical blocks flanking the arches. The central block carries an Italianate clock turret which acts as a delicate foil to the dramatic simplicity of the façade. In King's Cross Lewis Cubitt achieved functionalism long before the twentieth century thought of it; it was no accident either that his employer, the Great Northern Railway, gained a magnificent station at a fraction of the cost of some rivals' establishments.

Having spent a considerable fortune in getting itself incorporated by Parliament, there was no money for architectural frills. The station buildings were ranged down the departure side in contemporary fashion, again in severe yellow brick somewhat enlivened by an immense cornice and Venetian windows.

King's Cross was opened in 1852 at the same time as a similar idea was again being expressed in Paris at the Gare de Montparnasse, built in 1850–2 by Victor Lenoir. There the twin train shed had pitched roofs and the profile was reproduced along the top of the screen wall to form a roof line instead of in great arched windows as at King's Cross. Although this technique was adopted at a number of other large Continental stations, only George Berkeley used it again in this country. He was engineer to the London & Blackwall Railway, and when he designed the second Fenchurch Street terminus, opened in 1854, he carried his crescent-shaped train shed roof forward over the two-storey frontage block to form a curved pediment. It was an ingenious device, made all the more effective by a central clock. Beneath it, a series of seven tall round-topped windows articulate with doors and windows below, between grey-brick pilasters and rustication. While it lacks the drama of King's Cross, Berkeley's façade wears an air of quiet distinction.

By no means did all major cities enjoy imposing stations. Indeed, we have seen in Chapter 3 how poorly the Midland Railway served Sheffield for many years, and while few towns of its size were quite so badly off for so long, a number of them suffered some very mean stations until well after mid-century or longer. Among the big companies the Great Western and those lines within its sphere of influence were particularly notorious in two respects, the first the result of I. K. Brunel's early policy of building separate platforms for up and down trains, not in the conventional manner on opposite sides of the line, but on the same side, as shown in Fig 5. As the platforms were complete with all facilities, it meant there had to be two of everything. In effect they were like two separate stations and some quite important places were served in this way, among them Reading, Taunton, Exeter and Wolverhampton Low Level. Each platform had its separate wooden train shed and station building. At Reading and Taunton the station buildings were square, two-storey blocks, the former of no distinction but at Taunton wearing a modest Georgian air with some stone dressings to door and window openings and a parapet. At Exeter they were single storeyed with an awning running around three sides, and a low hipped roof rising behind a parapet to a slender, decorative cupola, looking rather charming.

It quickly became obvious that with rapidly growing traffic the criss-crossing of trains over the central points created a problem, and most of the stations did not last too long before being rebuilt in more normal fashion. Reading, however, lasted incredibly long. It had a wooden connecting platform added about 1861, by which time it was already a byword for

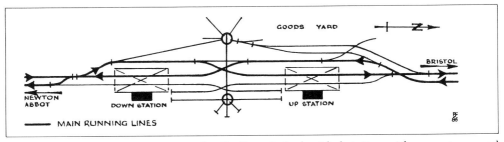

Fig 5. Exeter station, 1847; an example of a Brunel single-sided station with separate up and down platforms

inconvenience and delay, but was not rebuilt until 1896–7. Wolverhampton was built as a one-sided station as late as 1854 but slightly differently, with one long platform and shed, and a single range of buildings sited in the middle. Why a practical and far-sighted engineer like Brunel should have adopted such a system is not clear. His sketchbooks, preserved in Bristol University Library, show the single-sided station that was built at Slough, but the other through stations illustrated have conventional opposing platforms, including four replacement layouts for Reading of about 1853 which suggest that by then he appreciated the single-sided plan's short-comings. He said it prevented passengers mistakenly boarding a train going in the wrong direction, and avoided their having to cross the line. Otherwise these stations avoided nothing except unnecessary expense.

The other feature of Great Western notoriety was what has been called the 'Brunel barn', comprising a wooden train shed with an office building alongside, sometimes more substantial but frequently constructed of timber as well. That they were well built is undeniable, for they lasted a long time. Many small town stations and nearly all the main stations had one or more of Brunel's sheds and the company continued to build and add to them after his death, sticking to his basic design. They will be considered in more detail in Chapter 8.

The first Oxford terminus was a small wooden shed which lasted from 1844 to 1852 before being relegated to a goods depot. Its successor, opened on extension of the line northward, was another wooden barn but the overall roof had been removed by 1893. Like Banbury, it was one of the last important Great Western wooden stations to survive many years of bitter complaints. It might be thought that the company would have done something special for a city like Oxford, as it did at Bath and Bristol. Perhaps the GWR was getting its own back for the initial opposition to the railway; certainly Oxford paid the price for a long, long time, until 1972. If only the Oxford, Worcester & Wolverhampton Railway had been serious about building the independent station it illustrated in its prospectus, then Oxford would have had something really worthy of the city.

Even the capital was not immune. The Great Western's so-called temporary terminus opened in 1838 continued in use for sixteen years, in direct contrast to the grand scale of the rest of the line to Bristol. The first terminus was a wooden island platform beneath a wooden roof open at the sides. It stood on the west side of the Bishop's Road bridge, which was built by the company (Fig 6). To save space, carriages were transferred to adjacent lines by traversing tables, presumably hand-worked. The station entrance, booking hall, waiting room and offices were in the arches of the bridge. Some time before 1840, two more platforms were added for arrivals, and the original one was then reserved for departures. In 1851 the directors decided to build a separate departure station on the east side of the bridge, which would not only have been incredibly messy but would effectively have divided the station into two distinct parts. They thought better of it and instead authorised an entirely new station between Bishop's Road and Praed Street, the present Paddington, which was opened in 1854.

Elsewhere, Leeds started off with a well-designed station, as one would expect from Francis Thompson, the architect to the North Midland Railway. Located in Hunslet Lane some distance from the town, the two-storey brick building alongside the departure platform was fronted by a long and handsomely arched arcade at the head of stone steps, surmounted by the arms of Leeds, Sheffield and Derby in stone by the noted sculptor, John Thomas. Opened in 1840, it had a short life. Midland Railway trains from the south started using the central Wellington station in 1846, and in 1851 Hunslet Lane became a goods station.

Wellington was described in 1851 as being 'one of the finest central railway stations in the kingdom',[5] although this may have been intended to

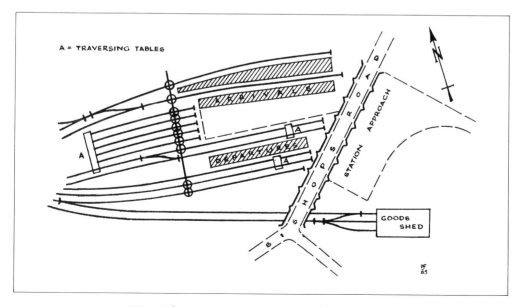

Fig 6. The temporary station at Paddington, 1845

apply more to its location than its appearance and accommodation, which at best appear to have been meagre and after the closure of Hunslet Lane must quickly have become inadequate. A writer in 1903[6] commented that it was then in the same condition as when it was built (1846) except for a new platform on one side, although a comparison of large-scale plans of 1847 and 1882 shows that it had grown from two to four platforms, was longer and had a larger frontage block. His further comment that it was still one of the most convenient stations with 'ample platform accommodation and ample circulating space' is hardly borne out by his accompanying plan and photographs. Before the Queens Hotel of 1863 hid it, the 'frontage' was merely a collection of wooden booking office and refreshment room buildings beneath the gable ends of the train shed. More alterations took place after 1882, but the station remained anything but impressive.

Leeds Central, a short distance away, was worse. It started off in 1848 as a temporary station in a converted warehouse, until a grand scheme by Hawkshaw for a large station used by four railways could be implemented at an estimated cost of £258,000 (the original plan of 1846 would have cost a cool £½ million.) Failure to agree led in 1849 to a third plan, this time at a quarter of the cost of Hawkshaw's, and the much reduced station was opened in an incomplete state later that year, in which form it languished until an accident in 1855 precipitated virtually entire rebuilding. This was finished in 1857, in such a cheese-paring fashion that Leeds was left with one of the country's meanest stations for a big city.

Edinburgh suffered, too. While three of its stations were at least contiguous, none of them seems to have possessed architectural pretensions appropriate to the Athens of the North. In 1850 the entrance to the North British and Edinburgh & Glasgow railways' combined station was on Waverley Bridge, spanning the tracks. It was of modest appearance, single-storeyed with a Roman arcaded front and matching windows. The buildings of the adjacent Edinburgh, Perth & Dundee Railway station in Canal Street were in a rather more severe Italianate style. With piecemeal additions, Waverley station lingered on in public disgrace until rebuilding in 1869–73, repeated again in 1892–1900. The fourth station, the Caledonian Railway's in Lothian Road, was a temporary building with a small iron shed and an unimposing canopied entrance, opened in 1848 and intended to be replaced by a grand Italianate station designed by Tite 'on a scale that would do no discredit to the magnificence of the great City of Edinburgh'. The Duke of Atholl laid the foundation stone with great ceremony in 1849 and that was as far as it got, the shed and single platform having to make do until the line was slightly extended to the end of Princes Street in 1870 and a second 'temporary' station erected, described by Sir William Acworth in 1890 as 'a wooden shanty'. Fortunately it was burned down in that year and was at last replaced by a large, well-designed station more fitting for Scotland's capital.

6

Early Layouts

So far we have paid little attention to the layout of the station, although it is the most important feature to which the architectural elevations must come second. The first purpose-built termini, Crown Street at Liverpool and Liverpool Road at Manchester, had a single platform alongside the station building which contained first- and second-class booking offices and waiting rooms, and accommodation for staff (see Fig 3 in Chapter 4). It was not long before it was realised that one platform was inadequate for arrivals and departures and, as we have seen, the Liverpool & Manchester Railway soon moved its Liverpool passenger operations to Lime Street where separate platforms were provided, facing each other behind the screen wall with the passenger entrance and offices along the departure side, and a separate exit on the arrival side, both with accommodation for cabs. The term 'platform' is here used in the loose sense to describe what was at first no more than a few inches off the ground and at many stations not above rail level; Rugby in 1838 had platforms only 7in high. Carriages were fitted with footboards in the same way as road coaches to enable passengers to clamber up from the lineside, and only very gradually were platforms increased in height. It was not until the 1870s and '80s that platforms level with the carriage floor started to come into use, and they still remain a peculiarly British institution.

There was no space for a separate arrival platform at Manchester because the space opposite Liverpool Road station was occupied by the large warehouse which still stands, so a separate arrival station was built in 1837 on the other side of the bridge crossing Water Street, on a space where hitherto passengers had alighted. Apparently there had been no facilities of any kind there, apart from a shed erected in 1833 and a sloping ramp down to the street which was also used for the carriages of those passengers who wished to take their own on the train, or even to travel in them, on a flat truck attached to the rear. Provision for loading private carriages was a feature of railway stations for many years and the term 'carriage dock' lingered on long after the practice ceased.

G. T. Andrews' Gateshead terminus of 1844 had a curious single-sided layout with the arrival platform occupying some two-thirds of the train shed at the inner end and the departure platform recessed into the remaining third, the rest of it being in the open (Fig 7). It will be seen from Fig 8 that

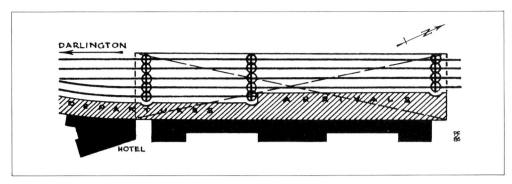

Fig 7. The single-sided terminus at Gateshead (Newcastle & Darlington Junction Railway) 1844

Euston was laid out as a side station with the buildings along the departure side completely detached from the entrance arch and screen. The same applied at both of the Curzon Street stations in Birmingham. It is interesting to note that had the Great Western used Euston, for which land on the west side was provided, and assuming a similar layout was adopted, the central section would, in effect, have been the forerunner of the island platform with tracks on both sides; it did, in fact, become so in 1846 when the strain on the station's outgrown resources was eased by building two platforms on the west side for Yorkshire traffic via Rugby and the Midland Railway.

The station building at Euston was a single two-storey stuccoed block containing what became the usual offices, including separate first- and second-class entrances, booking offices and waiting rooms. Carriages and cabs entered through the Doric Arch and passengers alighted alongside a colonnade. The low platforms were of timber and arriving passengers left the station through a gate beyond the easternmost lodge. Within a year of

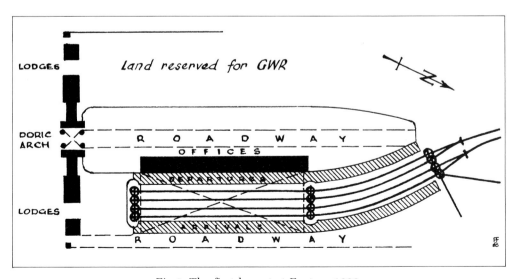

Fig 8. The first layout at Euston, 1838

opening, the station was extended at the outer end by a larger departure building, again with a colonnade, a feature adopted with similar layouts at Bricklayers Arms and Manchester London Road. The screens featured at these stations and others were different in that they were built on to the end of the train shed, whether they were simply walls like Liverpool Lime Street, Bricklayers Arms and, later, King's Cross, or buildings erected across the head of the tracks.

Bridge Street, the first Buchanan Street and Queen Street stations in Glasgow, and Lothian Road in Edinburgh also had buildings only along the departure side. Hull Paragon was the same, but on a far grander scale, the screen building across the inner end being an hotel opened in 1851. Hotels are dealt with in more detail in Chapter 9, although we can mention here that at Paddington Brunel used the same principle. Opened in 1854, Paddington comprised three departure and two arrival tracks with the station buildings along the departure side as they are today. Two platforms were provided on each side, one of each pair being an island and apparently used for auxiliary purposes such as attending to carriage lamps, with lifts to underground lamp rooms.

At London Bridge there was joint use of a single booking office and other facilities, except by the Greenwich company which had, in effect, a separate station (Chapter 5), but at most joint stations each company provided its own facilities in full, like Manchester Victoria, or at least separate booking offices like Manchester London Road. Liverpool Tithebarn Street had a block of offices along both sides of the station; the East Lancashire Railway's were alongside the arrival platform on the east, which was used by both companies' trains, and the Lancashire & Yorkshire's were along the western side. Each company had two departure platforms.

Southampton Terminus was deceptive. The approach to Tite's four-square frontage block gave the impression that the train shed stretched back behind it, whereas the entrance building actually stood at an acute angle to the outer end of the departure platform (Fig 9). Behind his Tudor façade at Bristol Brunel was characteristically ingenious. Because the line from Bath rose to a bridge across the Floating Harbour a short distance from Temple Meads, the terminus was built on arches which Brunel put to good use. It was a two-sided station with the customary entrance on the arrival side, reached from a narrow yard through the left-hand archway in the façade. Passengers ascended stairs to the platform while their conveyances drove out by a one-way system through one of the arches under the station to emerge on the arrival-side exit road. Between the centre tracks in the train shed, chutes were provided through the arches underneath, down which enginemen could throw ashes from their locomotives, an efficient means of disposal which lessened the fire risk in what was largely a wooden superstructure. Other arches were used as stables and various station offices. Extending into

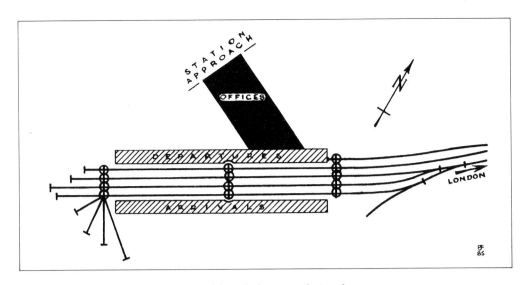

Fig 9. An early double-sided terminal; Southampton, c1847

part of the frontage block on the arrival side was an area where engines could draw forward and stand after being released from their trains, reached by a sector plate from which they could also gain an exit line. Water was supplied from an elevated tank on the adjacent corner of the station.

In 1841, nearly a year after the opening of the Great Western station, the Bristol & Exeter Railway arrived at Temple Meads from the south at right angles to the Great Western, to which for the first few weeks turnplates were the only means of transferring vehicles until a connecting curve was completed, as shown in Fig 10.

The Bristol & Exeter's own two-sided station, also at right angles, was not opened until 1845, the same year as the 'Express Platform' was built on the connecting curve so that through trains no longer needed to reverse into or out of one of the main stations. This highly inconvenient layout lasted until the 1870s (see Chapter 8), leading one to wonder why an engineer of Brunel's vision did not build a through station for both companies on the lines of the Tri-junct station at Derby. He was, after all, engineer to both, and when he was designing Temple Meads construction of the Bristol & Exeter was well under way. The answer is probably that for all his forceful character Brunel, no more than any other engineer, could only do what he could persuade his directors to sanction. There was a great deal of parochialism among early railways and it is significant that the original Bristol & Exeter board contained no Great Western directors.

The extensive use of turnplates in early stations, apparent from the accompanying diagrams, was supplemented at Paddington and Bristol by traversing tables which moved a vehicle sideways from one pair of rails to another. Both methods enabled the early four-wheeled carriages to be easily moved about the station by hand or by horses without the need for a

locomotive. As larger vehicles were built and with the more general
introduction of six-wheeled carriages in the early 1850s, more pointwork
became necessary, although turnplates continued in use for transferring
short vehicles like carriage trucks, horseboxes and baggage vans. They were
scattered about the station with what today seems like careless abandon,
regardless of main running lines and platforms (which required recesses to
accommodate them), and some remained in use until remarkably late. The
sidings shown in Fig 14 criss-crossing Rugby station in 1851, are good
examples; G. P. Neele, recalling journeys in 1857–60 in his *Railway
Reminiscences*, refers to the main lines having turntables across which trains
jarred when entering the station. The plan of Chester in Fig 13 shows two
still in use in 1876 on bay lines to give access to sidings.

A feature of early terminals was the lack of safe means of walking from one
side to the other. Passengers, of course, rarely had to; the stations were
designed for arriving and departing, with separate entrances and exits, not
for changing trains. If on the odd occasion passengers might need to do so,
they could always walk out of one side and back in through the other,
although there seems little doubt that they, like the staff, walked across the
rails if they wished and in some cases there was no alternative. Sir Francis
Head in *Stokers and Pokers* of 1849 wrote about walking, or rather

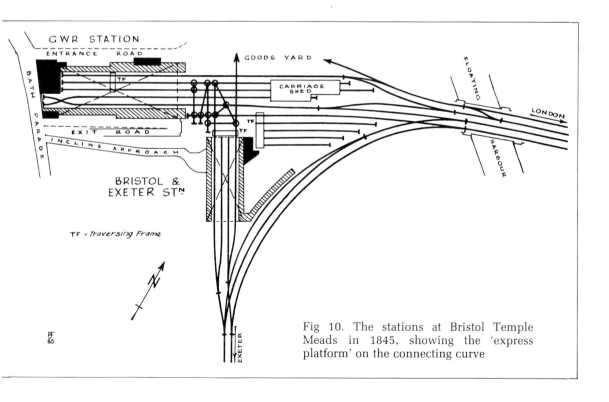

Fig 10. The stations at Bristol Temple
Meads in 1845, showing the 'express
platform' on the connecting curve

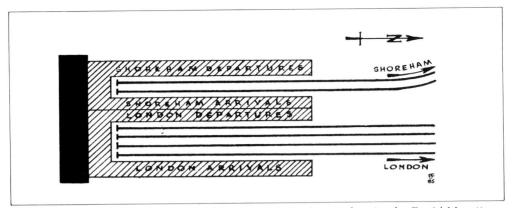

Fig 11. Conjectural basic layout at Brighton in 1841, from a drawing by David Mocatta

scrambling, across five sets of rails 'on which are lying, like vessels at anchor in a harbour, crowds of railway carriages waiting to depart,' to reach the departure platform at Euston. At Paddington the tracks extended beyond the inner ends of the platforms to a series of turnplates used for manoeuvring horse and carriage trucks. To provide access between each pair of platforms, Brunel designed moveable bridges which could be hydraulically lowered and retracted under the platforms when a train occupied the track.

A platform across the head of a station did not become at all common until the 1850s, although it first appeared at Nine Elms in 1838, followed by Brighton and York in 1841 and Bricklayers Arms in 1844. As Brighton (Fig 11) and York (see Fig 4 in Chapter 5) were also used for changing trains the cross-platform was a necessary innovation, and when the hotel was built at York it became the first station to have the U-shaped building plan. Brighton was the first to have more than two platforms, a central platform being provided for the Shoreham line which diverged almost immediately outside the station. A curious single-line tunnel under the station led back from the Shoreham branch to the low-level goods yard on the east side, but seems to have been disused after 1854. Nine Elms and Brighton were the first true 'head' stations, where passengers entered and left through a building at the end of the tracks instead of at either side, a type of layout that obviously was more convenient and became increasingly common.

The single-sided principle was applied to many large through and junction stations. The first large station designed for changing trains was the celebrated Derby Tri-junct station of 1841, those of the North Midland, Midland Counties and Birmingham & Derby Junction railways all meeting at that point. It comprised a single through platform with a recessed bay at each end for trains starting or terminating at Derby, and numerous turnplates on five cross tracks – two cutting through the platform – giving on to seven sidings within the station itself. Two of the cross tracks are shown on a contemporary plan from which Fig 12 is taken, leading out through two of the arches in the long screen wall, presumably for loading horses and carriages, although engravings of the same period show carriages being driven into the station for loading.

The use of the train shed for sidings on which coaches could be stabled was common, whether at a single- or a double-platform station. Manchester Victoria had five sidings opposite its single 852ft long platform line, one end of which was used for Manchester & Leeds trains and the other by the Liverpool & Manchester. It was, when built, the largest station in the country. Paddington also had five storage sidings, with a subway beneath for staff, one of the earliest examples; King's Cross had as many as fourteen. Even St Pancras, opened in 1868, was provided with six sidings beneath the station roof. An odd arrangement in the very confined space at Glasgow Queen Street placed coaches in stalls formed by alcoves in the walls along one side and reached by series of turnplates, requiring three movements to get vehicles in from the running lines.

Other single-sided stations followed: Chester, Carlisle, Huddersfield and Perth were among the largest, although an account of a meeting to consider Tite's plans for Carlisle indicates that it was originally intended to build a two-sided station with both a subway and a footbridge, either of which would have been an early example of this feature.[1] At Perth the layout was complicated by the opening of the 'Dundee Dock' in 1862, a bay platform leading from the Dundee curve and terminating at right angles to the main station (p 167). It ended the need for Dundee local trains to reverse in and out of the main platforms. Newcastle was a giant single-sided station with two through lines, three bays at one end, five at the other, two carriage sidings and the usual complement of cross tracks and turnplates, all on a curving site beneath Dobson's overall roof. At all of these places most of the siding space eventually became used for additional platforms, while central

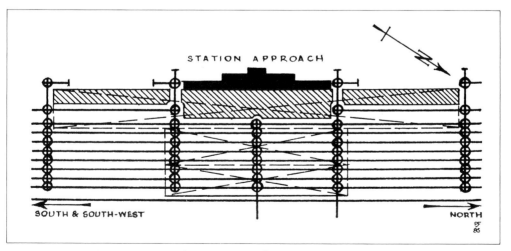

Fig 12. Francis Thompson's Derby Tri-junct station of 1841

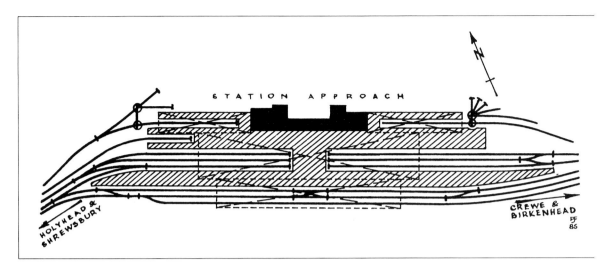

STATION APPROACH

N

HOLYHEAD & SHREWSBURY

CREWE & BIRKENHEAD
FF
85

Fig 13. Chester General station in 1876, little changed since Francis Thompson designed it in 1848

scissors crossovers were installed on long through platform lines to enable two trains to occupy them simultaneously without one blocking the other, as at Chester (Fig 13). The single platform was used for trains running in opposite directions until additional through platforms were built, when the scissors could be restricted to single-direction running which considerably simplified train operating.

The primary purpose of the large stations at Derby, Chester, Carlisle and Perth was to act as a junction where many passengers required to change trains, for which they were specifically designed from the outset. Others, like Crewe and Rugby, grew as the result of events and initially were quite small. Only when the Chester & Crewe and Manchester & Birmingham railways joined the Grand Junction line at Crewe in 1840 and 1842 respectively was the small roadside station provided with proper platforms, although there were only two, located on the north side of the Nantwich Road bridge. They were given full-length ornate canopies. The Manchester & Birmingham had its own separate station some little distance beyond, short of the actual junction which was made by a single-line connection through a gate. Only the up platform is shown with a canopy in A. F. Tait's engraving of 1848, having a high concave outer edge decorated with panels stated to incorporate carved oak figures above the iron columns. By this time the station had been widened to take four tracks, when presumably the down platform had been moved back and the other canopy not replaced. After the works opened in 1843, Crewe started to grow as a railway town as well as a junction, but the station had to suffice until it was completely rebuilt in 1867.

Much the same story applies to Rugby, although there the misery of an inadequate, outgrown station lingered on until 1885–6. The first station was well outside the town on the Newbold Road, the main road leading north, where the bridge under the London & Birmingham Railway was given Gothic embellishments, to Pugin's disgust. The station was only a wooden shed, according to Thomas Roscoe built in the Swiss style with a large projecting roof.[2] Despite being the better part of ¾ mile away, the trustees of Rugby School gave £1,000 towards the cost of the bridge to ensure that it harmonised with their new school buildings.

That was in 1838. Two years later the Midland Counties Railway entered Rugby from Leicester, but because of the topography its junction was made facing London some ½ mile beyond that end of the station. The London & Birmingham had no choice but to move their station, though the company not unreasonably insisted that if the Midland Counties wanted to use its line to reach London they must pay for the new station, which the Midland Counties did in return for £100 a year rent from the LBR which, moreover, retained sole control. For the London & Birmingham it was not a bad bargain. The site of the second station of 1840 was immediately to the west (that is, at the Birmingham end) of the present one and in 1848 comprised two very unequal platforms, that on the down side only 111ft long, but on the up side well over three times that length (Fig 14). The London & Birmingham was by now part of the London & North Western Railway and had offices on the down side. The Midland Counties was a constituent of the much larger Midland Railway which occupied buildings on the up, or southbound, side:

> Each platform had a bay at the north end, and the up side one at the south end also, and there was a short island platform in the centre, at which the Leamington trains were unloaded. From about the middle of the up side a level crossing was made across to the down side, and although accommodation existed for crossing the line in safety, by means of an overhead gallery, this level crossing was a constant temptation to people to take a short cut, and many sad accidents resulted, the worst of which happened on 15th March 1883 when a party of seven was caught by a train . . . The platform in places was very low and it was quite an acrobatic feat to climb in and out of the carriages . . .[3]

Rugby went on growing in size and importance as a railway junction and, until new industries were set up at the end of the century, to a considerable extent was a railway town with which the station did little to keep pace. Some tinkering with passenger facilities was done from time to time, and the *Railway Chronicle* of 6 June 1846 optimistically forecast 'the most extensive and magnificent in the kingdom,' but the layout of 1851 shown in Fig 14 remained essentially the same until complete reconstruction in 1886 (Fig 15), despite a number of proposals by the North Western to improve it. Part of the problem lay in the fact that the old station was to a large extent Midland property, and after the opening of their direct line to London in 1857 Rugby became of relatively little importance to the Midland.

After the 1880s the series of important junctions on the London & North Western main line between Euston and Carlisle had no equal for large,

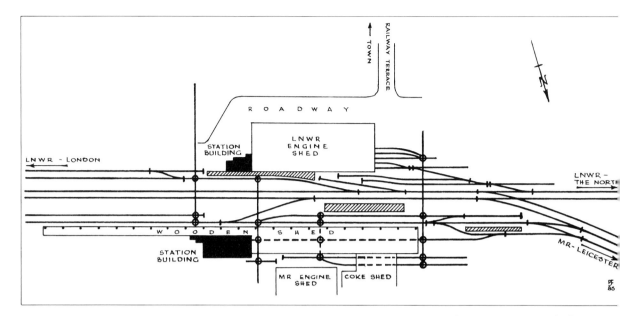

Fig 14. The second station at Rugby, as enlarged by 1851. See Fig 15 for comparison with the third station

spacious stations – internally, that is; Rugby, Stafford, Crewe and Preston were anything but imposing from the outside. On the East Coast main line, for instance, only York and Darlington were in the same class. We shall see in Chapter 8 how York until 1877 was an awkwardly located terminus, while Darlington before its complete rebuilding in 1885–7 was a hotchpotch of makeshift enlargements and additions to the original wooden shed of the early 1840s which Queen Victoria criticised in 1849 for its shabby

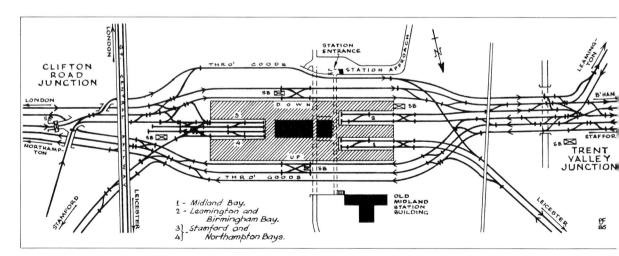

Fig 15. The new Rugby station of 1886, from a drawing c1910. Compare with Fig 14. The overall roof has been omitted for clarity and horizontal distances are heavily compressed

appearance 'in the place which gave birth to the railway system'; fair comment, we would say today. Other prominent railway workshop towns which were also junctions – Swindon, Doncaster, Ashford and Eastleigh – had by comparison fairly modest stations, none with more than four through platform faces. Indeed, Doncaster had only two until 1877 and then three until the London & North Eastern Railway partly modernised it in 1936–7 and created a fourth.

By the 1850s and '60s, then, the rapid growth in passenger traffic virtually ensured that nearly all Britain's existing principal stations were at least one step, if not several, behind the railway operating department's requirements. Only some of the newer stations were at all adequate, while the others suffered from underestimated traffic growth when they were built. From inadequacy it is a short step to the curious, although passengers using London Bridge station, both then and since, would have employed a stronger term. Its disorderly development is a fascinating story, but to its users until 1979 it was sheer frustration. Only too well did an architectural writer in 1914 describe it as comprising 'relics of the intermediate barbarism between the prophetic courage of Euston and St. Pancras and the mean modernism of St. Marylebone'.[4]

To fully summarise the extraordinary development of London Bridge we must trespass into later periods, after starting with the London & Greenwich Railway which, it will be recalled from Chapter 5, was opened on a viaduct in 1836. Land on the north side was acquired for future use by other railways intending to occupy the site, the first being the London & Croydon which in 1839 built its own terminus alongside with an entrance and booking office below. It joined the Greenwich line on the south side of the viaduct at Corbett's Lane Junction, Bermondsey, so its trains had to cross to the other side to enter their terminus. In 1841 the London & Brighton Railway arrived on the scene, running in over the London & Croydon's tracks which were widened in the following year. To avoid delays caused by the conflicting crossing of trains from one side of the widened viaduct to the other, the London & Greenwich reluctantly agreed to exchange stations with the London & Croydon, but not the arches and land on which they stood, thereby immediately initiating legal chaos. Also, in 1842 a fourth railway arrived, the South Eastern, again using the London & Croydon's tracks. The three later companies formed a joint committee to build and manage the new station described in Chapter 5, opened in 1844. The Greenwich company was also involved and in the event did not actually exchange complete stations, only sites, when later that year it finally moved into part of the old Croydon station on the north side.

Ownership complications were slightly eased in 1845 when the South Eastern leased the Greenwich Railway, and more so in the next year when the London & Croydon and London & Brighton amalgamated to form the

London, Brighton & South Coast Railway. Although there were now only two companies on the site, they found frequent causes for disagreement, while the joint station was already showing signs of being inadequate for their traffic. As a result, the companies decided to demolish it and divide the land between them for two separate stations. So in 1850 the much-praised station came down after only five years' life and a wall was erected down the middle of the site. The South Eastern converted the Brighton company's former goods shed into a temporary station for Greenwich trains and the former Greenwich station, which was the original Croydon one, was used by the South Eastern's North Kent line trains.

The South Eastern took little time to build a new terminus, a 'head' station with a three-storey frontage block designed by its architect, Samuel Beazley. As well as running his architectural practice, he was an author, playwright and theatrical producer. The colonnade at Drury Lane Theatre was his work and he designed a number of the South Eastern's North Kent stations. His London Bridge terminus was unadorned Italianate in style, its gracefully curved ends and flat verandah giving it a Regency air that was probably regarded as old fashioned in 1851; the *Illustrated London News* did not admire it, comparing its stuccoed front unfavourably with its predecessor, particularly the prominently ornate clock set above a deeply bracketed cornice. Offices with shops beneath were built along the north side of the approach ramp and the old London & Croydon train shed was incorporated into the station. The Brighton company, meanwhile, was building its own station on the other side of the wall, partly opened in 1850 but, because of the decision to build Bricklayers Arms, not completed. Instead it was rebuilt yet again in 1853 on a larger scale, like its neighbour three storeys high, but set further back and much plainer, enlivened only by stonework in the rusticated quoins and the fenestration.

Demolitions and alterations must have been a constant accompaniment for those using and working at London Bridge, for in 1859 an Act was obtained by the South Eastern for the building of Charing Cross station and new lines from London Bridge to it and to the London & South Western Railway at Waterloo. Major disruption again took place while a viaduct with five high-level platforms was built along the northern side of the station, partly on the site of the original London & Croydon terminus. The new portion was opened in 1864 and from 1866 also served Cannon Street trains. In 1879 the Brighton squeezed two new short platforms into the outer end of its station, after which things were rather quieter until 1893–4 when the South Eastern rebuilt its station yet again, with additional platforms on the north side but retaining Beazley's frontage block and the 1851 main line terminal platforms, the latter for conversion to a Continental goods depot. Important widening of the approach viaducts in 1899 gave eleven lines into the station, and in 1902 the Continental depot in the middle of the combined station was pulled down to make space for four further platforms, making a total of twenty-one terminal and six through platforms. They were somewhat lower than the Brighton station, thereby creating three distinct levels. From then on there were no more major changes until 1928 when, at long last, the Southern Railway pierced the dividing wall and London Bridge became one station.

The curious components of the old Waverley Station at Edinburgh give another insight into early station layouts. The cramped site in the narrow valley and the obstructive attitude of the town have been referred to in Chapter 3. The North British offices were at the east end and it seems that in 1847 the Edinburgh & Glasgow opened their own, even though the station was operated by a joint committee. It will be recalled that the Edinburgh Leith & Granton Railway opened a station at a right angle to the General station, as it was sometimes called, with only Canal Street separating them (Fig 16). This line formed the route to Fife and the north east via the Forth and Tay ferries, and after leaving the very short platforms immediately entered Scotland Street tunnel which took trains by gravity down a 1 in 27 gradient for ¾ mile under the New Town. Upward trains were hauled by a

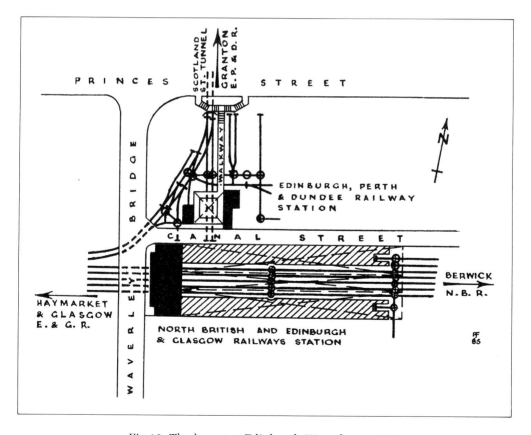

Fig 16. The layout at Edinburgh Waverley in 1852

stationary engine and rope. The small train shed was at a low level, overlooked by the booking-office building on the east and refreshment rooms on the west. They gave on to a curious balustraded walkway around all four sides of the exterior of the train shed roof, with steps down to the interior. Another elevated walkway extended on arches alongside the running line to two flights of steps at the opposite end, leading up to Princes Street – forerunners of the famous Waverley Steps at the present station.

By 1852 the main entrance and booking office for the General station were on Waverley Bridge, apparently serving both North British and Edinburgh & Glasgow companies, with two platforms and five lines of rails extending through a train shed towards North Bridge. A connecting line to the Canal Street station curved sharply from west to north. The Edinburgh, Perth & Dundee Railway, as the owners of Canal Street had now become, was taken over by the North British in 1862, which acquired the Edinburgh & Glasgow in 1865. By 1860 the North British appears to have also built a small terminal, quite separate, at right angles to the Canal Street station on its north side. In 1868 Canal Street was closed following the opening of a new line to Leith avoiding Scotland Street tunnel, thus enabling the North British to acquire the site of the Waverley Market which was relocated on the Canal Street site. This gave the North British land for expansion and in 1874 an enlarged station was opened. That became inadequate so rapidly that by 1890 it was attracting fierce criticism. It was not helped by the severe bottlenecks caused by tunnels at both ends and, of course, the sacrosanct Princes Street Gardens beyond the western tunnel, but a decade later the new Waverley station at last gave the North British and the citizens of Edinburgh a station adequate for the traffic.

Waverley well illustrates the reluctance of railway managements to embark on large-scale improvements, already referred to and exemplified in our own time by London Bridge. Although the shortcomings of the early single-sided stations were quickly recognised, for instance, many of them lasted far too long, even though the site might not be unfavourable to change, because of the capital cost involved. Perhaps this was one of the penalties of being pioneers, although had competition not been so obsessive in some cases the twentieth century might well have been bequeathed a more convenient, less expensive legacy.

7

Taking the Train

We have a fair view of what stations were like to the traveller in the first thirty years of the railway age. It is not complete in every detail, but is sufficient to be able to build up a picture of conditions as they were up to around 1860. Thereafter much more is known as stations began to assume the forms that in many cases are still familiar, or were until quite recently; far more has been recorded and we also have photographs to help. But descriptions and illustrations of early architectural features, train sheds and layouts are patchy and vary in the amount of detail. There is emphasis on London stations, less relating to the provinces, and little was noted about internal decor and appointments, so we have to rely on plans and guidebooks of the period and what has remained to be recorded in more recent railway literature.

Public facilities at all the main stations were provided strictly on a class basis. For his higher fare the first-class passenger enjoyed not only superior accommodation on the trains but at the stations as well. Second-class travellers were kept quite separate, but after gradual acceptance of third class started in the 1840s, they were occasionally privileged to share the first-class rooms at smaller stations. It was a long time before third-class passengers were considered to need waiting and refreshment rooms at all; for them the platform was good enough. The Midland Railway, originator of many improvements, was first to abolish second class in 1874 when third-class passengers automatically succeeded to the accommodation.

The building through which the station was entered would be fronted by a yard or forecourt, probably having entrance and exit gateways for carriages and cabs, corresponding to the arrival and departure platforms, although sometimes the outgoing passengers left by a completely separate exit. Vehicles would draw up beneath a large *porte-cochère* or alongside a colonnade where passengers could alight to enter the booking hall without getting wet in bad weather. The term 'to book' comes from the stage-coach practice of issuing paper tickets torn from a book and remains with us still, despite the introduction of Edmondson card tickets from 1846–7 and the recent renaming of booking offices as ticket offices. Nine Elms had an open counter for the issue of paper tickets, but generally the separate booking office with a pigeon-hole window or grille was adopted from the start. At the larger stations a semi-circular wooden office projected into the main hall, as at Newcastle and the second Liverpool Lime Street, or rectangular with rounded corners, like King's Cross – where a plan of 1852 calls it 'Pay Office' – sufficiently large to contain a number of windows for different classes of travel or destinations, each with a small wooden barrier in front allowing only one person to use the window at a time. Generally the booking halls themselves were at first fairly unpretentious, and the description in *The Midland Counties Railway Companion* of 1840, although saying nothing about its appearance, gives a typically detailed description of how the booking office was arranged at Campbell Street station, Leicester:

> In the central part of the station is the booking office, over which is the audit office, occupying the whole of the range of windows under the portico. The entrance door on the left is for second and third class passengers, and the corresponding one on the right for first-class. The passengers enter the booking office by the door nearer the entrance and, having obtained tickets, pass into the hall by another door, and from thence to the platform; the booking office being divided into two parts by an elegant iron railing.

The London & Croydon Railway's London Bridge terminus of 1839 had a booking hall 30ft by 60ft and 22ft high, more handsome than most with two rows of Doric columns supporting the ceiling, finished in a new form of polished cement resembling marble. King's Cross had a lofty hall alongside the departure platform, occupying the full height of the building with a panelled ceiling and a gallery on ornate iron brackets connecting the upper floors on either side. The original Euston had separate first- and second-class

booking halls, the latter doubling up as a waiting room, while the short-lived London Bridge Joint station had one hall with a partition down the middle separating second-class passengers from first-, although the actual office was common to both sections. There was strict segregation; passengers entered by separate doors and reached the platform by separate corridors with their respective waiting rooms leading off. Other stations had completely separate booking halls for the two classes, like Manchester Liverpool Road where they were on the ground floor with their own stairs to waiting rooms on the floor above. There were two fireplaces in the first-class booking office but only one in the second-. The Liverpool & Manchester Railway did not cater for third class until 1844. At Nottingham's second station, opened in 1846, the booking halls soon became inadequate yet remained unchanged for nearly sixty years when a writer recalled the second and third class as 'a small hall a few yards square with only three ticket windows, and on busy days, which were frequent, most vexatious delay occurred before one could book. Three other ticket windows, in another narrow hall, was also the provision made for first-class passengers.'[1]

As stations were extended they might be provided with more than one entrance, requiring extra booking offices. Birmingham New Street eventually had two main line and two local booking offices, each one duplicated for the London & North Western Railway and the Midland, eight all told, while Perth had six, two for each company using the station. Provision of separate company booking offices at stations used by more than one railway was, of course, quite normal. Newcastle had a North British booking office by virtue

The three north-end booking offices at Perth – one for each of the joint companies – some time after 1911. The details of the 1884 roof can be seen, with the new 1911 roofing on the right (*Perth & Kinross District Libraries*)

of that company's running powers over the North Eastern's line from Berwick, 67 miles away. Carlisle Joint station had a large booking office at the main entrance with separate windows for the main line companies using the station, and a similar one on the island platform. The small Maryport & Carlisle Railway, however, always jealous of its independence, maintained its own booking office near the bay where its trains started. Chester had separate London & North Western and Great Western offices, and the booking offices at the original Glasgow Bridge Street station for the Glasgow, Paisley & Greenock and Glasgow, Paisley, Kilmarnock & Ayr railways even had their own separate staircases up to the platform. A third entrance for third-class passengers was added in 1847 when the Greenock line's successful cheap fares policy made segregation socially desirable.

Such multiplicity of booking offices and companies' routes could create confusion. Three prominent boards side-by-side outside Wolverhampton High Level station advertising possible destinations by the London & North Western, Great Western and Midland railways presented three alternative routes to several towns including Birmingham and London. George Measom described the facilities at London Bridge in his *Guide to the Brighton and South Coast Railways* in 1853:

> The southern part is occupied by the booking offices of the Brighton and South Coast Railway, while the centre, facing the approach road, forms the Dover office, beyond which is the North Kent booking office; and on the north of this again, nearest Tooley Street, is the office of the Greenwich Railway . . . Every arrangement for the accommodation of travellers is most complete . . .

One wonders.

Huddersfield presented no such problems. The original LNWR and Lancashire & Yorkshire booking offices were easily identifiable in the small pavilions at each end of the façade, some 400ft apart. But how many unwary passengers missed a train by choosing the wrong one?

There were some quite handsome booking halls, the one at Brighton matching the frontage, with a panelled ceiling on iron columns and divided into booking offices for the main line to London and the Shoreham branch. Separate ladies' and gentlemen's waiting rooms led off each. Cambridge was equally elegant with two large ceiling panels and a dentilled cornice supported by two circular columns. The separate first- and second-class entrances at Euston were done away with when the Great Hall was built in 1846–9. With the Doric Arch it transcended all other British station entrances and nothing has surpassed it since.

In the same way that the Euston Arch symbolised the supremacy of the railway, particularly the London & Birmingham, the building of the Great Hall was a gesture marking the creation in 1846 of what was then the world's largest railway company, the London & North Western. It was formed by the amalgamation of the London & Birmingham, Grand Junction and Liverpool &

Manchester companies – the last two had already joined forces in the previous year – and the Manchester & Birmingham Railway. Philip Charles Hardwick, son of the designer of the Arch, was the architect of the first British station concourse in a separate building that became a feature in Europe and America but was not repeated here.

The original design appears to have been a vaulted hall in Roman style, but was discarded in favour of an Italian Renaissance interior which was much more up to date. Sir John Summerson conjectures that the design may have been partly influenced by the vestibule of the Berlin Opera House and partly by the Palazzo Massimi in Rome.[2] It has been called the largest waiting room in the British Isles, but was in fact much more than that. At 125ft 6in long, 61ft 4in wide and 62ft high, the deeply panelled plaster ceiling was believed to be the largest unsupported ceiling in the world. Copied from the church of St Paul's-outside-the-Walls in Rome, it was rivalled only by the earlier ceiling of the nearby St Pancras parish church and the later ballroom ceiling at Buckingham Palace. John Thomas carried out rich sculptural work on the double reverse voluted brackets (consoles) that supported the beams, and provided eight decorative panels in relief, two at each corner, representing London, Liverpool, Manchester, Birmingham, Carlisle, Chester, Lancashire and Northampton. They were in line with a series of deep clerestory windows, which gave the hall plenty of light, above a prominent cornice supported at each end by 20ft tall Roman Ionic columns. Below, a gallery ran round all four walls supported by smaller, matching consoles and having an iron balustrade incorporating scrolled gas lamp standards. Under the gallery a series of round-headed arches on each side led out to booking halls, the London & North Western's on the east or right-hand side and a smaller one for local services and Midland trains via Rugby on the other. Each was lit by an impressive cupola supported by brackets resting on lions' heads, topped by a glass dome. The south end formed the entrance from the Arch through five round-headed openings, and facing it at the north end was a fine curved double staircase leading up to the equally magnificent Shareholders' and Board Rooms (see Chapter 9). Over the Doric doorway at the head of the stairs, Thomas provided a large sculptured group prominently featuring Britannia, the emblem calmly appropriated by the LNWR for its coat of arms although the Grand Junction had earlier used her on its company seal. Some of the ceiling panels were perforated, concealing hot-water pipes to promote ventilation, and there were radiators at floor level.[3]

The cost of this gigantic and glorious piece of railway exhibitionism was £150,000. It would have been more had not there been considerable economising in materials and finish. The frescoes which Hardwick planned for the walls were dispensed with. Instead the panels were cement rendered and painted grey to look like granite. The columns had white marble bases and caps but otherwise were also rendered to imitate red granite, although

The booking hall at Hull Paragon in its original condition in 1958 (R. E. G. Read)

underneath they were brick. Those at the north end at the top of the stairs collapsed during erection, killing three workmen. They were only 2ft in diameter and at the inquest it transpired that the bricks were laid on edge, doubtless as a further economy, so the columns' instability is not surprising. Hardwick's specification left the actual method of construction to the contractor, William Cubitt. Criticism was directed at building such slender columns in brick, although William Tite and another prominent architect, Edward Blore, gave evidence in favour of brick construction, properly laid.[4] They were rebuilt with iron stanchions as cores. In 1852 a statue of George Stephenson by E. H. Bailey was placed at the foot of the staircases.

The Great Hall was slightly offset to the west of the line of the Arch and, grand though it was, effectively divided the station into two distinct parts, forming an island between them which thenceforth was a barrier to rational development and the principal cause of confusion in Euston's subsequent layout. Not all contemporary observers were impressed by the grandeur. Samuel Sydney, writing his *Rides on Railways* in 1851, said:

Comfort has been sacrificed to magnificence. The platform arrangements for departing and arriving trains are good, simple and comprehensive; but the waiting rooms, refreshment stand, and *other conveniences* are as ill-contrived as possible; while a vast hall with a magnificent roof and scagliola pillars, appears to have swallowed up all the money and all the light of the establishment. The first-class waiting room is dull to a fearful degree, and furnished in the dowdiest style of economy. The second-class room is a dark cavern, with nothing better than a borrowed light. The refreshment counters are enclosed in a sort of circular glazed pew, open to all the draughts of a grand, cold, uncomfortable hall, into which few ladies will venture. A refreshment room should be the ante-room to the waiting room, and the two should be arranged with reference to the booking office and *cloak-rooms*, so that strangers find their way without asking a dozen questions from busy porters and musing policemen.

Sydney was ahead of his time; we have had to wait for British Rail to combine waiting and refreshment rooms. The circular or oval counter marked the first appearance of the English bar where one can stand to drink or eat and became common at stations long before it was used in pubs. Even at the most primitive village inn customers' wants were met by serving maids, and it was the railway station refreshment room that inaugurated a new way of selling drinks.

Large stations had the same class division for eating and drinking as for booking offices and waiting rooms, although it was a long time before third-class passengers were catered for. The first station at Manchester Victoria was a notable exception, where third-class travellers were privileged to have their own refreshment room and bar in the basement. Brunel's sketches of the Swindon refreshment rooms, made in 1840, show three designs, all with a central servery, a partition dividing first and second class and a central spiral staircase to the kitchens in the basement. E. T. MacDermot's *History of the Great Western Railway* illustrates one of the rooms about 1850, showing an oval counter, with walls and ceilings decorated with Arabesques and wooden columns painted to look like inlay. Elsewhere some had a long counter along one side of the room, but whatever their shape they were laden with steaming and hissing tea and coffee urns, sandwiches under glass domes and cakes and pies piled on tiered stands. Behind would stand a kind of reredos of shelves and mirrors reflecting glasses and bottles of more interesting wares.

Greater attention was paid to decorating refreshment rooms than waiting rooms. Francis Thompson at Cambridge produced a well-proportioned room with a heavily dentilled cornice and decorative mouldings off-setting the plain ceiling, while at Chester he provided more elaborate plasterwork and decorated woodwork. Derby's refreshment room, which the *North Midland Railway Guide* of 1842 merely described as handsome, was more restrained, in keeping with the exterior, and limited to delicate cornice decoration and a panelled wooden dado matching the door and window casings. John Dobson's columns and pilasters, a splendidly coved ceiling lit from a large central lantern light, and moulded wall tiles at Newcastle can still be partly seen beneath the dark paint intended to hide them. Originally the first-class room, it had a bar at one end and a separate ladies' refreshment room at the other. Unfortunately Tite's rather magnificent rooms at Perth and Carlisle are no longer used by the public. Perth's Corinthian columns, deep panelled ceiling and marble fireplace happily are being restored after many years as an engineers' store, but the Tudor splendours at Carlisle lie behind locked doors, replaced by a buffet on the platform. The old room had two huge stone fireplaces, quite baronial in character, each with its Latin motto carved in Old English letters under the mantel. Loosely interpreted, one devoutly reminded passengers that 'God has made for us these places of rest', and the other, more ominously, 'I will cause you ever to remember this place'.

The very first railway refreshment room is claimed to have been opened by the London & Birmingham Railway at Birmingham Curzon Street. *The Times* of 18 September 1838 reported that part of the 'magnificent Station house in Birmingham has recently been licensed as an hotel . . . so that passengers, if they think proper, may be accommodated with every good thing without leaving the company's premises.' There was, of course, the Gartsherrie Inn built by the Garnkirk & Glasgow Railway in 1832, but that was rather different, and claims have been made for a refreshment room at Rugby where from 9 April to 17 September 1838 passengers changed from train to road coach while the final section of railway to Denbigh Hall, near Bletchley, was being completed. It also seems possible that the Grand Junction Railway may have had a refreshment room at its temporary Birmingham terminus at Vauxhall, opened in 1837. It certainly had one at its own Curzon Street station in 1839.

At all events, the L&BR refreshment room in the building alongside the departure platform at Curzon Street was certainly very early, and when the Queen Hotel was added to the frontage building in 1840 it was moved into the ground floor. It was a long room with a three-panel ceiling supported by two rows of elaborate Corinthian columns, and in its day must have been quite splendid. Sydney rated it much better than Euston: 'A capital table d'hote is provided four times a day, at two shillings a head, servants included, an arrangement extremely acceptable after a ride of 118 miles.' Sydney seems to have forgotten that he would also have stopped for refreshments at Wolverton where, until the introduction of dining cars, all London & North Western expresses had 10 minutes' halt. The refreshment rooms there were immortalised by Sir Francis Head in *Stokers and Pokers* (1849) when invaded by a horde of passengers to devour vast quantities of Banbury cakes, Queen cakes, pork pies, brandy and stout. The Queen stopped there, too, on her first journey on the London & Birmingham when she travelled from Watford to Tamworth via Hampton on 28 January 1843.

Refreshment rooms were leased to contractors, and at stations like Wolverton, Swindon, York, Normanton, Preston and Carlisle the compulsory stop was usually part of the terms of the lease. In the early days a refreshment

The former refreshment room at Birmingham Curzon Street in 1935, used as goods offices but retaining original decoration (*Author's Collection*)

stop was considered by the companies to be necessary every 50 miles or so, which initially took about two hours to cover. But as speeds increased, the railways found that reduced journey times made some of their compulsory eating stops unnecessary. After the introduction of dining cars in 1878, they quickly became an anachronism. None was more so than at Swindon where the Great Western was obliged not only to stop all its trains, but to refrain from making any other refreshment stop between London and Bristol that might reduce the Swindon trade. Because the company somewhat unwisely had granted a 99-year lease, its termination proved to be an expensive business. The contractors for their part had built and maintained the refreshment rooms in return for a peppercorn rent, and made a handsome profit from their captive market. As Acworth commented in 1889, when the rooms started to decline after a period when they had, in his opinion, been one of the best in England, the company could have put pressure on the lessees. He suggested sardonically that if the profits were restricted to a mere 200 per cent the Great Western might gain by a reduction in the value of the lease – a reference to the company's repeated efforts to terminate it on reasonable terms. Getting rid of the 10 minutes' stop eventually cost the company the incredible sum of £100,000 when it finally managed to buy out the unexpired 45 years of the lease in 1895.

Jokes about refreshment room fare, stale sandwiches and soggy cake go back to the beginning of rail travel. The food at the Swindon rooms was subject to complaint for many years; in 1842 Brunel himself complained

about the coffee, calling it bad roasted corn and avoiding using the rooms
whenever he could:

> . . . really the prices in some of them are much too high. Sixpence for a cup of tea
> which cannot cost 2d. (300 per cent profit) is perfectly extravagant. At Wolverton
> they allow a small bun with it; but it seems it is not the case at all places. For on
> our taking one of the smallest biscuits, value some fraction of a halfpenny, there
> being no buns at the Derby station some time back, one of the knights of the towel
> insolently demanded and received a shilling for it and the tea . . . The quality too,
> of the articles at some of the refreshment rooms is anything but what it should be;
> it appears to follow the inverse ratio of the price.[5]

Charles Dickens parodied the railway refreshment room in 'The Boy at
Mugby' in his story *Mugby Junction*, published in 1866. Whilst the scenes he
described were not necessarily based on Rugby but were an accurate account
of the activities at any large railway junction, 'The Boy' was based on an
actual experience there when he had fallen foul of the imperious refreshment
room manageress who refused him milk and sugar until he paid for his
coffee. So we are regaled with The Boy's account of the establishment 'what's
proudest boast is, that it never yet refreshed a mortal being', where the tea-
urn also did duty as soup-tureen (the contents being much the same) and,
upon announcement of the imminent arrival of a train, the young ladies
forming the staff skipped across the line from one room to the other to 'begin
to pitch the stale pastry into the plates, and chuck the sawdust sandwiches
under the glass covers'.

The arrangements at Rugby were known to be inadequate, for in 1850 the
London & North Western had considered a report from the General Manager
pointing out that there was only one room for all passengers and that
workmen, labourers and company employees were in the habit of frequent-
ing the bar. Like the station itself, there was no real improvement until the
rebuilding of 1886. Not all catering was of such a low standard, however, and
long-distance services such as the Anglo-Scottish trains could be much
better provided for. The extensive refreshment rooms at Normanton, for
instance, offered passengers on the Midland's Scotch expresses a six-course
dinner for 2s 6d, although the feat of catering organisation in providing it for
a train-load of passengers within the space of 20 minutes had to be equalled
by the gastronomic feat of consuming it in the same time. The *Manchester
Guardian* of 27 November 1847 noted without comment that trains stopped
there to give passengers time to lunch or dine, 'usually . . . a quarter of an
hour'. The same activity on the West Coast route at Preston, described by a
writer recalling the days before dining cars, reached its peak between 2.00pm
and 3.00pm each day in July and August. The two down expresses arrived
from Euston at 2.20pm and 2.50pm respectively, while the corresponding up
trains arrived at 2.05pm and 2.20pm. 'The impetuous charge of hungry
passengers endeavouring to get through half-a-crown's worth of food in 20

minutes, and scalding their throats with hot soup in the process, was a sight in itself worth seeing . . .'[6]

As journeys lengthened with the growth of the railway system, full meals like these became more in demand, as distinct from light refreshments, and the larger refreshment rooms provided a waitress service in an area set out with tables and chairs. By mid-century separate dining-rooms were common, and at some large stations they gained a sufficiently high reputation to attract a regular lunchtime clientele of local people. The new Aberdeen Joint station restaurant, opened in 1915, quickly gained a high reputation among local business men. The dining-room at the new Rugby station had much to live down but quickly did so, and after the British Thomson-Houston electrical factory opened nearby in 1902 many of its senior managers dined at the station and went on doing so into the 1920s. Latter-day dining and refreshment rooms were given elaborate decor in keeping with current fashion; the simplicity or restrained elegance of earlier interiors gave way to High Victorian opulence in the 1870s and '80s, typified by the dining-room at Manchester Exchange, built in 1884, where the diner was almost overpowered by the heavy plaster decoration, Minton tiled walls and massive woodwork. The charmingly Edwardian room at neighbouring Victoria, dating from the 1901–4 reconstruction, with its coloured glass dome, could hardly have been in greater contrast, while in London station restaurants like the Surrey Room and the Windsor Bar at Waterloo, and the Pillar Hall Restaurant at Victoria (latterly known as the Chatham Restaurant) were popular meeting places. The upstairs tea-room at Glasgow Central had its devotees, too, while by using the external entrance outsiders could enjoy a good north country tea at moderate prices (according to a contemporary description), among the potted palms and basket chairs of the *art nouveau* tea-room and café at York without going on to the station. The passenger requiring sustenance between trains rarely had to look far, either. The platforms of the big stations were liberally provided; Birmingham New Street, for instance, had five refreshment rooms and three dining-rooms, while Newcastle had a dining-room in addition to one first-class refreshment room and two for second and third class. Liverpool Street even had a separate 'Ladies' Dining Room'.

Trouble with catering contractors in the early years was not restricted to Swindon, and the requirement for intensive provision of food during short periods at intervals through the day, combined with a monopoly, made many of the contractors indifferent to quality, while the railway company was first in the firing line of complaints. Trade at stations not favoured with a lunch stop could sometimes be uncertain, though. There were problems over leasing the rooms at Glasgow Bridge Street, which after three years in 1858 were converted to waiting rooms, only to be reopened as refreshment rooms in 1870 until they finally closed through lack of patronage in 1890. The first

One could still dine at Cannon Street in 1954. The rooms entered from the concourse were in the former hotel (*R. C. Riley*)

catering contractors were often proprietors of local hotels; they were the only people with suitable experience, but some of those whom they employed soon gained sufficient expertise to set up as specialist railway caterers. In 1882 the London & South Western Railway let all its refreshment rooms to one contractor, called Simmons, followed in 1888 by the most well known of all the railway caterers, Spiers & Pond. They had started in Australia and their first British contract was for Farringdon Street refreshment room on the Metropolitan Railway in 1863. Later that year they gained the contract for stations on the London, Chatham & Dover Railway and its successor, the South Eastern & Chatham, until 1905. Other large station refreshment rooms under their control were Manchester London Road and Bradford Exchange, while they held the Cheshire Lines Committee contract until 1906 when the Great Northern took over the catering. The GNR was one of the partners in the Cheshire Lines and, like one of its co-partners, the Midland, had for some years been gradually taking refreshment room catering into its own hands. Most of the large companies gradually adopted this practice, generally in conjunction with their hotel departments, and the Midland's reputation, here, as in so much else when it came to passenger amenities, was ahead of many of the others. Neele comments, looking again at Preston:

> The dining arrangements at first were of the rough and ready order, a hot and perspiring woman stood at the top of the table doing the carving, which required some energetic work on her part to supply the customer, all anxious to lose none of their allotted time. Subsequently the North-Western Company took this department into their own hands, and a manifest improvement by dint of constant pressure soon developed itself, many of the Directors who had watched the French restaurants at roadside stations, bringing their impressions to bear . . .[7]

Significantly the London & South Western, which had no hotels, used contractors until they became part of the Southern Railway, when Spiers & Pond went on to manage catering on the former LSWR lines until 1930.

During the nineteenth century and the first part of the twentieth, North European emigrants crossed England on their way to America. Back in the early 1840s, the Newcastle & Carlisle Railway conveyed German emigrants across the north of England to Carlisle, whence they were taken by canal boat to Port Carlisle for a ship to Liverpool where they made their final embarkation. As more railways were completed, other east coast ports were used, and a plan of Hull Paragon station in 1887 shows special emigrants' waiting rooms, kitchen and dining-room, and their own internal booking office. They were still used in 1930, although to a less extent. Neele refers to the special through trains conveying Scandinavian emigrants from Hull to Liverpool where there was equivalent accommodation at Tithebarn Street station – 'extensive barrack waiting rooms', he called it, conjuring up a grim picture of mass emigration.

Queen Victoria's first train journey took place from Slough to the temporary Paddington station in 1842. When the Great Western and the London & South Western railways completed their branch lines to Windsor, both companies built special royal waiting rooms at their stations. On the opening of the permanent station at Paddington in 1854 a royal suite was provided in the main block of buildings alongside the departure platform. The rooms were finished in pale salmon with gilt mouldings and grey silk panels on the walls, and furnished with French furniture. The outer doorway was surmounted by a crown, and the door on to the platform had the royal arms on one side and the GWR's on the other. They can still be seen on Platform 1 at Paddington.

When she travelled by the London & South Western the Queen used Nine Elms. After it closed to regular passenger traffic in 1848 and became a goods station, she went on using it rather than transfer to Waterloo. She liked its privacy. She could arrive with the minimum of fuss, and it was easily accessible from the palace. The royal saloons were kept there and when the LSWR converted the station to carriage workshops in 1854 they replaced it with a special royal station built close by in Wandsworth Road. It had a single platform and survived until the 1890s.

Bricklayers Arms was similarly used for occasional royal trains after regular passenger traffic ceased in 1852. It was mainly for visiting royalty arriving from the Continent, again because of its convenient location, and a royal waiting room was provided. It was last used in 1863, after which the new Charing Cross station was nearer and more appropriate. The drive across Trafalgar Square and up The Mall was much more impressive, too.

The London, Chatham & Dover station at Victoria had a royal suite in the old entrance block in Hudson's Place, again mainly for foreign visitors. The rooms were decorated in white and gold. When the Great Hall was built at

Euston in 1846–9, a parcels office block was included alongside new platforms. The south end incorporated royal waiting rooms with a private entrance from Cardington Street. In Greek style, with white and buff walls and painted panels, the two rooms had French windows on to the platform through which the royal party could step direct to the train. They were not used very much and eventually became an extension to the parcels office.

Ordinary waiting rooms tended to be plain, and in later years their bareness gave them a music hall reputation approaching that of the refreshment room sandwich. Nonetheless many of the benches were upholstered, which is more than can be said of European and American stations. An attempt was made at Glasgow Bridge Street to make the first-class waiting room more attractive by leaving a daily paper there, but as the attraction quickly transferred itself to the newspaper the gesture did not last long. In any case most early railways allowed news-vendors on to their stations, where they would set up a trestle table or a portable stall that could be closed up. At first there was little attempt at control until in 1839 a seller of guidebooks at Euston complained to the London & Birmingham that his man had been ejected by the staff. He was thereupon given official approval, although there was still no control over what was sold or the vendors' behaviour. Letters in the press led the companies to gradually put proper contracts out to tender.

The first station bookstall contract was let by the London & Blackwall Railway to William Marshall at Fenchurch Street in 1841. He was followed by his son, Horace, who opened bookstalls at Midlands and South Wales stations on the Great Western and lines it acquired in those areas. He also sold sweets, sandwiches and bottled beer. Also in 1841 Walkley & Son obtained a contract for bookstalls on the Bristol & Exeter Railway. It was 1848 before the London & North Western realised that the authorised Euston news-vendor was on to quite a good thing, whereupon his contract was terminated and a new one advertised for all the company's main stations. The successful tender went to W. H. Smith & Sons who were then newspaper distributors. The previous vendor's protests were ignored and he was forcibly removed so that the first railway bookstall could be established. Two weeks later, Smiths gained the Midland Railway contract, followed by others, so that by 1852 they had over sixty standard bookstalls. For some years the Great Western was an exception, as in 1849 the contract for bookstalls between London and Bristol was given to F. C. Wheatley.

Smiths' uniformed platform newsboys became famous, each with his large basket, and were featured on their hanging signs and posters. In Scotland, however, Smiths encountered tough competition from John Menzies of Edinburgh and had only one bookstall, at the North British station in Edinburgh, until 1857, when they withdrew and left Scotland to Menzies. Smiths also withdrew from the LNWR and the GWR in 1906 because the rents demanded were too high, and Wyman & Sons took over, eventually acquiring some 350 stalls. The name W. H. Smith became linked with books through their railway bookstalls, from which they went on to open their well-known high street shops, although at one time it was very noticeable that these tended to be located only in towns where Smiths did not have the station bookstall contract.

Like the bar and the bookstall, the public lavatory had its origin on the railway station, generally providing a much higher degree of sanitation than the often communal privy that most ordinary people were forced to use at their homes. The class distinctions exercised over waiting and refreshment rooms were sometimes applied to the loo as well; Euston in its early days had first- and second-class 'Gents', but not Ladies. Since railways provided the first public conveniences, it is probable that they also installed the first penny-operated locks, of which Messrs Lockerbie and Wilkinson's patent seems to have acquired a near monopoly. At Glasgow Bridge Street in 1874 there was installed a 'self-acting register of persons using WCs for one penny'. As time went on the Gents' loos at big stations incorporated hair-dressing saloons, as a few still do, and it was common to find bathrooms. Newcastle at one period not long ago had four but these, like dining-rooms, have now almost become a thing of the past.

Strict control was exercised over cabs. Generally the main arrival platform at a terminus had a cab road alongside it where empty vehicles could stand after discharging incoming passengers. Until the London Cab and Stage Carriage Act, 1907, only railway-licensed cabs could use the London termini except Waterloo, which was open to all-comers at a penny a time, and in this way the companies could ensure that only reputable cabs were used. Even after the Act took over licensing, railway company regulations had to be observed. Usually some kind of circulatory system was instituted, using separate entrances and exits. As stations were enlarged or rebuilt, some had special subways or bridges to bring cabs to the arrival platforms without criss-crossing those on the way out, and some are still in use although the tendency now is to try to keep taxis outside the station and let the passenger walk. Brighton still has its old cab tunnel, just wide enough for a horse-drawn vehicle, running beneath Platform 9 where half-way down it does a tight U-turn and emerges between Platforms 7 and 8.

Nowadays the process of 'taking the train' has been speeded up. The stations – with one or two notable exceptions – are easier to negotiate, and the fast-food principle dominates catering. Inter-city journeys are incomparably faster. Only buying a ticket at a station is more tiresome, thanks to credit cards, cheques and the complications of electronic self-accounting ticket machines in the ticket office. The old-time booking clerk who issued a ready-printed, quickly-punched Edmondson card in exchange for cash was indisputably quicker.

8

The Great Iron Halls

The traditional great railway station evokes a mental picture of sunlight, smoke and steam mixed with a suffusion of sounds; squealing brakes as a train comes to a halt, carriage doors slamming, iron barrow wheels rumbling, shouts and whistles as another train prepares to depart; an amalgam of sights and sounds created by a great glass arched roof that forms both sounding board and lighting effects. The passing of steam has been accompanied by some of the station roofs that were built for the age in which it reigned, but enough survive to explain to younger generations why and how they were built. To older folk a large station with anything less somehow seems inferior, just as it did to the citizens of Sheffield and some other important towns nearly a century ago when they saw that long-awaiting new stations had mere awnings over the platforms instead of a proper roof; a roof which symbolised that material of the Victorian age which made it all possible, iron.

Sir Joseph Paxton's hall for the 1851 Great Exhibition in Hyde Park demonstrated to the world how iron and glass could be used to make a large yet well-lit building. Its spatial beauty, enhanced by the decorative capabilities of iron itself, was quite unlike anything seen before and earned it the name the 'Crystal Palace'. It was, of course, by no means the first large iron structure. Cast iron had started to enter general use in the late 1780s, accelerated by the Napoleonic Wars when shipbuilding had first claim on timber. John Nash, the celebrated Regency architect, used iron to imitate stone columns at Carlton House Terrace and in Regent Street, and in 1815–21 iron construction received the seal of acceptance in the Prince Regent's Royal Pavilion at Brighton. The canals used iron extensively for bridges and aqueducts, and mass-produced ironwork was used in textile mills, factories and even churches. After the wars big advances were made in manufacturing sheet glass, enabling curved shapes to be given to the large conservatories that were becoming increasingly popular in the gardens of the wealthy.

Paxton's own conservatory for the Duke of Devonshire at Chatsworth led the way in 1837–40, followed by the great Palm House at Kew Gardens, 1844–8, designed by Decimus Burton and executed by Richard Turner of Hammersmith Ironworks, Dublin. Equal advances in the foundryman's art showed that cast iron could not only be structurally pleasing but could carry

Even a sunny day did little to pierce the gloom at Leeds Central, seen here in 1957. Few mourned its demise (*Author*)

applied decoration that became increasingly intricate as the century progressed. Ultimately no design seemed too delicate to be reproduced. What the Crystal Palace did was to publicise to the world a technique that hitherto had not been commonly appreciated; more importantly it showed how the new principle of prefabrication enabled ironwork to be erected cheaply and quickly. Above all, it made iron fashionable.

Before the 1850s station train sheds generally had fairly low, pitched (that is sloping) roofs, two or more side-by-side being necessary to span more than two or three tracks. Cheapness and speed of construction were the main considerations so, unlike some of the elaborate frontage buildings, plain simple sheds were felt to be quite adequate. The term 'train shed' today seems an imperfect, almost demeaning term to apply to the great iron halls that followed, but 'sheds' the first buildings were, in the sense of a single-storey shelter for trains, and the term has stuck.

As the name implies, the function of the first train sheds was to cover the trains, not necessarily the passengers. Between the arrival and departure platforms of a terminus, at least two extra sets of rails were laid for remarshalling vehicles by manhandling them on turnplates, as described in Chapter 6. They could also be used as sidings for cleaning and storing coaches under cover. King's Cross had as many as fourteen, which came in useful when space was needed for more platforms, and as late as 1868 the new St Pancras station had six.

Because agricultural practice offered the only common examples, engineers drew on the designs of the great tithe barns and granaries to span the widths required for the early train sheds. The very first one was like that, built of timber by the Liverpool & Manchester Railway at Liverpool Crown Street station shortly after it was opened in 1830. Queen-post trusses were supported on one side by the platform canopy, which itself rested on twelve iron columns, and on the other by a screen wall. Some 30ft across, it seems to have been an afterthought resulting from realisation that a carriage shed was needed. The roof over the Grand Junction Railway's temporary Birmingham terminus at Vauxhall (1837) had wooden king-post trusses, again on iron columns set along the edges of the platforms which were mainly uncovered.

For a few years, the combination of iron columns and wooden trusses was the accepted design, although iron was used to reinforce the roof timbers when greater widths were covered. Holme and Cunningham's roof at the first Liverpool Lime Street station in 1836, spanning 55ft, had the joints reinforced with iron straps, and the columns had shallow curved brackets meeting at the centres to create the attractive segmental arched arcades that became a feature of many train sheds. At Lime Street the open spandrels of the brackets had simple diagonal struts; at later stations these spaces were used for decorative ironwork when it was realised that the train shed could be given a touch of elegance. The three low wooden-roofed sheds built side-by-side to span 74ft at the London & Southampton Railway's Nine Elms terminus in the capital, opened in 1838, had iron arcades of this kind.

A few other wooden-trussed train shed roofs were built, as shown in Appendix 2, but in general after the early 1840s new stations of any importance had iron roofs except on the Great Western Railway where, thanks to Brunel, the wooden roof reigned supreme until well into the twentieth century.

The longevity of Brunel's pitched timber roofs and their continued construction by his successors has already been noticed in Chapter 5, but before turning to the development of the iron roof it is appropriate to pause for a look at the more important examples. A number of reasons have been advanced for Brunel's choice of timber at most of his larger and some lesser stations: cheapness, ease of construction, simplicity in renewing components without recourse to large-scale rebuilding; even, at Plymouth North Road, soft ground. It has been suggested that mistrust of cast iron and the high cost of wrought iron confirmed Brunel in his preference for a traditional material, leading him to design so many wooden bridges, viaducts and train sheds that he has been described as the greatest timber engineer this country has known.

Originally Cardiff, Swansea and Birmingham Snow Hill all had Brunel's wooden sheds and buildings, some with quite wide spans. The Swansea roof stretched across four tracks and, after the addition of a second shed alongside in 1879, lasted until the late 1920s. Birmingham lasted until 1871 when it was moved to Didcot and re-erected as a carriage shed, a purpose for which it was much more suitable. Plymouth had two stations of this type, the first at the Millbay terminus opened in 1849 and the second, nearly thirty years later, at the new North Road station opened in 1877 where the Great Western built a pair of 46ft wide sheds in much the same fashion, each covering a platform and a single track, with the through lines running between them. The facing sides of the sheds were open on iron columns; later on sections of the roofs were carried downward to form awnings over additional outside platforms. To Plymouth it must have seemed that times on the Great Western had hardly changed, particularly when they made comparisons with the London & South Western's far superior stations at Friary and Devonport.

Bath and Bristol received special treatment, having roofs without trusses in which the structural system was deliberately concealed. Both were on viaducts and had masonry side walls. Constructed on the cantilever principle, the main rafters rested on a series of iron columns close to the platform edges. Each column acted as a fulcrum, the rafter extending backwards to form an aisle between the column and the wall to which it was tied internally by a vertical rod. Horizontal ties between the row of columns and the wall were boarded under. At Bath the span was 60ft, and deep concave panels covered the junctions between rafters and columns. This roof was demolished about 1897 and replaced by awnings.

Bristol Temple Meads is much more elaborate. The platform columns form neo-Tudor arcades, and to match the external styling the whole shed was given a medieval appearance by introducing mock hammer-beams with richly carved pendants and mouldings instead of the concave panels at Bath. The principals were plated with iron and the 'hammer-beams' were held together with iron straps instead of joints. The length of the original shed is 290ft and, as has often been pointed out, the 72ft span is 4ft wider than the genuine hammer-beam roof at Westminster Hall. Light entered through a line of glazing down each side, later augmented along the ridge. The tracks alongside the engine standing area at the inner end, referred to in Chapter 6, were under a mezzanine floor supported by iron columns between the tracks, making the space beneath dark and cavernous. It was not a very practical arrangement. Apart from the fire risk, engine smoke made it even darker and percolated up through the floorboards into the offices above. One was a large drawing office with extensive glazing to give good natural light.

Temple Meads is widely admired for its magnificent Tudor styling, now happily being restored after years of neglect, although pundits from Pugin onward have criticised it as imitation. As pure architecture this may be so, although no more than a lot of Victorian work, but for all its later inconvenience and rapid obsolescence the concept was unique and the execution masterly. Bristol and Bath were the first attempts to give architectural treatment to train sheds, and despite being a sham, Temple Meads had lasting style.

At the same time light iron roofs were being tried with considerable success. Charles Fox designed two 40ft wide spans, 200ft long, at Euston for the opening of the first part of the London & Birmingham Railway in 1837. Fox was a resident engineer under Robert Stephenson and went on to become well known as a partner in Fox, Henderson & Co who made and erected much railway and other iron work, including the Crystal Palace, for which Fox was knighted with Paxton and William Cubitt. Fox's Euston sheds had light wrought-iron trusses on slender cast-iron columns and arcaded brackets decorated with reducing circles. This feature appeared again at Nine Elms in the following year and was copied to such an extent that it became a distinctive characteristic of many British stations. A number of examples still remain. The contrast at Euston between the plain sheds and the massive bulk of the Doric Arch attracted a good deal of critical attention. In later days they were low and dirty but at the time they were built, when the trains themselves were much smaller, their height was not so disproportionate and their simplicity imparted an elegance that was enhanced when gable screens were fitted later. When locomotives started to burn coal instead of coke, lingering smoke became a nuisance. A commentator in *The Engineer* declared that 'there ought to be more space between the engine funnel and the ridge of the roof than there is at Euston.'[1] Later additions were somewhat higher and in 1872 the original roofs were jacked up 6ft and pedestals inserted. Euston-style roofs were built, with variations, at stations all over the London & North Western system, becoming larger and heavier as time went on, but still displaying many of the original features, the most prominent being the vertically glazed gable screen with its delicately curved transom which became as familiar on the LNWR as Brunel's wooden roofs on the Great Western.

The train sheds at the two Curzon Street stations at Birmingham were similar to Euston, but when only two years later, in 1840, Francis Thompson's Derby Tri-junct station was opened a big jump forward was perceived. It was a through station and the roof had three sections, the longest at 1050ft being over five times the length of Euston. It was praised for the airy elegance imparted by 22ft tall fluted columns to which horizontal iron beams instead of spandrel brackets gave an added impression of height.

The outer line of the roof rested on a brick screen wall pierced by a series of arched windows. The walled shed was also adopted at Manchester Victoria of 1844, at that time the largest station in the country, and by Tite at Carlisle and Perth, both completed in 1848, although Carlisle was actually opened in 1847. These side walls not only provided much better weather protection than the earlier open-sided sheds, but gave greater resistance to the thrust of the roof and from this time onward appeared at many stations, both termini and through. Thompson did the same at his Leeds Hunslet Lane terminus and at Chester. Parry's *Railway Companion from Chester to*

Holyhead (1848) credits the Chester train shed design to Wylde, considering it 'one of the most elegant yet constructed'. The rear screen wall comprised a brick arcade of part-open and part-blind arches, and the octagonal station master's office on the central cross-platform, with its tent-like pagoda roof, added a touch of whimsical charm.

The extraordinary speed at which the railway system expanded created a quite unforeseen problem of rapid obsolescence of stations, particularly terminals and junctions. Growth in traffic and the continually improving techniques for dealing with it meant that a station could become both too small and out of date in a very few years. One solution was to take separate goods lines along the centre of a station with a platform loop on each side. Stoke-on-Trent and the Midland station at Nottingham were designed in this fashion from the outset in 1848, each with a three-span roof across all four tracks. When it was realised that there was no point in roofing over the two through lines, the middle span was often dispensed with, as was done in the 1860s when the LNWR rebuilt Stafford and Crewe.

The narrow width of platforms created another early problem, aggravated by the rows of columns holding up the roof, frequently close to the edge and a hindrance to the movement of barrows, luggage and mailbags. Before rebuilding was started in 1861, the original Grand Junction station that still served Stafford, described as 'little better than . . . an unimportant roadside station', was so restricted that the horses used for shunting carriages often had to mount the narrow and crowded platforms to the 'considerable terror and confusion to timid passengers'.[2] Closely spaced iron columns also increased the risk of collapse in the event of a collision, so engineers began to turn their attention to the possibilities of the arched roof in order to gain greater height and width, and at the same time improve on the poor aesthetic appearance of the low-pitched sheds.

The first arched roof was built at the Shoreditch terminus of the Eastern Counties Railway. It was no more than the substitution of pitched sheds by semi-elliptical ribs clad with corrugated iron, and otherwise was constructed to the conventional plan of three columned aisles, the widest of which was only 36ft. It was, however, a step forward in that the spans were clear, with no ties or trusses. The central span was raised above the side aisles on clerestoreys. The station was opened in 1840 but the roof was not completed until about 1844.[3]

At this time John Dobson was embarking on the design of a remarkable train shed to complement his as yet unbuilt monumental frontage block at Newcastle Central. Arcaded in three 60ft spans formed of deep semi-elliptical ribs, like Shoreditch, the central aisle was higher than those at either side, the arcades being created by the usual spandrel brackets but in this case surmounted by rectangular wooden panels concealing bracing.

The ribs were made from curved sections produced by specially designed

The dramatic curves of Dobson's roof at Newcastle Central are attractively emphasised by new cladding and contrasting colours in 1978 (*G. W. Buck*)

bevelled rolls that were the first of their kind. Dobson was able to gain platform space by using strong longitudinal members on columns 33ft apart under every third rib, a method copied later at Paddington and York. The culmination of Dobson's design, unique among those that had gone before, was the remarkable exercise in curves. It was the first large station to be built on a sharply curved site, a difficulty which Dobson turned to aesthetic advantage by designing the ribs and spandrel arcades to form an integrated pattern of receding arches curving away into the distance in a spectacular vista that was entirely novel. The rear wall of the frontage block was also curved to fit the 800ft radius of the roof, with arcaded doors and windows complementing the roof arcades. At the back of the station the screen wall was curved, so that from wherever one stood the effect was of a series of curved, arched arcades in iron or stone. When it was opened in 1850, not for nothing was Newcastle called the finest station in the country. After the Queen performed the official ceremony on 29 August, stone roundels containing the heads of Victoria and Albert in relief were placed on the wall overlooking the concourse, although the date, 28 September 1848, is wrong; that was the day she opened the High Level Bridge. Edward VII's head was added after he opened the King Edward Bridge in 1906.

At a time of rapid technical progress, new achievements were short-lived, and in 1849 a train shed was completed at Liverpool that, although less spectacular, was more daring and far-reaching in its consequences. Already Lime Street station was inadequate, and on behalf of the London & North

Western Railway which had succeeded the original Liverpool & Manchester, Joseph Locke prepared a scheme for rebuilding. The old wooden roof of 1836 had to come down and he planned to replace it with roofs of the Euston type until Richard Turner proposed a segmental-arched, crescent-trussed roof which would cross the 153ft 6in of the new station in one great leap. Turner, who had completed the Kew Palm house in the previous year, pointed out that with a single-span roof there would be no columns to obstruct the platforms. Locke was sceptical and despite Turner's protests insisted that such an innovative design needed full-scale tests. Two bays were erected and at the second attempt were successfully tested at Dublin, resulting in Turner getting the contract which he completed in ten months. John Cunningham designed the outer gable screen with scroll-work and large wheel motifs, while the inner end was closed by Foster's Lime Street screen wall retained from the earlier station.[4] It was the widest single-span roof so far erected and marked the point in Britain when the train shed started to become the dominant feature of the large station. Imposing frontages would continue to be built, but more frequently as hotels than as expressive symbols in their own right.

By 1850 timber was no longer used for station roof trusses except for some relatively unimportant ones and, of course, on the Great Western, although several small arched roofs of laminated timber had been constructed in the north. So it may be said that the laminated wooden ribs of Lewis Cubitt's great double-arched train shed at King's Cross, opened in 1852, were the swansong of timber as a principal structural element in large station roofs. Laminated ribs had been used in Germany at the Munich Hauptbahnhof in 1849, where 80ft spans sprang direct from the platforms to support a tangentially pitched roof, and Paxton also used laminated wooden arches for his transepts at the Crystal Palace which could well have served as Cubitt's model. It is known that he had to hurriedly redesign King's Cross when the Euston-type roof at the Great Northern Railway's temporary Maiden Lane terminus, opened in 1850, showed signs of weakness.

The ribs were made up of sixteen 1½in boards screwed and bolted together and covered with an iron band, placed 20ft apart, forming two 105ft spans, 800ft long and 72ft high. They sprang from iron shoes attached to the brick side walls and the elliptically arched centre wall. Having no ties, they gave an appearance of lightness to the boldly simple design, aided by glazing over some 75 per cent of the curved surface. On the west side the thrust was taken by the office block, while the wall on the east was buttressed by the heavy timber roof of the cab rank alongside, later replaced by more offices. Deterioration of the timbers, thought to be caused by insufficient seasoning and ventilation, dictated replacement of the eastern train shed ribs by iron ones in 1869–70, and on the west side in 1886–7. Rectangular glazing in the outer gable screens matched the arched openings in the façade.

William Cubitt, Lewis's uncle, was the engineer. He had been closely concerned with the remarkable degree of prefabrication that was essential to the erection of the Crystal Palace in the astonishingly short period of nine months. It was made possible by a unique and highly organised system of supply and assembly that was quite revolutionary. Cubitt put his experience to good use at King's Cross where speed also was essential. As soon as Lewis's designs were accepted by the Great Northern board, he was able to start fabricating the ribs on the ground, using large chocks to obtain the correct radius, and then hoist them into place. The Palace also opened engineers' eyes to the creative possibilities of iron structures, and the next thirty years witnessed the construction of many spectacular iron buildings and roofs, from market halls, shopping arcades and pumping stations to iron bandstands, park pavilions and conservatories.

The year 1854 was an important one for iron roofs. In Chapter 5, we have already noted George Berkeley's new Fenchurch Street station, the London & Blackwall Railway's modest terminus tucked away in a City of London side street that was notable for its frontage roof profile. During the summer two other stations were opened within a few weeks of each other, vastly different yet both equally radical in the design of their train sheds: Birmingham New Street and Paddington. Of the two, New Street was the greater technical achievement in that the elliptical roof covered in one span the unprecedented width of 212ft at the widest point. With tunnels at each end limiting the lengths of the platforms, it was absolutely vital that every foot of space should be used, which the single span ensured. It was not easy, as one side had an irregular curve so that each of the thirty-six crescent trusses was of different length and therefore of different depth.[5] Its designer, E. A. Cowper of Fox, Henderson & Co., translated the design of Turner's Lime Street terminus roof into one for a through station, springing at one side from W. J. Livock's office and hotel block and on the other from broad iron columns to reach a height of 75ft to the crown of the arch. The truss outlines were repeated in the upper part of the gable screens, with vertical glazing over a horizontal transom below.

New Street was purely functional; Paddington less so but highly decorative. The original shed has three spans, the widest 102ft 6in, and is divided laterally along its length by two 50ft wide transepts clearly derived from the Crystal Palace. They were intended for traversers to move carriages sideways from one track to another but were never used for that purpose. The elliptical ribs are supported on deep cross-braced longitudinal girders with a plain iron column beneath every third rib, following Dobson's principle at Newcastle. But instead of resting on the top of the girder, the ribs reach down to the bottom flange in a clasping action to which decorative wooden pendants were attached. The absence of ties, a later cause of trouble, added to the very fine vaulting effect of the transepts. For the decorative work

Looking south beneath Cowper's roof over the LNWR side at Birmingham New Street in 1905. The narrow platforms, famous footbridge and elevated signal box are well in evidence. Compare with Snow Hill (page 132) (*V. R. Anderson Collection*)

Brunel called in Sir Matthew Digby Wyatt, a noted architect and designer. Both had served on Great Exhibition committees and were very familiar with Paxton's work, of which Brunel was a great admirer. In addition to the transepts Paddington's was the first large station roof to use Paxton's system of ridge-and-furrow glazing in a series of straight transverse inverted W-sections over the central half of each span, the outer portions being clad with galvanised iron.

Wyatt's share of the work has often been dismissed as ornamental frills to Brunel's grand design, but it is much more than that. Without it Brunel's aisles, although still impressive, would look bare and sterile. Foliated cast-iron plates bolted to the lower portions of the ribs provide a repetitive decorative effect, and the upper sections have patterns of shaped holes, partly to lighten them and partly to take scaffolding for maintenance purposes. The gable screens are decorated with gracefully curved iron strips creating Moorish patterns of tracery, a style also followed in the capitals.

These effects demonstrate the strong partnership between the two men. The terms of Brunel's offer to Wyatt were phrased in a manner indicating that they fully understood one another.

Wyatt was also responsible for the decoration of the office block wall along the main departure platform which directly complements his work on the roof. The cross-bracing of the longitudinal girders is filled with delicate iron filigree above a long arcade of round-headed doors and windows bearing elaborately moulded decoration in spandrels, panels and friezes, all looking and feeling like iron but in fact cleverly executed in very hard, smooth cement that has withstood time and war damage to a remarkable degree – a great tribute to the workmanship of Brunel's day. Looking out across the transepts from the first floor are two singular iron-and-glass oriel windows, each with a smaller one on either side. These compositions are framed by elaborate cement rustication and pilaster strips decorated with incised Moorish floral patterns, each within a great semi-circle of outsize applied valancing emphasising the blind end of the transept, again in cement. This side of the station must have looked particularly fine when it was new, and sympathetic repainting in recent years has restored something of the original dignified exuberance which 130 years of accretions has not managed to

Cannon Street from the river, c1905–10, showing the towers, great gable screen and signal box spanning the tracks (*National Railway Museum*)

destroy. Brunel and Wyatt might not be over-pleased if they came back today, but they would not be too disappointed either.

New Street held its record for the world's widest span for fourteen years, although the design was copied. Despite being less than twenty years old, Liverpool Lime Street by the early 1860s once more was too small and was rebuilt for the third and final time. Tite's office block was left for the time being but Turner's roof had to go. William Baker, chief engineer of the LNWR, replaced it in 1867 with a wider one of 212ft span, and in 1874–80 his successor, Francis Stevenson, with E. W. Ives, added a second span of 191ft alongside. Meanwhile, two other single-span, crescent-trussed roofs competed in height instead of width, designed by Sir John Hawkshaw for the South Eastern Railway at Charing Cross, opened in 1864, and Cannon Street in 1866. They were the South Eastern's reply to the rival London, Chatham & Dover Railway's extension into central London at Victoria in 1862, and were built on arches at the ends of bridges on the north bank of the Thames. Seen from the river they looked enormous, Charing Cross towering up 98ft and Cannon Street 106ft above the rails. Massive side walls supported the roofs, those at Cannon Street terminating in the pair of Baroque towers which still remain Thames-side landmarks. They housed water tanks for hydraulic lifts in the station. Meanwhile in 1862 the LCDR's Victoria station, designed by Sir John Fowler, opened with a twin-span, segmental-arched roof of considerable lightness and elegance. Trusses were dispensed with in favour of light iron tie rods arranged polygonally between radial iron struts, forming a graceful arc beneath the latticed ribs.

In 1874 Fowler, with W. M. Brydone, repeated his design with a single-span version at Liverpool Central. The ribs were spaced as far apart as 55ft due to difficulties caused by adjoining buildings ('one of the boldest designs of its kind', said Walmisley approvingly[6]). The last and only remaining single-span station roof of this type was designed by the engineer-in-chief of the North British Railway, James Carswell, for the reconstruction of Glasgow Queen Street. It was the NBR's reply to the challenge of St Enoch, and for the smaller and very restricted site it was an ideal choice for a light, airy roof with the right degree of grandeur. As at Liverpool it stands at the mouth of a tunnel above which a magnificent gable screen admits radial patterns of light, contrasting with the darkness beyond. Undoubtedly Queen Street is the most handsome station interior remaining in Scotland and visually is one of the most satisfying left in Britain.

In terms of widths and heights, the single-span roofs of the 1850s and '60s pointed the way to the ultimate at St Pancras, opened in 1868. Here three main factors influenced the design. Foremost was the Midland Railway's overwhelming desire to enter London, primarily to gain access over its own metals instead of someone else's but also, and nearly as important, to demonstrate beyond doubt that a provincial railway could out-perform the

London-based companies. The satisfaction gained from cocking a snook at the capital is nothing new, particularly when your deadliest rivals – in this case the London & North Western and the Great Northern – are near neighbours on Euston Road.

The site presented difficulties. The Fleet River, which acted as a main sewer, flowed across it and could not be disturbed; the Midland wanted a link with the Metropolitan Railway (the present Circle Line) which meant putting it in a tunnel under the station; and, thirdly, the current 'state of the art' exemplified by New Street, Charing Cross and Cannon Street had to be bettered. Anyone wishing to study the history of St Pancras in detail should read Professor Jack Simmons's *St. Pancras Station* in which the methods of overcoming these problems are fully examined.

The company was fortunate in having two remarkable men leading the project: James Allport as general manager, and William Henry Barlow as consulting engineer. To reach the terminus in Euston Road, the line into London had to cross the Regents Canal, the same obstacle that had bedevilled Robert Stephenson's approach to Euston, necessitating the steep descent from Camden, and William Cubitt's into King's Cross where he had burrowed beneath it. Barlow decided to bridge the canal and use the height gained to build, in effect, a two-storeyed station with the passenger accommodation on the upper floor, thereby avoiding too steep a descent, and beneath it warehousing space required for the important Burton-on-Trent beer traffic, reached by hydraulic wagon lifts.

To meet all these requirements, Barlow drew up the daring plan of spanning the station with a great single-arched roof springing from ground level and using the first-floor deck to tie it horizontally, thereby dispensing with trusses. In this way he avoided the cost of the massive side walls needed at Cannon Street and Charing Cross in favour of lighter screen walls, at the same time increasing the height-to-width ratio to give him the widest span allowed by the site, 243ft. Down below he gained maximum storage space by building his deck from iron plates supported by a grid of girders on iron columns and brick plinths instead of the more usual brick arches. The grid's dimensions were based on the size of the standard beer barrel. By rejecting an aisled roof with columns, Barlow was also able to avoid deep foundations down the centre of the station, particularly over the tunnel which would have needed reinforcement, although he still had to place the Fleet River in a large iron conduit.

In designing the ironwork, Barlow was assisted by R. M. Ordish, an engineer extensively experienced in structural cast-iron work who had advised on Birmingham New Street and the Crystal Palace. The latticed ribs of the train shed rose 110ft to the crown of the arch, which was slightly pointed to increase wind resistance, although Barlow was not unaware of the dramatic effect of the clear Gothic outline. So the great roof stands today, the sweep of its curves unimpeded by struts and ties, the platforms free of columns; a vast hall lofty enough to lose smoke and steam. Only three other single-span train sheds exceeded it, all in the United States: the Pennsylvania Railroad's at Jersey City and Philadelphia Broad Street, and the Reading Railroad station in Philadelphia. But none of them was as high.

In Britain two more were built having a similar appearance but smaller and on rather different principles: Glasgow St Enoch sadly has now gone, but Manchester Central remains, at the time of writing being restored as an exhibition hall. Curiously, from London they were both reached from St Pancras so that at each end of his journey the traveller found himself in a counterpart, in much the same way as in the early days Curzon Street and Euston matched. Although neither St Enoch nor Manchester Central was owned by the Midland that company had a strong influence over their construction.

St Enoch was built by the City of Glasgow Union Railway, a joint venture by the North British and Glasgow & South Western railways with both of whom the Midland had dominant partnerships in Anglo-Scottish services that competed with the London & North Western and Caledonian's. It was the Midland that decreed that the Caledonian was not to be allowed to share the station, and after 1896 the North British relinquished its share, leaving the GSWR in sole possession. We have seen in Chapter 3 how, when it was

In early BR days a train hauled by an LMS 2P 4-4-0 emerges from Glasgow St Enoch beneath the great radial gable screen (*Royal Commission on Ancient Monuments, Scotland*)

Manchester Central in 1964, with a corner of Trubshaw's Midland Hotel on the right (*Manchester Central Library*)

opened in 1876, St Enoch was the first station to do justice to Glasgow. The roof was 198ft wide and 83ft high, springing from platform level but not tied by the floor which was partly built on a brick undercroft. Instead the latticed ribs were anchored to cast-iron beams embedded beneath the outer platforms, the thrust being taken by brick arches or solid ground. The profile, too, differed slightly in having a rounded crown instead of a pointed arch, although it was still Gothic in outline. Fowler acted as consulting engineer with James F. Blair. A second and smaller span, 140ft wide, was added in 1904, designed by the GSWR's chief engineer, William Melville, and trussed on the Queen Street model.

The Midland's influence at Manchester Central was more direct as the company was one of the three railways jointly forming the Cheshire Lines Committee, which also owned Liverpool Central. Several writers, regrettably including the present one, have attributed the design to Fowler but contemporary sources do not mention him. Walmisley states unequivocally that 'the whole work was *designed* [my italics] and carried out by Mr. L. H. Moorsom, to the satisfaction of the engineers of the Midland, Great Northern and Manchester Sheffield & Lincolnshire Railways', and it is they who signed the drawings: Andrew Johnson for the MR, Richard Johnson for the

GNR and Charles Sacré for the MSLR. Their names also appear on the drawings reproduced in *The Engineer* in 1880, with the comment that Moorsom, resident engineer of the Cheshire Lines Committee, was responsible for 'the immediate superintendence of the work'.[7] Moorsom was the son of the early railway engineer, Capt W. S. Moorsom, and had also carried out the new roof at Manchester London Road. His obituary is just as unequivocal as Walmisley, stating that he 'designed and constructed' Manchester Central.[8]

Although the crown of the roof is curved like St Enoch's, the rectangular glazed gable screens and sloping roof above the spandrels formed between the lower ribs and side walls superficially give a greater resemblance to St Pancras. The span is 210ft and although, like St Pancras, the station has two storeys with the lower floor originally a goods station, it is built on brick arches and the ribs terminate just below platform level on large anchor plates bolted to masonry footings. Opened in 1880, Central immediately became and remained the most impressive of the city's stations. It could be said that it followed the American and Continental fashion of making the train shed inner gable part of the façade, except that at Manchester it *was* the façade. The original plan to follow St Pancras and St Enoch and build an hotel across the front was changed in favour of a site across the street (see Chapter 9), so the temporary entrance through low wooden offices became permanent. They had the sole, if somewhat negative merit of not hiding the magnificent roof so that alone among big city stations in Britain the Manchester Central train shed completely dominated the approach.

After its remarkable effort at Paddington, the Great Western seemed to retire from the contest exhausted. Its only other impressive roofs were at the second Birmingham Snow Hill of 1871, a pair of semi-circular crescent-trussed sheds unique on the GWR, and the very fine single-span Gothic arch built by Francis Fox[9] over the new through platforms at Bristol, opened in 1878, where the interplay of horizontal and vertical curves can still be admired. Built on the sharp curve between the original Great Western and Bristol & Exeter lines, the roof required a span of 125ft. By using a pointed arch, Fox was able to have a rise of 31ft 3in from the springing on side walls, in turn enabling them to be kept low and, with the aid of looped-up ties, dispense with buttresses which in any case were prevented by the nature of the site. It was a very economical roof, and although Fox was employed by the Bristol & Exeter Railway – which amalgamated with the GWR in 1876 while work was in progress – one wonders whether the Gothic form was influenced by the Midland which was the third joint owner, or whether it was merely intended to harmonise with Brunel's original terminus. Matthew Digby Wyatt did the French Gothic frontage and interiors, and the extensive ornamental detailing that went with them, so he can probably be credited with the roof detail, particularly the distinctive Gothic glazing bars in the

Gothic in iron 1: Francis Fox's curved Gothic roof makes an imposing backdrop for Castle class engine No 7017 *G. J. Churchward* on a train at Bristol in 1960 (*Russell Mulford*)

gable screens and the screen on the pitched extension to Brunel's old roof erected simultaneously.

At the same time the North Eastern Railway uncharacteristically was 'going Gothic' at Middlesbrough, where in 1877 it replaced its old Italianate station with what Meeks calls 'the most Gothic of train sheds'. There were two spans, one fairly low and narrow and the main one with, to quote Meeks again, 'a 5:4 ratio of width to height, the most vertical proportions ever applied to a train shed. The significance of this is not minimised by its relatively small dimensions – 74 feet wide by 60 feet high; as in the 13th century, the most characteristic examples are not necessarily the largest.' The ribs were of latticed wrought iron forming clear spans, and deep gable screens were fitted. W. W. Tomlinson credits the design to William Peachey, the current North Eastern company architect, although Meeks attributes it to Cudworth without saying which one. William Cudworth was engineer for the Darlington district of the NER at that time, and his son, William John, who had spent four years studying architecture in London, was his assistant, so the work could have been a collaborative effort with Peachey having ultimate responsibility.

While engineers like Fowler and Barlow were extending the limits of technology, there were others less adventurous who kept to more conventional methods, although in doing so one designer achieved one of the most dramatic structural vistas to be found in any station. By 1865 the North Eastern Railway, after years of prodding by its East Coast route partner, the Great Northern, finally conceded that something would have to be done about York. The 1841 terminus was inadequate and the need to reverse through trains in and out (twice if they were going to Scarborough) was intolerable. Accordingly an Act for a new through station was obtained in 1866, although even then there were more years of delay while the North Eastern went through a difficult financial period. At length a start was made in 1874.

The new station was placed on a sharp curve and designed by the NER's architect, Thomas Prosser. He retired shortly after work started and was followed in quick succession by Benjamin Burleigh, who died in 1876, and William Peachey who completed it during his equally short period of office. Burleigh and Peachey made detail changes to Prosser's design which followed the principles adopted by Dobson at Newcastle and Brunel at Paddington. Every third rib is placed over a thick foliated Corinthian column, the intermediate ones 'clasping' the longitudinal girders, as at Paddington, with heavy decorative pendants below. The ribs form five-centred arches of clear span, tapering from the base and given added

York station when it was new – from the catalogue published by the builders, John Butler & Co of Stanningley Ironworks, Leeds (*Author's Collection*)

lightness by quatrefoil holes that match the pierced patterns in the girders which rest on shallow spandrel brackets. Cast into the spandrels are the white rose of York and the NER's heraldic device.

The roof comprises a main span 81ft wide and two smaller ones of 55ft on either side, while on the east side of the station a further 43ft span covers bay platforms at each end, separated by the central entrance block. The York roof lacks the lightness and grace of Newcastle and Paddington, displaying all the florid elaboration typical of the period and, despite being 20ft narrower than Paddington's widest span, is much heavier. In fact, for its date it was rather old fashioned, as Walmisley implied in his comment that on such a sharp curve a single span would have been preferable so that there would be no columns to obstruct the signals or the guard's view of his train. However, without them we should be unable to admire the skilful interplay of curves and arches sweeping to a majestic conclusion at the three eccentrically centred arcs of the radially glazed gable screens – a masterpiece of visual geometry. The final touch lay in the Gothic styling of the wooden glazing bars in the screens, a familiar bit of York's unique character that was lost when they were replaced by plain aluminium in 1972.

There can be no doubt that for many railways it was important to extract the maximum grandeur from their train sheds, and as the gable screen was the first thing the passenger saw from outside and in, and gave the shed much of its character, the design was a matter for great care, resulting in fascinating variety. To provide maximum shelter from the wind, the screens needed to be deep; at the first Aberdeen Joint station they reached down to within a few feet of the carriage roofs. Radial glazing was always effective: Glasgow Queen Street, the LCDR side at Victoria and Bradford Exchange were outstanding examples. One of the most artistic was designed for the small two-platform terminus at Dundee East which was virtually all roof and little else. Its highly ornamental fan-like screens did much to make up for the complete absence of a frontage building, although in later years the frontage screen was covered by stepped vertical boarding, creating a curious appearance.

At Cannon Street and Charing Cross the gables were particularly imposing, especially when viewed from the river (page 112). The prominent vertical glazing at Cannon Street was offset by a deep, diamond-lattice frieze around the curve of the roof and a matching horizontal girder below. White-painted radial boarding behind the lattice work gave added effect. At some stations shelter was sacrificed for artistry, although economy doubtless was not too far from the designers' minds as well. Shallow gable screens at Liverpool Lime Street do no more than shield the trusses, forming delicate sickle shapes that enhance the gentle curves of the platforms. The radial screens at Glasgow St Enoch, although deeper, were also sickle shaped and made a major contribution to that station's distinction. A particularly elaborate

Cabs wait beneath the fine, newly-painted arched roof at Bradford Exchange around the turn of the century. The large number of coaches and empty platforms probably indicate that the photograph was taken on a Sunday. (*J.B. Hodgson/LYR Society*)

effect was made at the Blackfriars Bridge station of the London, Chatham & Dover Railway, which lasted from 1864 to 1885; the crescent-trussed roof was deliberately disguised as a pitched roof by a sloping gable, partly glazed and partly boarded, with applied circle motifs. The extent of the aesthetic contribution the gable screens made can be gauged by looking at station roofs where they have gone, leaving them with a bare, empty appearance like Rugby and Huddersfield, or where replacements are in unsympathetic modern materials, as at Carlisle and Fenchurch Street. At one station at least, though, screens were omitted from the outset. The Great Northern Railway was not given to frills, and the grand gesture it felt was needed for its incursion into Midland territory at Leicester was strictly tempered with economy. Although the twin-arched train shed at Belgrave Road station (1883) might have given the impression of a mini-King's Cross, closer inspection revealed a degree of bare simplicity that included dispensing with gable screens entirely. Even then the station was larger than anything the traffic ever justified; one half as big would have been more than adequate and might possibly just have paid for itself. It finally closed in 1962.

The great arched roofs could only have been built with the help of moveable timber staging that ran on rails along the length of the site. The system was first used at Birmingham New Street, stretching across the full width and profiled to the curve of the roof ties. Sheerlegs mounted on the top platform hoisted up sections of each 25 ton truss for fitting into place. The same method was used at St Pancras, first with one staging and then two so that at the height of the work three or four ribs were being assembled per month. Erecting the scaffolding itself was a major task, filling the cross-sectional area of the roof with a vast trellis of timber baulks weighing over 1,000 tons. It was inched along by a host of men wielding crowbars in unison to the beats of a gong. The staging for Manchester Central had twenty-eight wheels running on seven rails and was long enough to allow two ribs to be erected simultaneously, using steam cranes to lift the sections.

Considering the degree of pioneering construction that went into these large station roofs, their long lives were a tribute to their designers. There can be no doubt that like so many Victorian structures built without the benefit of the detailed scientific analysis and research that goes into preliminary design work today, they were, by modern standards, 'over-engineered' with a margin of error that would not be tolerated. There were failures of course, although they were surprisingly few. Joseph Cubitt had the double misfortune to see his roof at Bricklayers Arms collapse twice. It fell shortly before the opening in 1844, killing one man and injuring nine more, due to a defect in construction, and a second time in 1850 after a column was hit by the buffer of a vehicle on a turntable, bringing down two of the three spans.[10] The properties of cast iron were not always fully understood, giving rise to its use for unsuitable components such as the end pieces and struts of latticed, longitudinal girders in the new roof at Manchester London Road in 1866. A 90ft section collapsed during construction, thought to be due to a combination of over-long girders for the type of fixing and narrow supporting bearings on the columns. Strong winds may have caused excessive deflection as all the wind ties had not been fitted, leading to the fracture of an end casting. James Brunlees, reporting on behalf of the coroner's jury, suggested that had the roof been completed it would have 'balanced' and all might have been well.[11] As it was, thirty men were injured of whom two died. An adjoining bay was also in a precarious state so it was pulled down in spectacular fashion by a pair of locomotives. Imperfect fixing of girders was also responsible for the entire 100ft span roof being blown down in a gale at Blackburn in 1861, while sixteen spans of the new Huddersfield station roof collapsed during erection in 1885, just after a train had left and killing four men. Again there was no wind bracing in position. It was considered that the struts may have been inadequate and there were defects in four of the columns.[12] Subsidence of made-up ground was alleged as the reason for the collapse of the roof during its erection at the Caledonian's Lothian Road station, Edinburgh, in 1869, although the official cause was given as a flaw in the iron.[13]

When Brighton station was extended in 1861, a 50yd length of 58ft wide new iron roof being erected next to the old collapsed into the cab rank at 5.30 one morning. It was fortunate that owing to the early hour no one was about, but the noise woke up a goodly part of Brighton.[14] The most spectacular roof failure occurred in 1905 at Charing Cross when Hawkshaw's gable screen, 70ft of his roof and part of a side wall fell in. From the first unusual sounds to the final collapse took about twelve minutes, allowing the thirty-odd men replacing some glazing time to scamper to safety, although three men were killed in a train standing underneath and three more who were working in a theatre alongside the station when the wall crashed down into it. No criticism was levelled at Hawkshaw, the cause being attributed to a faulty constructional weld in a wrought-iron tie that had weakened during forty-one years of strain. However, the railway company took no chances, getting Handyside & Co of Derby to demolish the rest and replace it with ridge-and-furrow roofing similar to that used in extensions to Euston, and the station was closed for three and a half months.

When the large arched roofs were being built in the 1860s, there was considerable argument for and against them. Walmisley, in the paper to the Society of Engineers in 1881[15] on which his book was based, listed three advantages of the wide single-arched span: it gives freedom from internal supports and uninterrupted space for movement, there are no valleys in which snow can lodge, and it provides grander architectural effect, although that could be a matter of taste. *The Engineer* hopped from one side of the controversy to the other. In 1866 Cannon Street was 'a magnificent realisation of what a great railway terminus of the English metropolis should be',[16] but twelve months later it was declaiming that Charing Cross and Cannon Street 'completely eclipse the churches in the Strand when viewed from the river' in a leader that was generally critical of the cost of large roofs. While conceding that Euston was low and dark and the multiplicity of pillars was an inconvenience, the writer felt that there was a big difference between those and just a few columns 'for the purpose of curtailing what would otherwise be a roof of gigantic proportions'; he concluded that 'there is no possible utility in constructing a roof of dimensions similar to those of the future St. Pancras station'.[17] A year later, a few weeks before St Pancras was opened, its opinion had hardened still further. Another leader headed 'Monster Station Roofs' asserted that height rather than usefulness seemed to be the objective, ascribing to St Pancras a 'gigantic rotundity' and comparing Charing Cross with the back of a large fish. In settling the question of single versus multiple spans, the writer added, the sole object should be light, air, space and ventilation, but not at the expense of dispensing with intermediate columns, which was too great. The 'dingy row of low sheds' at Euston was roundly condemned, Fenchurch Street was 'so bad as to be past condemnation' (it was only fourteen years old), and Shoreditch 'might be remodelled with benefit to everyone, including the company'. The LCDR station at Victoria was held up as a model, along with the Brighton company's new roof at London Bridge which was claimed to be 'the best and cheapest in the city'[18] (p 168).

There can be little doubt that the more ambitious railways regarded big station roofs as a status symbol worth considerable financial risks to achieve, while others were more concerned with economy even to the point of downright ugliness. The motives of the Midland at St Pancras and by proxy at St Enoch and Manchester Central have already been alluded to; in its bid for West End and City traffic, the South Eastern at Charing Cross and Cannon Street was prepared to spend enormous sums to outdo its bitter rival, the London, Chatham & Dover, at Victoria and Ludgate Hill, and succeeded very handsomely, although admittedly in the latter instance it was not difficult. Yet beyond its termini most South Eastern stations were a disgrace. The London & North Western represented the other view. Although self-styled 'The Premier Line' and 'the oldest passenger railway in the business', whenever possible it saw no point in building anything more than variations on its Euston sheds, for choice following Sir Charles Fox's stated maximum of 50–60ft spans because they were cheaper. And thus they duly appeared, at Stafford, Crewe, Preston, Huddersfield, Holyhead and Swansea Victoria.

Other railways followed their own less stereotyped policies as both types of roof continued to be built until the end of the century. The more important ones are listed in Appendix 2, of which Francis Fox's 132ft wide single-span pitched roof at Exeter St Davids is notable as the widest of this type attempted in Britain. It was built in 1864 to replace the South Devon Railway's old Brunel double station and because of its extreme width the complex light iron trusses were difficult to erect. William Bell's high semicircular roofs on the North Eastern Railway also are worth singling out for their family characteristics at Darlington Bank Top, Stockton and Hull.

In the midst of this surge of varied development, one station stands in the same front rank of great train halls as Paddington and St Pancras. Liverpool Street is closer than any other to the analogy of the railway cathedral made by *Building News* in 1875, the year in which it was finally completed. *The Engineer*'s strictures on the old Great Eastern terminus at Shoreditch, or Bishopsgate as it was renamed in 1846, were well merited. The station was too small and too far out even then, yet the cost of cutting through the densely packed areas and into the City would have daunted an affluent company, much less the penurious Great Eastern. Even when it did face up to it, eleven years elapsed between obtaining an Act and a fully operational new terminus, not helped by two years in Chancery.

The design was entrusted to the company's engineer, Edward Wilson, in close association with Fairbairns, the great Manchester ironworkers and structural engineers who supplied the roof. When they took on the job,

Gothic in iron 2: looking through the transept at Liverpool Street in 1974, with two of the Edwardian tea-rooms on the left (*G. W. Buck*)

Fairbairns were paying 10%; when it was virtually complete they went into liquidation, partly due to market forces but, as the directors said, mainly in connection with a single large contract. It could only have been Liverpool Street.

The station is in two sections, the original or western train shed being partly a head station with short platforms for suburban trains, and partly a side station with much longer main-line platforms stretching back alongside the office block. This desire to gain the advantages of both types of layout made the station very awkward when eastward extensions became necessary, just as happened at Euston nearly forty years before. The train shed combines two 109ft main spans of tapering, cantilevered latticed trusses carrying pitched roofs, with narrower side aisles of transverse ridge-and-furrow roofing. Something of Liverpool Street's cathedral-like effect is gained from the two striking rows of tall columns between the main spans, only 5ft apart, with radiating spandrel brackets in richly pierced patterns, like webs of iron lace. Each column is built up in cluster form around a central rainwater pipe, although unfortunately the foliated decoration on the capitals was removed in 1956. A vaulted transept at the head of the suburban platforms covers a concourse, breaks at the narrow centre aisle and then continues to intersect the main-line roof. From the head of the station, these 76ft high vaults framing the filigreed arcades of the aisles make the most dramatic contribution to the station's high visual impact. The pointed arches of the side roofs co-ordinate with blind Gothic arcading on the western side wall, in buff brick trimmed with red. Tripartite lancet openings pierce the tympani.

The eastern side wall dates from the 1894 extension by John Wilson, nephew of Edward, and W. N. Ashbee who had been appointed Great Eastern architect. The open red-brick, white-trimmed arcade of semi-circular arches matches the blind arcading on the far side along Bishopsgate. Although similar in outline, the roof is lower and more subdued than its brethren. Columns supporting the four narrow spans carry latticed, longitudinal elliptical brackets. There is no transept. A simple transverse roof covers the eastern concourse.

In recent years one of the station's other distinctive features was lost when the shallow elliptical valancing was removed from the outer end of the western train shed, which otherwise was devoid of any kind of screen. It was as though the fanciful design was intended to relieve the majestic solemnity within, and its spiky silhouette is missed.

One can speculate whether this exciting visual exercise was worth it. For all its beauty and grandeur, the western train shed was undoubtedly a very complicated structure, built when the technology of simpler, wider spans was well developed. Apart from knowing that moveable scaffolds were used in erection, we have no details of how it was put together, and it would be interesting to be able to compare the cost of, say, the contemporary arched roofs at Liverpool Lime Street and Central after allowing for their smaller areas. Certainly Liverpool Street caused something of a stir, mostly complimentary, and it did all the Great Eastern hoped for and more, to the extent of needing enlargement twenty years later. Even so, it would have been more convenient had it been built on a high level as originally intended, instead of in an expensive excavation made merely to facilitate a through line to the Metropolitan Railway that was hardly ever used. Avoiding the high cost of construction and maintenance, not to mention starting trains up a 1 in 70 gradient from the station, would have considerably eased the Great Eastern's financial burden. It did not make a reputation for Edward Wilson, either, for he sought little publicity and died two years after his station was finished, hardly known even in his profession.

The mansard roof, which has two slopes on each side of a central ridge, the lower one steep and the upper one shallow, was used at only one major station. Thomas Prosser, the North Eastern's architect, employed it for the Leeds New station, opened by that company jointly with the London & North Western in 1869, in two spans to which a third was added in 1879. The trusses were of complicated design, and straight-pitched longitudinal and transverse extensions at each end made the whole roof even more so to the point of ugliness. The only other station of any consequence to have this type of roof was the original Dundee West (1862), and the Adolphus Street terminus in Bradford, completed in 1855 to the designs of John Fraser, the Great Northern Railway's resident engineer. Mansard only in outline, its roof pitches rested tangentially on tied arched ribs springing from platform level.

The idea of a tangentially pitched roof was not used to any great extent; the Midland built two spans at Sheffield and a single one at Bath Green Park in 1870, both to a similar pattern of arched ribs on columns with side aisles following the pitch of the roof. William Bell tried one at the North Eastern's new Sunderland station, opened in 1879, where he used pierced semi-elliptical ribs to support his pitched roof. Inside he completed the illusion that it was an arch by fitting curved soffit boarding. The largest roof of this type was designed by H. E. Wallis for the reconstruction of Brighton station in 1883, together with an iron *porte cochère* that practically obscured Mocatta's façade. With the Midland side at Birmingham New Street, (Chapter 10), it was the last of the dramatically curved arched roofs. New Street was considerably narrower and lacked the broad elegance of Brighton's stately columns and elliptically cantilevered trusses that were a less elaborate version of those at Liverpool Street. Among the pitched roofs built at the end of the century, Nottingham Victoria, completed in 1900, stands out for its airy, spacious quality.

The final type of overall roof evolved from Paxton's ridge-and-furrow technique in the same year that the Crystal Palace was finished, 1851. Under Fowler's direction, Fox, Henderson erected an elliptical roof of 83ft span, presumably on crescent trusses, for the Manchester, Sheffield & Lincoln-shire's new station at Sheffield Victoria, employing ridge-and-furrow glazing. Despite the example of the Palace, this combination of ridges and furrows with a curved roof was rare at railway stations. Sheffield predated Paddington by four years, where in any case only the central parts were glazed with straight sections sloping to an apex, and with the exception of Leicester Campbell Street other ridge-and-furrow station roofs were horizontal. The Sheffield roof was not long lived, being replaced by a conventional straight-pitched shed in 1867. The roof at Campbell Street replaced the original narrow Midland Counties Railway train shed of 1840 when the station was enlarged in 1857–60. Crescent trusses carried longitudinal ridges and furrows of irregular section over the platforms at each side. Along the centre over the four tracks transverse ridges and furrows on louvred upstands formed a continuous clerestorey to let out steam and smoke, broken in the middle of the station where there was longitudinal glazing right across, possibly an alteration made when further improvements took place in 1878. This unusual roof lasted until the new London Road station at Leicester was built in 1890–5.

Also erected in 1851 by Fox, Henderson was the first horizontal ridge-and-furrow roof at the little Rewley Road station for the LNWR at Oxford, but for some reason the system thereafter was widely used for awnings but did not recur as a major roof for nearly twenty years. Robert Jacomb-Hood's roof for the London, Brighton & South Coast Railway's Victoria station of 1860 incorporated a form of ridges and furrows but they were 50ft broad, more like a series of transverse pitched spans running across the station on latticed girders. A single row of intermediate columns down the middle of the cab road kept the platforms clear of obstructions.

It was 1892 before narrow ridges and furrows appeared again, requiring only light supporting girders and closer to the Paxton style, first on the Euston extensions completed in that year and followed by new roofs at Stoke-on-Trent, Charing Cross and finally the great twentieth-century rebuilding of Waterloo where there are nearly twenty acres of it, very efficient but lacking the glamour of the arched roof. With one exception broad ridges and furrows became a peculiarly Scottish design associated with the Edinburgh consulting engineers Edward L. I. Blyth, his nephew Benjamin Hall Blyth Junior and George Miller Cunningham. They practised successively as Blyth & Cunningham, Cunningham Blyth & Westland and Blyth & Westland. They designed the new two-span roof at Lothian Road station, Edinburgh, in 1869, but were best known for their horizontal ridge-and-furrow roofs that were planned to combine the advantages of broad spans without the expense of high arches, which they were known to dislike, and they did much work for the Caledonian and North British companies.

The commonest type comprised deep ridge-and-furrow bays running transversely across the station on even deeper trussed girders between substantial side walls. The ends of the bays were hipped and slated or glazed, and heavily patterned end screens were a hallmark. The earliest roofs of this kind were two built for the first major reconstruction of Edinburgh Waverley in 1874. They flanked a central block of offices and an approach road sloping down from Waverley Bridge, and were linked at the east end of the station. James Bell, the NBR chief engineer, was credited with the entire work and there appears to be no record at Blyths that they were involved, although the design was very much in the style that became associated with them. Blyths designed a similar roof for the extensions to Perth General station in 1885, with square-patterned end screens, although the old two-bay roof of 1848 was left in place until Caledonian-type awnings took its place in 1911. The type appeared again when Dundee West was rebuilt in 1889, almost identical to Perth, and at Edinburgh Princes Street in 1894 where the irregularly tapering site added a dramatic quality to a roof that at its widest spanned 183ft. Blyths were responsible for all these, and went on to excell themselves with a gigantic specimen at Leith Central in 1903 with a maximum span of 220ft, the widest of this type to be built, which can still be seen towering above the roof tops from the head of Leith Walk a mile away. The North British intended the station to take some of the pressure off Waverley by using it for starting and terminating its Edinburgh–Glasgow and some long-distance services, but in the event did not do so. Consequently, like Leicester Belgrave Road, the station was far larger than the local traffic warranted, and its spacious accommodation and four broad platforms represented something close to the ultimate in railway company optimism. It was closed in 1952.

In Glasgow, Blyth & Westland incorporated longitudinal ridges and furrows in the rebuilding of Bridge Street station which was completed in 1879. It served as a prototype roof for Glasgow Central, opened in 1882 with a maximum span of some 213ft, but for the major extensions of 1901–6 they reverted to their more customary transverse roofing in a modified style that moved away from characteristic heaviness by having a semi-elliptical bottom flange. The impression of lightness was aided by total glazing and attractive fan windows in the side wall and the opposing arcade that joined the new roof to the old, which itself was extended at the south end by six bays of the new-style roofing.

Blyths' Scottish influence materialised south of the border at Carlisle when the 1880 enlargement of the joint station necessitated replacement of the old twin-span roof. Here, too, lightness was achieved by using delicately curved longitudinal trusses braced by circular hoops to carry broad, fully glazed transverse bays, terminated by deep end screens of Gothic glazing that matched Tite's original buildings. They gave a character to Carlisle station that since their removal has been much the poorer. The commissioning of Blyth & Westland for the job indicates the dominant influence of the Caledonian; had it been left solely to the London & North Western there would probably have been simply an updated version of the Euston roof. Blyths last big station roof was for the final reconstruction of Edinburgh Waverley, completed in 1900 and forming the third station on the site. It still had to be kept low, although again it was quite light, and five intermediate rows of columns were provided – slender fluted pillars with delicate Corinthian capitals that helped to give an impression of height.

Only one such roof was built by English companies, the LNWR and the

GWR for their enlargement of Shrewsbury Joint station between 1890 and 1904. R. E. Johnston, engineer for the joint lines, widened the bridge over the Severn to take platform extensions that were roofed on the Blyth system with 150ft span trussed girders, so low that Central signal box needed a special flat roof to fit beneath them. Here again Blyths' records do not indicate any involvement. The pair of ridged sheds over the older part of the station were retained until about 1932 when they were replaced by awnings, and in 1963 the newer roof was replaced as well.

The Midland built three notable longitudinal roofs, quite different from Blyths', in which the glazing was fitted to the diagonal braces within trussed Warren girders which could therefore be lighter as they had no superstructure to carry. This method formed a compact, economical roof of neat appearance. After a trial run at Ilkley on the Otley & Ilkley joint line in 1888, the system was used for the rebuilding of the much bigger stations at Bradford Forster Square (then called Market Street) in 1890 and Leicester London Road, completed in 1895. The latter was spoilt by deep, arched wooden end screens at the north end that do not appear to have lasted long.

The deep, heavy-trussed roof at Shrewsbury, added in 1904 and removed in the 1960s, photographed in 1955 (R. E. G. Read)

In 1885, W. Jacomb built a remarkable longitudinal ridge-and-furrow roof for the London & South Western's new Bournemouth East (now Central) station, 43ft high and spanning 95ft. It is carried on deep, diagonally braced girders supported by huge foliated iron brackets springing from heavily buttressed brick screen walls, and as a style remains unique.

Three other remarkable roofs remain to be mentioned for their singularity. Reconstruction of Rugby by the LNWR in 1886 produced an unusual combination roof which dominates a station that visually has nothing else to offer. The bays at each end of the single broad island platform have pitched roofs of the LNWR's conventional Euston pattern, but the central portion is formed by lofty transverse ridges and furrows resting on the lower flanges of deep plate girders that reach out over the through lines to terminate on brick side walls and further girders. The object was to allow central crossovers to be installed between the platform and through lines so that a train could enter or leave one end while a second train occupied the other (Fig 14 on page 82). Vertically glazed side screens matched the gables, but like them have long since been removed. There were similar screens at Crewe and several other stations on the same system.

A combination of roof types also marks the Lancashire & Yorkshire's largest station, at Manchester Victoria, where by 1904 a series of extensions culminated in a station in two distinct parts. The through platforms have a massive roof, of which only part survived war damage, comprising 57ft wide arched transverse bays carrying tangential glazing and, horizontally across the top, narrow ridges and furrows running longitudinally, each bay having its own set. Completed in 1883–4, they are a unique, if cumbersome design, tremendously elaborate for the area they covered. The terminal section of the station has three pitched roofs dating from 1877 to 1904, the oldest having a span of 128ft. The curved ridges impart to the trusses a more graceful appearance than is usual with this type. Between the two portions of the station lies a section of hipped ridge-and-furrow roofing. Until 1934 there was an 87ft span pitched roof, dating from 1864, covering the through lines and the long platform to Exchange station, linking up with the 1884 roof.

Lastly came the Great Western's final fling – or more accurately its only fling since the extension of Bristol Temple Meads – in the complete rebuilding of Birmingham Snow Hill for the second time. Completed in 1912, the new station embodied all the latest thinking on a large through station, with broad island platforms, separate goods lines down the middle and a novel ridge-and-furrow roof of shallow-pitched bays 36ft wide. Each fully glazed bay was carried on a latticed truss having an elliptical lower flange, and had a prominent ventilator along the ridge. There were fourteen of them, carried on latticed girders 276ft long at the widest point, supported on a row of steel stanchions along each side. There were two more rows down the centres of the platforms, which were so wide that the stanchions

The Great Western's final fling: Birmingham Snow Hill looking north in 1933. The roof trusses over the centre tracks were left unglazed to let out steam and smoke from goods trains passing through the station (*LGRP, courtesy David & Charles*)

caused no impediment to the working of the station. The longest unsupported span was 103ft and the stanchions were encased with ornamental iron plates. Great care was taken to articulate the ornamental soffits of the bays with the glazed-arch screens that acted as side walls. To let out smoke and steam a 22ft gap was left over the through lines down the centre, where the facing ends of the roof bays had frilly elliptical valancing to match the profile. The roof as well as the station buildings was decidedly Edwardian in character, quite different from any of its predecessors and a fitting finale before the great railway mergers of 1923. Even more remarkably it was built without interrupting traffic by using moveable staging, one side at a time. The roof at Snow Hill was designed by W. Armstrong, the Great Western's new works engineer, and erected by E. & C. Keay who brought the 90ft main girders ready assembled from their works at Darlaston, 10 miles away, on special rail wagons.

Responsibility for design, manufacture and erection of station roofs and other ironwork varied; sometimes the whole job might be entrusted to a large firm under the general supervision of the railway company's engineer or consultant, or it might be divided into a number of contracts and sub-contracts employing local firms. One of the most famous names associated with stations, going back to the days of the Crystal Palace, was Fox, Henderson & Co of Smethwick who numbered Paddington, Birmingham New Street, Liverpool Tithebarn Street and the first station roofs at Bradford

Exchange and Sheffield Victoria among their achievements. Equally well known were Andrew Handyside & Co of Derby who erected a succession of arched roofs of increasing size at Bradford Adolphus Street, Middlesbrough, the Central stations at Liverpool and Manchester, and Glasgow St Enoch, among others. They were responsible for the 1907 roof at Victoria and manufactured a wide range of iron goods. Many a Midland Railway lamp standard bore their name. The great bridge builder whose name will always be associated with the Forth Bridge, Sir William Arrol, built the roof designed by Blyth & Cunningham for Carlisle, and less-remembered firms also did important work, such as Lucas Brothers of Lowestoft who not only were contractors for the Charing Cross, Cannon Street and Liverpool Street roofs but built the Albert Hall. The North Eastern Railway went to John Butler & Son of Stanningley Ironworks near Leeds for its roofs at York and Leeds New stations; Glasgow engineers P. & W. McLellan did the roofs for the reconstructed Bridge Street station and the original part of Central, and later for the final rebuilding of Edinburgh Waverley. The Great Western favoured a Cheltenham firm, Vernon & Ewens, to erect Francis Fox's roof at Bristol, and the arched roofs at Penzance and the 1871 station at Birmingham Snow Hill, which they also designed. The name of Mabon & Co of Ardwick Ironworks, Manchester, which supplied the second roof at Sheffield Victoria, lives on, cast into iron columns at Manchester Victoria, and the part the Butterley Company played is proudly displayed on the roof ribs at St Pancras.

The Victorians were proud of the great train halls, seeing them as symbols of their new power, steam, in a way which has few parallels in modern technology. They were very quickly copied all over the world, as railways spread, and were regarded as status symbols not just by the railways but by the world's cities and by the firms that built them. They inspired the world of the arts, too: painters, writers and, in the twentieth century, film-makers have found in the railway station a setting in which to portray an infinite variety of human experience. Jean Dethier demonstrated these and many other responses to the 'volcanos of life' in his exhibition and book *All Stations*. Frith's painting vividly captures the crowded animation of Paddington as a train prepares to depart, while Monet was stimulated by the effect of smoke and steam under a great arched roof; in the world of literature many writers have used the station for a scenario, and film-makers have seen the vigorous atmosphere of a large station as an ideal setting for drama. At least one musical piece has also featured a station: the opening chorus of Offenbach's *La Vie Parisienne* is set on a station platform.

9

The Grand Manner

From the late 1850s architectural ideas entered a period of rapid and continuous change. Classical styles were on the way out, Italian Renaissance was becoming coarsened and Gothic was definitely 'in', boosted by the new Houses of Parliament. As Pugin's influence waned, High Victorian Gothic of the 1870s and '80s looked more to France and Italy for inspiration, while a growing popularity of Dutch and Flemish forms led to the so-called Free Renaissance style which was not really a style at all but a mixture of many. Even the architectural press had difficulty in applying descriptions, and there was plenty of robust Victorian criticism of this free mingling of styles which we now call eclecticism. *The Builder* put it more bluntly: 'Deliberately to take the features of various styles and bundle them together is the only way to produce monstrosity and a sort of architectural chaos.' Although all new work was not as bad as that, there was a lot of vulgarity and brashness as architects strove to satisfy clients' desires for bigger and better monuments to their power and prosperity. The period was the one that gave our city centres the appearance which most of them largely retain today, despite modern redevelopment programmes, and the railways were well to the fore in adding their quota. For them competition, not achievement, was now the guiding precept, and there were architects in plenty ready to design monumental frontage buildings to equal the engineers' train halls within.

For the wealthier travellers it was the age of the grand hotel that developed directly from railway enterprise when the companies realised that the inns and taverns of the coaching days were inadequate for the growing travelling public. The first hotel expressly for rail travellers was built by Lord Crewe close to the station bearing his name shortly after the Grand Junction Railway was opened in 1837. Queen Victoria stayed there in 1848, apparently well satisfied, when fog at sea forced her to make her first Anglo-Scottish rail journey. The London & North Western Railway took over the Crewe Arms Hotel in 1864 and enlarged it in Jacobean style.

The London & Birmingham was the first railway company to build a hotel, in two blocks named the Victoria and the Euston on either side of the approach to the Doric Arch, hiding the outer lodges. Philip Hardwick designed them in plain Georgian fashion, apparently quite amenable to ruining the total aspect of his station little more than twelve months after its opening. One side catered for first-class passengers and the other contained 'dormitories'. The sacrilege was completed in 1881 when J. M. McLaren linked the two buildings from the first floor upwards in a so-called French style, forming a low bridge over the access drive and entirely shutting off the Arch from view. In 1840 the LBR company built the Queen Hotel adjoining the classical front to Birmingham Curzon Street, spoiling its symmetry.

In 1841 the Midland Hotel was opened opposite the station at Derby, designed by Francis Thompson on an H-plan with the entrance between the wings and intended to resemble a country house, which it probably did as it stood well outside the town. Later the main entrance was moved to face the station and a glass-roofed covered way was built. G. T. Andrews built the first hotel to actually adjoin a station at the Greenesfield terminus at Gateshead in 1844, with direct access to the platform, followed by the Royal Station Hotel at Hull in 1851 which was built across the head of the station. Its handsome front has recessed Doric and Ionic arcades, and was extended in 1903–5. The interior was planned around a well, lighting what is now the main lounge and reception, surrounded by an arched arcade. Andrews placed his York station hotel in similar fashion in 1853. Here the yellow brick front is quite plain, as were most of the interiors.

Having seen the success of the Euston hotels, when the decision was made to start on Paddington Brunel persuaded the Great Western board to build an hotel across the head of the station in the manner of Andrews at York and Hull but on a far grander scale. He saw it as a fitting commencement to a journey from London to New York via the railway to Bristol and thence across the Atlantic on his new steamships. The hotel was managed by a separate company of GWR directors and officers with Brunel as its first chairman, a financial device by which many railway hotels were built. P. C. Hardwick designed it and Prince Albert performed the formal opening in 1854. The Great Western Hotel set an entirely new standard in size and comfort; with 103 bedrooms and numerous suites, it was the largest in Britain, having cost in total some £60,000. The contrast with the station's severely plain frontage in Eastbourne Terrace was very marked. Hardwick chose the French Renaissance style of Louis XIV in which to clothe his hotel and gave it a high mansard roof between prominent corner towers to provide the right château-like appearance. Bedroom windows gave on to elaborate balconies, and over the iron *porte-cochère* four giant urns were untiringly supported by well-formed caryatids. Above the topmost cornice a large pediment enclosed sculptured figures, representing Peace, Plenty, Science and Industry, by John Thomas who also did other sculpture about the hotel. The balcony ironwork included the GWR monogram in the entwined letters that became so familiar a feature of station seats and other equipment, still much in evidence today; it was possibly the first use of this device. The GWR took the hotel into direct ownership in 1896 and during modernisation in

1936–8 most of the external decoration, apart from Thomas's pediment, disappeared along with remodelling of Hardwick's sumptuous interior in current Art Deco style. The richly decorated ceiling in the dining room, the statuettes and the elaborate motifs were all removed or covered up, and only some of the upstairs corridors now retain something of their original atmosphere. Typical Brunel innovations were electric clocks, private lavatories (but not baths) and hot-water pipes in linen cupboards.

In the same year the LNWR completed the first combined hotel and station entrance at Birmingham New Street. J. W. Livock designed a very restrained four-storey block in white brick with the station entrance through an arcade on the ground floor. It was named the Queens and North Western Hotel, later just the Queens, thus perpetuating the name of the old Curzon Street hotel. Two more floors, a pair of Edwardian domed towers and a new central foyer were added in 1911 and 1917. Pilasters on the rear wall supported Cowper's arched station roof, and at platform level an arched arcade led into refreshment rooms and other station offices in the hotel basement.

We have already mentioned in Chapter 8 the side-by-side pair of stations at Victoria, which were the next new ones in London. The original scheme was drawn up by the Victoria Station & Pimlico Railway to give four southern railways access to the West End by building a bridge across the Thames and a station open to all comers modelled on the American terminal station principle. It misfired and although the bridge was built only two companies used it. The station was leased to the London, Chatham & Dover Railway, with the GWR as a junior partner, opened in 1862, but in the meantime the other main participant, the London, Brighton & South Coast Railway, had opened its own station alongside two years previously. There was no communication between the two without going out into the street, and neither of the station frontages in Victoria Street was at all presentable. The Chatham's building containing the booking office was round the corner in Hudson's Place, a pleasantly modest Italianate building in yellow brick with some quiet stone rustication, while the LBSCR station was dominated by the seven-storey bulk of J. T. Knowles's overbearingly pompous Grosvenor Hotel, built in yellow brick with a bulging convex roof crowned by a pair of large cupolas sprouting immense spikes. Heavily ornamented stone dressings include sculptured heads of long-forgotten politicians and other notables amid plentiful vegetation. It was independently owned until 1899 when the

---

The Queens Hotel at Birmingham New Street in the 1920s. Designed by J. W. Livock in 1864, the towers and top two floors were added later. The station was entered through the arcade on the left (*British Rail*)

City commuters leave the 'Brighton' side at Victoria in the late 1900s. The original Grosvenor Hotel is in the background and the 1907 extension nearer the camera (*National Railway Museum*)

LBSCR bought it, only to lease it to Gordon Hotels one year later. Even so, it was the Brighton's reply to Paddington and its interior retains much of the original grandeur, including one of London's best hotel foyers from which a marble staircase ascends to arcaded galleries around three sides. The arched restaurant and neo-Tudor lounge are equally impressive. The Terminus Hotel that was built adjoining the Brighton's station at London Bridge was less successful, and in 1893 the company bought it for use as offices. It was demolished in 1941 after bomb damage.

The provinces could provide some of the best new work at this time, including a station that until recently has been overlooked. It was built in London Road, Nottingham, by the local architect Thomas C. Hine for the deceptively named Ambergate, Nottingham & Boston & Eastern Junction Railway, and bears some of the characteristics of his Thomas Adams lace warehouse in Stoney Street. In 1854, with little prospect of getting anywhere near Ambergate or Boston, the company was leased to the Great Northern which became the owner of quite the most elaborate station on that otherwise austere system. Opened in 1857 but not completed until 1858, with its triple-span train shed it eventually joined the ranks of over-large stations that never had the traffic their owners hoped for, and after 1944 was used solely for goods. The building rambles round a corner site, with a prominent stone *porte-cochère* fronting an arcade, a French gable and pavilion turret.

Henry Lloyd of Bristol designed a long stone façade that was a good example of wall treatment to go with Francis Fox's new train shed at Exeter St Davids, opened in 1864. A broken balustrade carried twenty-five classical urns above a projecting office building but was spoilt by the obligatory iron *porte cochère* and, later, the addition of a two-storey wing in 1911–14. Fox's roof was replaced by awnings at the same time, leaving a range of elevated wooden offices which, with the floor removed, now forms a curious kind of clerestory above the main down platform to which arched windows add a touch of elegance.

The new station at Manchester London Road that at length was opened after years of complaints and disputes between its joint users, the London & North Western and the Manchester Sheffield & Lincolnshire, incorporated a three-storey block facing a broad approach road sloping up from the street, designed by the Manchester architects Mills & Murgatroyd in a heavy and rather coarse Italianate style. Even so, by virtue of its commanding position the building formed the most imposing station front in the city.

It was an expensive time for the North Western. Between 1867 and 1880 it again rebuilt Liverpool Lime Street, and to front it Alfred Waterhouse designed a large hotel. He was a son of the city and a noted architect who had just finished Manchester Town Hall and later counted the ubiquitous red-brick corporate architecture of the Prudential Assurance Co among his numerous works. The North Western Hotel replaced Foster's screen wall and

The former North Western Hotel at Liverpool Lime Street in 1985, after cleaning and during conversion to shops and offices (*Author*)

a large part of Tite's side block, although a portion remained in Lord Nelson Street until 1984. The ground floor was mainly station offices and refreshment rooms, and above it five hotel floors terminated in a roof line that became a Liverpool landmark. Rows of dormer windows and chimneys sprout between spiky spires, spirelets and towers. The building's height is accentuated by strong vertical emphasis and completely hides the 1867 train shed. Stone roundels display the LNWR arms showing Britannia apparently seated on a lion with a background of a train on a viaduct, while a king and queen (Victoria and Albert?) guard the grand staircase windows over the entrance. It had over 200 bedrooms, although there were only 8 bathrooms and 37 toilets.

The strong vertical lines and towers that were fashionable in commercial architecture were softened by the lines of windows on the hotels designed by Edward Middleton Barry for the South Eastern Railway's new stations at Charing Cross and Cannon Street in 1865 and 1867. The capital was raised by forming separate companies to build them, which the railway took over later. The Charing Cross Hotel Co's hotel had 250 rooms, with a further 98 added in an annexe reached by a bridge over Villiers Street in 1878. Both hotels had undeniably exciting roof lines. Cannon Street's was considered to blend with the City skyline, together with the train-shed towers. The top two floors at Charing Cross were rebuilt in a sort of flat Georgian style following damage in World War II and attracted considerable criticism, although lower down the exotic balconies and pedimented doorways give some impression of what the original composition was like. When the Cannon Street City Terminus Hotel was built, it attracted condemnation of the cost of profuse external decoration that included gilded finials on the spires and the use of French craftsmen to apply zinc decoration to the roof.

The interiors were palatial. The City Terminus had fewer bedrooms than Charing Cross but specialised in catering for City functions and entertaining, to which the first and second floors were devoted, the ground floor containing the station offices. On the first floor the 36ft high Great Hall had Corinthian columns and arches containing coats of arms of principal cities beneath a heavily decorated ceiling. There were galleries at each end and two tiers of windows looked on to the station, double glazed to keep out the noise. The fireplaces bore the hotel company's monogram and the South Eastern's arms embellished the door pediments. Corridors of 10ft width were lit by an ingenious system of mirrors reflecting borrowed light. A boardroom, coffee rooms and restaurant occupied the same floor, and there were more on the one above. Bedrooms were on the third and fourth floors.[1]

There was less ostentation at Charing Cross, and the barrel-roofed entrance hall has been spoilt by a false ceiling and encased stair banisters, but at the time of writing the domed and panelled ceiling in the finely proportioned restaurant can still be enjoyed. Outside, Barry's conjectural replica of Queen Eleanor's Cross that stood in Whitehall until 1647 is at once a reminder of a medieval royal funeral procession and a quaint piece of Victorian railway architectural eccentricity.

The contemporary façade at Broad Street offered a complete contrast. Built as its city terminus by the North London Railway, a nominally independent suburban line controlled by the London & North Western, more than any other London station its mixture of styles reflected the advance of eclecticism. The overall design was by William Baker, the LNWR chief engineer, probably assisted by J. B. Stansby who became the company's architect. The styling may indeed be wholly attributable to him. The building was given added height by its position on the end of a viaduct, aided by dominant curved and sloping French roofs with a central clock and profuse decorative ironwork. No one seemed to know quite what to call it; Sir John Betjeman was nearest with his 'best Town Hall style of 1866' (it was actually opened in 1865). The white Suffolk brick front was not improved when a Portland Stone screen and two ugly footbridges across the forecourt were added in 1913.

Less elaboration on the same basic theme featured at the Great Western's new station opened at Birmingham Snow Hill in 1871, replacing Brunel's shed. A long, two-storey building on the down side with a mansard roof, an iron trellis and coupled-arch windows was matched by a smaller block on the opposite side in Livery Street. At the London end an hotel, built in 1863, was enlarged by J. A. Chatwin in 1870. It stood partly above the tracks which in 1874 were roofed over to extend the tunnel between Moor Street and Temple Row so that the Great Western Arcade could be built over the top. The four-storey hotel was French inspired with classical detailing on the taller corner blocks and a row of large ball finials along the parapet. A memorable feature was the prominent zig-zag effect of the pointed second-floor window hoods. The GWR acquired it for offices later and in the reconstruction of 1906–12 drove an archway through the ground floor to make an entrance to the new concourse behind it. A smart restaurant was opened on the ground floor.

Returning to the 1860s, renewed growing pains added to the periodic attacks on the London & North Western over the chronic inconvenience of Euston. Richard Turner, builder of the pioneer arched roof at Liverpool Lime Street (Chapter 8), published a scheme for a station. 'It seems so strange', he wrote, 'that this, the Parent Railway, and being the greatest in Europe, should have its station in the background so much as it is, and where the approaches to it are so very inferior as to convey to the mind of a stranger the most

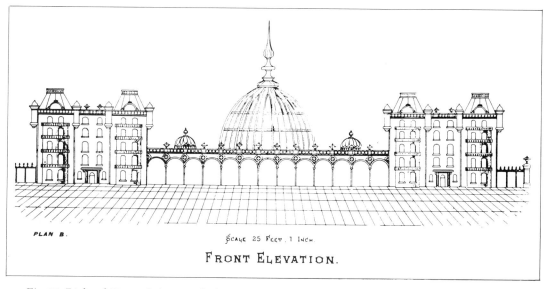

PLAN B.   SCALE 25 FEET. 1 INCH.

FRONT ELEVATION.

Fig 17. Richard Turner's iron-and-glass extravaganza proposed for Euston, c1860. The arcade was semi-circular and the flanking five-storey buildings were hotels (*ICE Library*)

unfavourable opinion of this City.' Recognising that Lime Street was again becoming too small, he recommended that his 1849 roof should be dismantled and re-erected at Euston in place of the four sheds, and that the mean streets that had grown in front of the station should be opened up to make a worthy approach from Euston Road. His plans show a large circular forecourt in front of a semi-circular glass-and-iron arcade designed in a Moorish style. Inside he planned a spacious booking hall beneath an enormous glass-and-iron dome some 80ft in diameter and 85ft high, surmounted by a huge 47ft spiked finial. With two small domes on either side, it looked like a cross between an iron Taj Mahal and a gigantic Victorian bird cage. On either side a five-storey hotel fronted on to Drummond Street, with French pavilion towers and corner turrets (Fig 17). He suggested that one side might charge 3s per bed for second-class passengers and the other 2s for 3rd class, while the existing Euston and Victoria hotels should be retained for first-class patrons. The new booking hall would be built on to the front of the Great Hall but the Doric Arch would have to go, perhaps, Thomas added piously, to a cemetery 'where it would answer admirably'.

Such an extravaganza at Euston would have 'rescued it from obscurity' with a vengeance, and we can see in it the influence of Turner's experience with Kew Palm House. Had even a small part of his scheme been executed, Euston would have been rid of a considerable disadvantage that it still suffers. Beneath the grand approach, Turner proposed that a pedestrian subway should link the main line terminus with a new station on the underground Metropolitan Railway, avoiding the five minutes' walk to Gower Street, now Euston Square on London Underground's Circle Line.[2]

After more rude comments such as *The Engineer* likening the Arch to 'a jewel in a swine's snout' standing 'amid mean dram shops and lodging houses'[3], the North Western did eventually, in 1870, make a proper drive from Euston Road, 80ft wide and flanked by a pair of sedate Italianate stone entrance lodges by J. B. Stansby. Cut in the rusticated quoins in gilt letters are 72 destinations that could be reached from Euston although only 37 were on the most direct route. Oddly enough, modern rationalisation of services has increased the number to 42. The station approach was certainly improved until the Arch at the far end was blotted out by the hotel link block. Between the lodges a statue of Robert Stephenson by Carlo Marochetti was erected, presented by the Institution of Civil Engineers.

These improvements were purely superficial, particularly when compared with the work going on down the road. In 1868 the Midland Railway had opened St Pancras and was now engaged in building an hotel. Not only was it the most important station to be built since the classical era of the Euston

High Victorian Gothic of Scott's Midland Grand Hotel at St Pancras, seen from the western entrance porch in 1968 (*Author*)

Arch, Huddersfield and Newcastle, but in purely architectural terms was, and remains, the supreme example of High Victorian Gothic. In 1865 the Midland decided to hold a competition for the design of an hotel and station offices. Eleven selected architects were invited to compete and Sir George Gilbert Scott's designs and estimates were accepted, although they were the most expensive. Among architects Scott's name was the most prestigious and the Midland obviously considered he was worth the money. For his part, Scott had been looking for a suitably important project on which to express his passion for Gothic that had been frustrated when Lord Palmerston, the Prime Minister, insisted on Italianate government offices in Whitehall, which he had recently finished. St Pancras fitted the bill admirably, although he did not use his rejected Foreign Office design or anything like it.

Although the Midland wanted its hotel to be the finest, it began to flinch as Scott's plans took shape. Towards the end he had to be restrained, which is why the niches on the front are empty. Even so the Midland Grand Hotel is an incredible building. From every external viewpoint it has a fantasy quality. The pinnacles and the 270ft high clock tower at one end of the majestically curved front echo the western tower and *porte-cochère* at the other; the glimpse of Barlow's roof through the great central arch gives a sense of anticipation and inside *does* relate to Scott's hotel, whatever critics may say. Over all, the sheer attention to detail impresses most, nearly all of which Scott designed himself – the carvings, the fine variegated brickwork and masonry, the linenfold oak panelling and carved stone railwaymen corbelling the arcading in the hammerbeamed booking hall. The interior of the hotel was, if anything, more lavish than the outside. The grand staircase ascending beneath its superbly groined vault still retains the original rich red wall covering decorated with golden fleurs-de-lys, faded though it is; the elaborate chandeliers made by Skidmores of Coventry, murals, marble-topped radiators in broad corridors, panelled bedroom doors with swivelling fanlights in trefoil and quatrefoil designs; all give an impression of what it was like despite partitioning of the great public rooms. Even the secondary staircases are quite grand. Everything down to the cutlery and table linen was specially designed, again most of it by Scott or under his close supervision, including Gillows's furniture. What did it all cost? £438,000. With the station, Professor Simmons estimates the total came to not far short of £1 million.

Apart from the technical press, the opening of St Pancras and its hotel had more impact as a tourist attraction than it had on Londoners. Because it had taken so long to build, they had become familiar with it well before it was opened in 1873. Furthermore there were now other new hotels in London,

The splendour of a first-floor drawing-room at the St Pancras hotel, shortly after its opening (*British Rail*)

each one trying to outdo the last in luxury so that palatial hotels quickly became accepted as part of the scene. Ever since it was built the Midland Grand has attracted praise and criticism in about equal proportions according to changing taste. Without doubt it is the greatest of Scott's works and a tribute to his tremendous ability, imagination, capacity for sustained effort and, above all, an immense self-confidence that went well into the realms of conceit. More faithfully than any other building, it reflects the spirit of the period and could never have been built without a man possessing those qualities. Robert Furneaux Jordan summed it up in his *Victorian Architecture* when he said:

> It is the St. Pancras Hotel that is most likely to be regarded as a symbol, not only of Scott himself, but of that whole mid-Victorian epoch. It combined in one building the romantic aspirations, the stylistic display and the solid philistinism of the sixties. With its variegated and strident materials, it is a most positive piece of design, not a mere essay in the Gothic style.

What was more, it did just what the Midland intended; it put Euston and King's Cross well and truly in the shade; the latter, it might be said, literally.

While the spires of St Pancras were rising above Euston Road, a lesser spire on a low tower rose over Liverpool Street when Edward Wilson's new terminus for the Great Eastern Railway was opened in 1874–5. The L-shaped weak Gothic front was enlivened by a spiky iron trellis along the roof, lancet windows and some fairly basic plate tracery. It was not a patch on the train shed. The hotel portion was built later in 1884 by Charles Edward Barry, brother of E. M. Barry and son of Sir Charles who, with Pugin, had been responsible for the Houses of Parliament. Its mixture of Renaissance styles which overpowers the station block was added to by Robert Edis's Edwardian Tudor-Dutch extension of 1901. Apart from the fine restaurant, in recent years spoilt by dim lighting and gimmickry, the Abercorn Rooms in the extension provide the more interesting interiors. The rich rococo work, murals and figured ceiling of the Hamilton Hall (named after the Great Eastern chairman, Lord Claud Hamilton), the mirrored walls of the Cambridge Room, and the robust Queen Anne oak panelling in the Essex Room offer an amazing contrast in styles of studied opulence. More extraordinary are the two Masonic Temples, one Grecian with marble pillars and the other Egyptian, with appropriately matching anterooms.

The only other railway hotel built in London before the end of the century was Lewis H. Isaacs's Holborn Viaduct Hotel at the London Chatham & Dover Railway's small City terminus, opened in 1877. Six storeys high, it presented a relatively plain yet dignified front beneath a French Renaissance roof.

Many railway managements preferred to build hotels a short distance apart from the station, on the Euston and Derby pattern, where they could be free from noise and dirt. The Great Northern at King's Cross faces the station in the same yellow brick, only the curving front giving interest to what is as uncompromisingly plain a building as many of the company's stations. Railways south of London were not very hotel minded and the London & South Western's at Southampton was the only one on its entire system. It, too, stood apart from the Terminus Station, featuring unusual circular dormer windows in a mansard roof and a large curved pediment over a figure of the Queen surrounded by railway and nautical emblems.

Arnold Mitchell built one of the best-located station hotels in 1882 for the London & North Western and Lancashire & Yorkshire Railways overlooking the valley of the Ribble at Preston, where gardens and a park stretch down to the riverside over which there are distant views. Yet the Park Hotel is close enough to the station to have been connected to it by a long covered footbridge (originally intended to be a subway) until it was sold for conversion into county offices. It shared with Perth the distinction of being a 'joint' hotel and externally bears strong overtones of the style of Richard Norman Shaw with a hint of Scottish Baronial.

The Royal Station Hotel at Perth is also unusual in having been built under a special Act of Parliament. Opened in 1865 by the Caledonian, North British and Highland railways, the mildly Scottish Baronial building was extended in 1890 and connected to the station by a covered way. The oldest railway-owned hotel is also in Scotland, the North British next to Queen Street station in Glasgow. Its Georgian front dates from about 1780 and the French roof was added later. The NBR acquired it in 1880 when they extended the station but wisely left the dignified frontage alone, which is more than can be said for the new owners under privatisation who have also for some reason changed the name to the Diplomat. The oldest hotel to have been built by a railway in Scotland seems to be the Station Hotel at Inverness, erected in 1855, possibly by the engineer Joseph Mitchell who built so much of the Highland Railway. Enlarged in 1858–9 and again in 1880, the interior contains an unusual two-tiered gallery around three sides of a central well, not unlike the Royal Station at York, gained by a fine T-shaped staircase.

Scott's work at St Pancras influenced at least three other English stations and one in Scotland. For the North Eastern Railway William Peachey designed a new station at Middlesbrough, opened in 1877, where the Gothic style matched Cudworth's roof and was stated to be a tribute to what was then the fastest growing town in Britain. Like St Pancras it had a terraced forecourt on arches. In nearby Sunderland the new station, opened in 1879, took the likeness further, with a tall, turreted clock tower, although neither had anything like Scott's vigour. An echo of his lavishness and attention to detail was certainly present at Bristol Temple Meads, although in a very different manner. In 1878 Matthew Digby Wyatt built an exuberantly French Gothic façade and interiors that went so well with Fox's pointed train shed on the old 'Express Platform' curve. The pale grey rock-faced stone, white dressings and crocketted spirelets made the central tower particularly striking beneath its French turret, and the long iron-and-glass verandah integrated equally well, repeating the quatrefoil theme of the platform detail. Viewed against Brunel's train shed, one almost feels Wyatt was trying to outdo his old friend with a Gothic fantasy unmatched outside St Pancras. The resemblance between St Pancras and the St Enoch Hotel at Glasgow, on the other hand, related solely to the site, which incorporated a sloping terraced approach, and the outline, which was tall with an erratic skyline. There it ended, for the dark red sandstone façade was not Gothic and made few concessions to gaiety; in fact it glowered. Perhaps there was Midland influence at work here as well as on the train shed because the designer was an Englishman, Thomas Willson of Hampstead, assisted by Miles Gibson who was local. When it opened its 200 bedrooms in 1879, it was Scotland's best and largest hotel.

This challenge from the Glasgow & South Western was quickly taken up by the Caledonian whose Central Station Hotel, opened in 1883, was seen to exceed the St Enoch and the old North British in both size and appointments. It started off as an office block which the Caledonian hastily converted in mid-stream when they saw the success of the St Enoch. Designed by Sir Robert Rowand Anderson, a successful Edinburgh architect, its style was described as Queen Anne, although that much abused term was a trifle stretched to apply to such a pile. The multi-gabled roof and attics are in the Dutch and Flemish manner, with a disproportionately low 129ft clock tower. The inconspicuous street corner entrance deceptively leads to a spacious interior where a broad staircase sweeps up to the Court Lounge, a fine domed room overlooking the station concourse.

Before leaving Scotland an accolade must be awarded to the frontage of the third Dundee West station, opened in 1889, but now demolished. After Tite's frontage at Perth was obscured by later extensions (Chapter 10), Dundee was the most imposing of larger Scottish station frontages, fully in the best Victorian Scottish Baronial tradition with stepped gables, pointed turrets and a lofty clock tower. It would have looked equally at home in a Highland glen.

A lot of the work during the century's final decades south of the border was mediocre. The outdated Italianate frontage of the new Manchester Exchange station of 1884 was a typical example; the heavy Free Renaissance of the rebuilt Liverpool Exchange station, for which the Lancashire & Yorkshire Railway held a competition in 1881, is another. The judges' initial choice for first prize-winner, Thomas Mitchell of Manchester, was ultimately placed third and in the end all forty entries were rejected amid accusations of favouritism. Mitchell's design was in a heavy French Gothic style, elevated above a terraced approach in the St Pancras idiom.[4] The fact seems to be that the LYR directors did not really know what they wanted, and in the end they

Scottish Baronial, Caledonian Railway style: the third Dundee West station, c1900 (*Dundee District Libraries*)

instructed the company architect, Henry Shelmerdine, to design an hotel. The result, completed in 1888, like the new pitched-roof train sheds, had none of the flourishes of Lime Street. Things might have been different. *The Engineer*[5] published the rejected design by Goddard & Paget of Leicester with an arched train shed by J. B. Everard. The drawing shows a Gothic front with a clock tower and spire over 200ft high that, had it been built, would have been Liverpool's reply to St Pancras, but the LYR was the wrong company for that kind of frivolity.

Three railways employed architects who carried out noteworthy work during the twenty years up to and just beyond the turn of the century, each of whom evolved a distinctive company style. W. N. Ashbee on the Great Eastern and William Bell on the North Eastern had less opportunity for major works, and their contributions were mainly at smaller stations. Apart from his involvement in Liverpool Street (Chapter 8), Ashbee's largest job was the rebuilding of Norwich Thorpe in 1886 in a cheerful red-brick Free

A lounge in the 1892 extension of the Royal Station Hotel at Newcastle, probably shortly after opening (*National Railway Museum*)

Renaissance style in which he used a large convex roof as the dominant element. Beneath it a handsome elliptically arched *porte-cochère* leads into an equally dignified booking hall, all very straight forward and good looking with none of the frothiness of, say, Broad Street. Likewise, Bell had only one large new work to his name, although he carried out extensive alterations and additions, including York, Newcastle and Hull. At Newcastle he also considerably extended the hotel which retains many of its older and newer features. He completely reconstructed Darlington Bank Top station with Dutch gables and a tall, well-proportioned clock tower in 1887. His plans to replace Andrews's old side entrance buildings when Hull was extended in 1905 were not proceeded with, and his new entrance alongside the hotel in Paragon Square was principally a large iron *porte-cochère*. It ugliness was deceptive, for it led into a very fine booking hall that is the chief glory of Hull station. The walls are covered in green and brown faience tiles above a bottle green dado, with arched openings. The 80ft by 70ft ceiling is divided into four panels with a lantern light in each, beneath which is a large oak-panelled booking office with twelve ticket windows, fluted pilasters and attractive little pediments picked out in green and cream (p 92).

Charles Trubshaw was the third man. As official architect to the Midland Railway, his scope was greater because, despite its progressive outlook, the company had fallen badly behind when it came to improving its larger stations. Its resources had been put into building the London extension, St Pancras, the new main line to the north between Kettering and Nottingham, and the Settle & Carlisle, all within seven years, so it did not seriously embark on major rebuilding projects until the end of the 1880s, coupled with a vigorous hotel policy.

There had been no real move to expand the hotel business between the opening of the Midland at Derby in 1841 and the Queens at Leeds in 1863. The latter was one of Trubshaw's first jobs for the company and stood in front of Wellington station – which was an improvement – to which it was joined by a glass roof over the intervening carriageway. There was a lengthy pause until 1885 when the Midland Hotel at Bradford was opened to Trubshaw's designs with floors of so-called fireproof construction. It dominates the adjoining Forster Square station, then called Market Street, which Trubshaw rebuilt in 1890 with a low, weak frontage block and glass-roofed *porte-cochère* behind an arcaded stone screen wall, the first of four stations like this. It is notable for the short polygonal domed pepper pot turret that became a favourite device in a number of his subsequent works and others of the period. At both Leeds and Bradford the Great Northern Railway responded to the Midland challenge by opening rival hotels named after the company, close by Central and Exchange stations respectively. Although they were separate, these and others like them at Sheffield and York were far more prominent than the nearby stations. They impressed by virtue of their size, and often the interiors were the more interesting, like the rich ironwork of the unusual three-tiered galleries and 'bridges' at York and the plaster-work ceilings in the Great Northern at Leeds by J. F. Bentley, who went on to design Westminster Cathedral.

In 1895 the Midland's Leicester London Road station replaced Campbell Street. The old one had been inadequate for years and anticipation of competition from the Manchester, Sheffield & Lincolnshire's planned extension from Sheffield to London created a sense of some urgency. Trubshaw's dome duly appeared on a low octagonal clock tower at one end of a long, massively arched *porte-cochère* in the favourite contemporary brown and buff terracotta that he used on so many of his stations. The entrance was divided into split-level arrival and departure sections and bestrode the railway alongside the road bridge.

In 1892 Trubshaw made the last of a string of alterations and additions that had accrued over the years on the front of Thompson's long-suffering building at Derby. In the 1870s an arched brick *porte-cochère* with stone dressings and a glass roof was built on to the entrance, but in 1892 Trubshaw took it down and re-erected it further out on the front of a new two-storey entrance block that had three-storey wings, pediments and balustrades, with a central clock and two wyverns, mythical dragon-like beasts that were the Midland's emblem. The wings, which had his characteristic hexagonal domed turrets, made an attractive composition with the transplanted *porte-cochère*, but on closer examination behind and around corners one realized what a hotch-potch of extensions it all was, and of little credit as the company's headquarters. Now it is disappearing and by the time this is published will probably have been replaced.

Sheffield had to wait until 1904 for enlargement. The Great Central continued to use its old station, rebuilding only the frontage in 1908 – and very half-heartedly at that – so the Midland could afford to take its time. Trubshaw adopted a similar basic form to Leicester but in rock-faced stone with numerous elliptical arched openings and without a dome, which made the long *porte-cochère* look incomplete. The interior is better; an inner Roman arcade with decorative iron grilles and stonework divides the cab road from a spacious booking hall and concourse. The original Italianate frontage block became a platform building.

The final station in the series was opened in the same year at Nottingham, and although it bears Trubshaw's stamp, the design was carried out by a local architect, A. E. Lambert. For some years Trubshaw must have been busy enough with Sheffield and his most important work, the Midland Hotel at Manchester, so probably he restricted himself to general oversight on the company's behalf. Nottingham's chunky red sandstone and orange-brown terracotta façade is typically Edwardian, and the turret could be vaguely likened to a coarse form of Baroque. Like the others, it forms a screen to a large *porte-cochère*, on a bridge in the Leicester manner, and the booking hall is lined with dark green tiles. Here there was real competition from the Great Central whose Victoria station had a much larger two-storey façade in a French Renaissance style, made impressive by a lofty clock tower. Opened in 1900, it was jointly owned by the Great Northern. Now only the tower remains, marooned in a shopping precinct.

Manchester's Midland Hotel was designed by Trubshaw in collaboration with William Towle, the company's hotels manager. Towle, who was subsequently knighted, was largely responsible for persuading the board to embark on high-class development. His son Arthur became hotels and catering manager for the LMS. Strangely, Manchester had no railway hotel and the others were not good. Towle aimed to put the city on the world hotel map by building a luxury establishment that would surpass the best in Europe and America. The intention to build on the front of Central station was abandoned in favour of an island site opposite, where Trubshaw reared up a vast and flamboyantly pompous six-storey edifice in red brick, polished granite and the inevitable orange-brown terracotta. He put his domes on corners, and a glazed covered way crossed the street to the station. It was opened in 1903, had 500 bedrooms, cost a cool £1¼ million and in innovative luxury had no equal.

The hotel was an early example of steel-framed construction and incorporated an air filtration system to get rid of Manchester's soot, an early form of air conditioning. Every room had a telephone and most had *en suite* bathrooms. There were Turkish baths, shops, a post office – the first in an hotel, with its own postmark – and, specially for the ladies, a Paris milliner's, a tea-room and suites where they could interview domestic servants. Diners could choose from four restaurants, including the Louis XV-style Grand Dining Room, and the Midland Hall was available for functions. The famous domed Octagon Court was finished in Grecian marble and the roof garden was stated to be the world's largest, while that essential adjunct to every grand hotel worthy of the name, the winter garden, was a popular meeting place for everyone who was anyone in the city. There was even an 800-seat theatre. Although the two men's work is in no way comparable, to Trubshaw the Midland at Manchester was what the Midland Grand at St Pancras had been to Scott thirty years before. Modifications have now removed the more exotic features yet, despite the advent of rivals in the post-war hotel boom, to many the Midland is still Manchester's most comfortable hotel.

Although less than ten years separated them, the Adelphi at Liverpool could hardly have differed more. The old Adelphi, a favourite of Charles Dickens, was bought by the Midland Railway in 1890 and, following the success of the Manchester hotel, Towle had little difficulty in persuading his directors to do the same in Liverpool, where the North Western Hotel at Lime Street by now was distinctly old fashioned. Trubshaw had retired so the new Adelphi was designed by Frank Atkinson who had impressed Towle with his work at Selfridges store in Oxford Street, London, with which there are affinities. The neo-classical touches on its white Portland stone façades suggest the influence of Lutyens and the restrained interiors – compared with the Midland – anticipated the Art Deco of the 1920s and '30s. Opened in 1914, it is smaller than the Manchester hotel, as planned extensions were not built, but the elegance of the Fountain Court and the Romanesque Hypostyle Hall captured a considerable degree of attention and, as yet, remain splendidly unspoilt.

Railway palace hotels reached their peak at the turn of the century. A London rival to the Midland was built to a similar plan across the road from Marylebone station, which was opened by the Great Central in the same year, 1899. Crouching behind the overpowering bulk of the hotel, the sedate little terminus had nothing of the grand gesture of St Pancras when the Midland Railway arrived in London thirty-one years earlier; the Great Central could not afford it and the traffic never warranted it. The train shed is low and modest, and the best parts of the station are the terracotta ticket hall, the mahogany and brass of the Victoria and Albert bars, and the delicate ironwork in the *porte-cochère* and the covered way to the Hotel Great Central. Robert Edis, who designed the Great Eastern Hotel extensions at Liverpool Street, built it on land leased from the railway to a company headed by Sir Blundell Maple of stores fame. Its uncompromisingly ostentatious exterior in red brick with a heavy overlay of terracotta is broadly French Renaissance and sports a central clock tower. Inside, a huge marble staircase lit by windows containing coloured arms of towns served by the Great Central led up to 700 bedrooms. The huge reception rooms were lavishly decorated, and the splendours of the Wharncliffe Rooms were the hotel's reply to the Abercorn Rooms at the Great Eastern. In the central well, patrons could sit in the colonnaded winter gardens beneath a glass roof or listen to an orchestra in the Palm Court, while gentlemen could confer in the wood-panelled, leather-seated alcoves beneath the rococo ceiling of the Smoking Room. Despite its having been used as offices since its purchase by the LNER in 1946, one can still gain some impression of its magnificence.

Two great hotels face each other from opposite ends of Princes Street, Edinburgh, symbolising the rivalry between the Caledonian and the North British railways. The second rebuilding of Waverley station in its deep valley in 1892–1900 gave the NBR no more scope for an imposing front than had the earlier stations, although it did its best at the grand manner with a very fine central booking hall. Lit by a glass dome and octagonal roof lights over elaborate iron grilles set in gilded plaster panels, an oak-panelled booking office stood surmounted by an elegant balustrade and surrounded by patterned mosaic flooring with the NBR's arms at each corner. Equally resplendent public rooms led off, and a bronze statue of John Walker, the NBR general manager from 1874 to 1891, stood in a corner. In flamboyance it almost, but not quite, equalled the incredible elaboration of the wooden refreshment room and office block, with its near-Baroque clock turret, that stood on the concourse of the Caledonian station. But nothing could draw attention to Waverley from the outside, so the company made up for it by building the North British Hotel perched alongside and above. The six-storey Edwardian French Renaissance building with its clock tower immediately became Princes Street's most prominent feature. Designed by Hamilton and George Beattie and completed in 1902, the 'NB' is connected to the station by a lift through three basements, a long corridor ending at a covered footbridge and a second lift down to the platforms. To obtain ideas the company sent a deputation on tour of Europe's best hotels, and the electrical equipment was designed by Professor Barr of Glasgow University. After the opening, attractions included a special NB Whisky blended in one of the basements. Despite these efforts the NB seems to lack the spacious quality of the

Caledonian Hotel which opened its doors a year later. It was built on to Princes Street station in pink sandstone by Peddie & Browne, with a giant Dutch gable, an elegant pediment over the entrance, and a wide T-shaped staircase leading from the roomy foyer.

After the building of Marylebone in London, the two Victoria stations were reconstructed, the LBSCR's in 1906–8 and the South Eastern & Chatham Railway's in 1908. The latter railway was formed as a working arrangement between the SER and the LCDR in an endeavour finally to resolve their long-standing enmity. The Brighton's reconstruction was total and included a red-brick extension to the Grosvenor Hotel with the station entrance and booking hall on the ground floor. The French styling, stone dressings and three large, curved pediments are quite different from the original Grosvenor alongside and have a little more dignity. Above a standard LBSCR-style *porte-cochère*, the eye is drawn to a large clock set in foliated and scrolled stonework between two large recumbent maidens. It contrasted with the large and quite elegant booking-hall interior, decorated with pretty art nouveau tiles, while the screen wall and carriage arch that Parliament stipulated must face Buckingham Palace Road was much the more dignified external composition. The Chatham company kept its original roof and Hudson's Place offices, but was not to be outdone on the Victoria Street side where the next year it unveiled its own new French creation. In white Portland stone by the company architect A. W. Blomfield (not to be confused with Sir Arthur or Sir Reginald Blomfield), it is smaller than the Brighton's façade but the four caryatids holding up two pediments are more robust than the Brighton's ladies. Called Second Empire, on its own it would look a pretty ostentatious piece of work were it not for the Grosvenor giving it a restrained air of determination not to be overwhelmed. Both stations had their complement of restaurants and other eating and waiting facilities, the Pillar Hall Restaurant, later renamed the Chatham Room, becoming a popular meeting place on the SE&CR side, while for functions the Brighton offered the Bessborough Rooms in the Grosvenor, named after the chairman.

There are similarities in appearance between the Brighton's Victoria frontage and the Lancashire & Yorkshire's in Manchester, completed in 1909, marking the conclusion of the final remodelling. William Dawes's façade has the same curved, shell-like pediments and heavy vertical rustication, topped by a balustrade along a flat roof. Now that the old offices opposite have been demolished and the site opened up, cleaned stonework reveals the full scale and detail of the building, although it still seems overbearingly heavy. A shallow canopy bears the names of British and foreign destinations, most of which can no longer be reached from the station.

The last great rebuilding, and the most overdue, was officially opened at Waterloo by Queen Mary in 1922 after fifteen years' work. The great curved front by J. R. Scott, containing the London & South Western's offices, contrasts with the almost clinical simplicity of the train shed and cannot be seen from anywhere in its entirety because the South Eastern's viaduct blocks the view. The great Victory Arch in Portland stone forms the LSWR's war memorial, bearing a sculptured group representing War and Peace watched over by Britannia – the style was well named 'Imperial Baroque', for it marks the final fling of railway imperialism. A series of elegant public rooms led off the huge sweeping concourse and although most of them are now used for other purposes or have suffered numerous revampings, the coved ceiling of the former booking hall is still in view and the little Edwardian pay kiosks in the former Windsor Tea Room, though shabby, stand at the entrances to the Travel Centre, sad relics of a former elegance that still partly pervades the marble columned cafeteria and the old Surrey Room that now serves as a staff dining-room.

To some extent the display that the railways bestowed on the public at their new stations and hotels was not matched in their own offices. Board and chief officers' rooms, by and large, were remarkably modest compared with the exhibited tycoonery considered essential in other business empires. Headquarters were usually at the main London terminus or, in the case of provincial companies, the historical base. Significantly, after it reached St Pancras the Midland still retained its headquarters at Derby. A few lines had their offices in separate buildings, as the little London & Greenwich did in the three storey building next to its 1836 London Bridge terminus. Designed by George Smith, it had classical outlines; the board room and offices were on the first floor and the booking office below. The North British head-quarters were in Waterloo Place, Edinburgh, although the Edinburgh & Glasgow's handsome little boardroom of 1842, upstairs at Haymarket station, still exists, nicely restored. The NBR Glasgow offices at Queen Street station were unusual in being in the former West George Street chapel, built in 1819 and acquired when the station was enlarged in 1855. Its Doric columns and pilasters made it the best looking part. Known as Wardlaw's Kirk after one of its pastors, the name stuck with generations of railwaymen.

According to the *Midland Counties Railway Companion* of 1840, the boardroom at Leicester Campbell Street had a ceiling 'beautifully decorated', including a 'superb bronze chandelier', and directors could watch the trains from an adjoining balcony. Among other early stations, Thompson's building at Chester afforded relatively plain office accommodation, while at Derby a long corridor gave access to senior officers' rooms that had panelled pilaster strips around the doors and windows, and marble or polished granite fireplaces in different sizes according to rank. The lofty ceiling in the 1862 shareholders' room had deep panels and the long boardroom of 1872 had deep coving decorated with diagonal patterns above a dentilled cornice, while the walls above the wooden dado were embossed with flower motifs. One wall was occupied by a large roller map of the company's system.

Mocatta's offices at Brighton and Andrews's at York, both of 1841, appear to have been as plain as Thompson's, but those designed by Brunel for the Great Western's Bristol committee at Temple Meads were as impressive as his station. The directors' entrance in Clock Tower Yard leads to a noble wooden staircase with crenellated newel posts and, at the top, a large ceiling boss. The secretary's room and the boardroom are connected by double doors; one has a marble fireplace and the other a great stone Gothic piece, and both have huge, elaborate ceiling bosses. There is an even larger one forming the centre-piece of geometrical panels in the Bristol & Exeter Railway's boardroom in S. C. Fripp's 1852 Jacobean office block across the road, lit by a fine curved-glass oriel window. The entrance is more impressive, too, with stone stairs, intricate iron banisters and an arcaded gallery around a well (p 158).

The GWR indulged in much less display at its Paddington offices fourteen years later. A long corridor overlooks the station roof except where Wyatt's

Seats of power 1: the Great Western boardroom at Paddington in 1911, with a wall map of the system on the right (*National Railway Museum*)

Seats of power 2 (*left*): the Shareholders' Room at Euston, laid out for a function, c1913 (*National Railway Museum*). Seats of power 3 (*right*): an elegant Moorish balustrade overlooks the entrance-hall stair well in the Bristol & Exeter Railway's offices at Bristol Temple Meads, as restored in 1984 (*City of Bristol*)

oriel windows look out across the transepts, and the boardroom and committee rooms are relatively modest, although they have been modified at various times. Tall wooden doors with the company crest and monogram on the pediments, wooden dados and chastely panelled ceilings are the main features. A scheme of 1881 to extend the offices included a 60ft by 40ft shareholders' room and a 100ft high tower;[6] had it been executed the plain Eastbourne Terrace frontage would certainly have been enlivened.

Smaller companies did themselves equally well on occasions. The proudly independent North Staffordshire Railway had a handsome oak-panelled boardroom behind the oriel window looking out over Winton Square at Stoke station. The ceiling was coffered and a curious balcony on two sides gave access to ranges of cupboards, probably for the storage of documents close at hand. Matthews & Laurie built the Highland's head office opposite the hotel and next to the station at Inverness in 1873–5, forming the third side of a square. The first-floor boardroom is now divided into offices but retains its coffered ceiling, decorated coving and pendant bosses.

The Great Eastern boardroom and principal offices upstairs at Liverpool Street, dating from 1873, are contrastingly modest. There are oak panels and marble or oak fireplaces, but otherwise they have an atmosphere more of rooms meant for working in than for display. Other former headquarters offices in London have gone; those at King's Cross, London Bridge and Waterloo were bombed, although some idea of the LSWR's standards for senior officers' accommodation at Waterloo can be formed from the former chief engineer's office, now a conference room, with its panelled ceiling and walls, brass chandelier and wooden panelled fireplace. The finest railway room of all disappeared with the Doric Arch in the demolition of Euston, where the magnificent Shareholders' Room stood at the head of the grand stairs leading up from the Great Hall of 1849. Paired Doric columns and richly decorated coving surrounded lofty ceiling panels decorated with large floral motifs. The oak-panelled boardroom with its Corinthian pilasters and columns lay beyond.

The final word in railway offices goes to the handsome block built by the North Eastern across from the old station at York in 1906. The design won Horace Field and William Bell a gold medal at the 1904 French Exposition. Nikolaus Pevsner called its great Dutch gables, banded chimneys, steep roofs and rows of superimposed dormers 'Grand Edwardian William and Mary'. Despite its grand manner, it has none of the floridness of contemporary railway hotels. The hexagonal stair landings and delicate balustrades exude an air of quiet dignity, the offices seem cosy and portraits of famous North Eastern men look down from the panelled walls of the boardroom and committee rooms.

The impact of the great station façades on the general public was less than the more dramatic train sheds. They were not so easily identifiable and symbolic, they did not possess the same recognisable railway style and, moreover, they had to compete with other large public and commercial buildings unless they were also part of hotels. Railway hotels were pre-eminently in a class of their own and much more likely to be a source of civic pride, whereas a station frontage block that was nothing else had to withstand comparison with the new town halls, museums, banks and commercial premises that were transforming town centres in the second half of the nineteenth century. Indeed, many station exteriors came to be considered at best as only in the second rank as the century wore on, and even the great classical and Gothic station entrances, imposing though they were, became assimilated fairly quickly into the local scene as other, newer buildings were erected, which may go some way to explain the railways' insensitive masking or mutilation of fine façades like those at Brighton, Derby and Perth.

10
Curing Chaos

In the last two chapters we have seen how the big stations built from the 1860s onwards resulted from a combination of fierce competition between rival railways and the inability of existing stations to handle the enormous expansion of traffic. Most of the brand new stations had sufficient space to cater for future traffic without major reconstruction, or were capable of expansion in a reasonably orderly fashion. The original layouts at Charing Cross and Cannon Street, for instance, sufficed with minor modifications well into the present century, and St Pancras was enlarged by the simple expedient of moving the carriage sidings out to Cricklewood which gave space for two extra platforms. York had no additions until 1900, when a wooden platform was built outside the main train shed, intended for special traffic or occasions of pressure but quickly brought into use for regular services. A broad footbridge was built to replace the old subway at the same time, and in 1909 William Bell added the art-nouveau tea-room that became such a popular feature, but otherwise the station changed very little until the 1930s. The same could be said of Liverpool and Manchester Central stations; an outside platform added to the latter in 1905 was the only real change.

As an example of orderly development, one can cite Manchester London Road, once the chaos of the early years was overcome. This was so chronic that in 1860 the Mayor of Manchester presided over a public meeting to discuss the inadequacies of London Road and Victoria stations, which were described as 'the shabbiest, dingiest and most inadequate and inconvenient that could be found in a town of third or fourth rate importance'. Crowding of the narrow platforms at London Road was alarming, and at times passengers had 'to thread their way through the congregated cans, paddling through intervening pools of milk' and were 'constantly perplexed, carried off in the wrong train or left behind altogether'. Victoria was as bad, where scenes at the third-class booking-office beggared description, 'aggravated doubtless by the stupid practice of issuing tickets only five minutes before the starting of the trains'.[1]

The LNWR blamed the Lancashire & Yorkshire, with which it shared the station, and only fully resolved the problem by building its own Exchange Station next to it in 1884. At London Road the Manchester Sheffield & Lincolnshire blamed the LNWR for dragging its heels after an Act for a new joint station had been secured in the previous year. When work did eventually start, the collapse of Moorsom's roof caused more delay, but at length the new station was opened in 1866, with a twin-span overall roof covering four platforms, two for each company. In 1881 the LNWR side on the west was extended by adding two more spans of similar design, which also enabled the MSLR to insert a further platform on its side, where they were lettered A-C and, until 1909, the North Western's were numbered 1-5. In that year the Styal line was opened, for which it was intended to add a further platform to which number 2 was allocated. It was not built, so London Road continued to have no Platform 2 until the designation system was changed in 1960 when the station was remodelled for electrification. The only untidy part comprised the platforms for the Manchester South Junction & Altrincham Railway, opened in 1849, jointly owned by the same companies and known to Manchester commuters as the 'MSJ'. In effect they formed a separate station at the outer end that was connected to the main station platforms by a footbridge, which also led to Mayfield station. The latter was a truly separate station on the other side of Fairfield Street, opened in 1910 for LNWR suburban traffic, although it saw greater use for milk, horse and carriage traffic and parcels than for passengers.

By the 1880s the four through platforms and four bays (two at each end) at Birmingham New Street clearly were inadequate for the trains of two companies. The London & North Western built what again was effectively a separate station alongside, with two semi-circular roofs over four sharply curved platforms. The Midland side, as it became known, was brought into use in 1885 but was not reserved more or less exclusively for Midland trains until 1889. The two parts of the enlarged station were separated by Queens Drive, which replaced a street. It was covered in the middle by ridge-and-furrow roofing, and there was more over sidings and docks on the south side of the station which virtually hid the new two-storey office block that formed a second entrance from Station Street. The famous footbridge, that from the outset also acted as a public footpath across the station, had been rebuilt with its well-remembered arched steps in 1874, and was extended across Queens Drive and the Midland side.

The orderly development of Liverpool Street referred to in Chapter 9 provided eighteen platforms, of which the two forming the principal main line platforms reached back to the hotel under which there were sidings, effectively splitting the station into two sections, a disadvantage that was only partly remedied by the long footbridge. Three delightful little Edwardian tea-rooms were built out from it, two in the western train shed and one in the east, their charming bow windows acting as a foil to the roof vaults above. The connecting tunnel to the Metropolitan Railway from the westernmost pair of platforms was no longer used after 1904, having seen less than six months' regular use, although the tunnel still exists.

The main departure platform at Paddington in the early 1900s. Apart from the wooden platform and gas lighting, the same scene with an IC125 train looks little different today. (*National Railway Museum*)

Other extensions made by adding a second roof span enlarged Liverpool Lime Street and Glasgow St Enoch, also mentioned in Chapter 9, and the same happened at Newcastle when two near-replicas of Dobson's roof were added in 1893–5 to provide a total of fifteen platforms. A second entrance and concourse that were provided at the east end became known as the Tynemouth Square, after the destination of trains using the adjacent bay platforms that served the coast lines. Similar work was done at Paddington in 1916 when a third roof of 109ft span was added to match Brunel's originals, the culmination of progressive alterations to provide extra platforms that started by dispensing with some of the carriage sidings in 1878. At the same time it brought the separate Bishop's Road station on the connecting line to the Metropolitan Railway a little closer to the main line station.

Further along the Metropolitan towards the City, King's Cross developed in a far less tidy fashion. The Great Northern's connection to the Metropolitan comprised separate tunnels for up and down lines on either side of King's Cross, opened in 1863, and in 1866 a separate platform called York

Road was opened on the up line short of the tunnel, although in the down or outward direction trains had to reverse into and out of the main station departure platform. The sidings in the main station gradually gave way to additional platforms, but for suburban departures a separate three-platform station with its own booking-office and overall roof was opened on the western side in 1874. Beyond it, yet another separate platform was opened in 1878 on the down line from the Metropolitan where it rose out of the tunnel, known as the 'Hotel Curve'. Although it did away with the tiresome business of backing into the main line station, the combination of the sharp curve and steep gradient created its own problems for drivers starting heavily laden trains. More platforms were added to both these stations, which from 1895 had their combined five platforms lettered A-E, giving them some sort of cohesion, but York Road, resited in 1877 when the main approaches were widened, continued to be quite separate with no direct access to the main line station, where the platforms were separately and confusingly numbered 1 and 2 arrivals and 1-5 departures. The front of the station was an equal mess, containing a clutter of wooden huts and buildings for a variety of purposes including the left-luggage office and a purveyor of garden furniture. Although a number were burned down in 1902, other equally squalid structures took their place, including, in the middle, the entrance building to the Piccadilly Underground station.

Suburban platforms at two of Glasgow's stations developed quite differently as the result of the construction of cross-city links. Backed by the Caledonian, the Glasgow Central Railway built a 7 mile east-to-west line of which 5 miles were underground, including a low-level station running at right angles to the outer end of Central station, and opened in 1896. It was the Caledonian's reply to the Glasgow City & District Railway of 1886, a subsidiary of the North British which had a similar low-level station on its own cross-city line underneath Queen Street. The extra passengers from Central Low Level exacerbated the already overcrowded main line station which had only eight short, narrow platforms and a small concourse. There was no real alternative to complete redevelopment, only twelve years after it had been built. A second bridge over the Clyde enabled the whole station to be moved outwards across Argyle Street, giving space for a much larger concourse. The old platforms were extended and four new ones built alongside, with a broad cab drive between. The entire scheme was drawn up by the Caledonian's dynamic Chief Engineer, Donald Alexander Matheson, whose idea it was to ease the flow of passengers across the irregularly shaped concourse by placing the heads of the platforms in a diagonal line and making all the structures curved. It was finished in 1906 with thirteen platforms and the most easily understood departure indicator in Britain: above the Caledonian Restaurant (formerly the main waiting-room) a series of thirteen windows – one for each platform – contained a canvas panel

The famous departure indicator at Glasgow Central, in 1979. It finally gave way to electronics in 1985. The curved buildings were designed to smooth the flow of crowds (*Author*)

displaying the destinations, placed in position from behind by a man who selected them from a rack. The system was only replaced in 1985.

The scrapping of Brunel's wooden train shed at Cardiff and widening to take four tracks had been completed by 1880, and in 1896 further extensions resulted in four through platforms and two bays with separate canopies and buildings in the Great Western's standard pedestrian style of the period. Two years earlier two platforms had been built on the Riverside goods branch, which curved away from the main line just west of the station. Although they adjoined the main platforms, for no apparent reason they were separately named Riverside station and were also used by the Barry and Taff Vale railways. The latter company's own station at Queen Street was far superior to the Great Western's, and had one of the most impressive frontages on Britain's smaller railways.

Ten years after it was opened, Leeds New station also had become too small. In 1869 it comprised a single through platform with two bays at each end for the North Eastern and LNWR respectively. In 1879 the through platform was converted to provide two more bays each and a new through platform was built further out, with an island platform beyond that, making eleven in all and requiring an additional span of overall roofing. Originally the approach was from the narrow courtyard running between the adjacent

Wellington station and Queens Hotel of the Midland Railway, but a completely new approach road was made at the same time, appropriately called New Station Street. Separate goods lines were also added outside the station.

Planned large-scale reconstruction, as opposed to extensions and additions, were frequently spread over a period of years, with the result that a scheme could be overtaken by events and again be too small even before it was finished. This happened at Bristol, where a start on work under the 1865 Bristol Joint Station Act was delayed by financial wrangling between the three companies until 1871, and even then it was 1878 before the job was fully completed. All the additional platforms were in use two years earlier, yet a Board of Trade report declared that the station was already 'clearly much less than adequate'. The work comprised Fox's roof over the old Express Curve platform and a new down platform opposite, together with an extension to Brunel's shed that enabled the original platforms to be more than doubled in length. A handsome Tudor booking hall, refreshment room and other offices were built in the angle. More space became available when the broad gauge was converted to standard in 1892, allowing two narrow island platforms to be squeezed into the through station and additional carriage sidings in the terminal portion. The latter were later converted to running lines, and crossover points were installed half way along, allowing two trains to occupy each platform. The Brunel shed came to be used for South Wales trains and the new section for Midland trains, while the platforms on the curve were used primarily for through services.

There was nearly always considerable reluctance to embark on complete rebuilding, not only on financial grounds but because of the disruption to traffic which, again with cost, was one of the reasons why so many schemes took so long to finish. Complete closure, such as that decreed necessary by British Rail for the 1985 remodelling of Crewe, could never have been entertained. Sheer force of circumstances dictated, for instance, the replacement in 1867 of the two Aberdeen stations (Chapter 3) by a single joint station which, because it had five bays but only one through platform, was quickly overtaxed. Although plans for rebuilding were prepared in 1883 all that happened was the addition of an extra bay. When in 1898 the Caledonian and the Great North of Scotland companies finally agreed on reconstruction, passengers had to endure further the low, congested platforms, slimy and smelly with fish, until 1913 while arguments with the town council and the Harbour Commissioners were resolved and work could commence. The four through platforms were long enough to take two trains each, and there were nine bays, all ready by 1914, although World War I delayed full completion until 1920, including a fine booking hall and a spacious glass-roofed concourse.

To be fair to the railways, local authorities were not always willing to co-operate once the decision to rebuild had been taken, although, as we have seen in the case of Edinburgh in Chapter 3, they could be vociferous enough in their condemnation beforehand, while railway companies' reluctance was often engendered by the difficulties of the site. A start on the Lancashire & Yorkshire's Tithebarn Street station reconstruction at Liverpool in 1886–8 was hindered not only by ditherings on the part of the company but difficulties in agreeing on the closure of streets, purchasing property, deciding on levels (which were awkward) and, not least, diverting the Leeds & Liverpool Canal. But when it was finished the new station's ten long platforms and ample concourse made it adequate for the rest of its life.

The same company's terminus at Bradford Exchange, which had already been enlarged in 1867, lingered on in a disgraceful state for far too long because of the confined site and difficult approaches which needed widening before work on a second rebuilding could start. E. L. Ahrons, writing in 1917, recalled conditions in the late 1870s, when the station had four platforms and a short bay at the end of a ¼ mile double-track tunnel on a falling gradient of 1 in 50. The station was also used by the Great Northern, and all arrival trains had to back out of the platforms into the tunnel, from which they returned to the departure platforms by gravity. The accompanying engine movements in and out of the tunnel were augmented by a shunting engine darting in and out of the adjacent goods yard:

> The resulting chaos which occurred several times daily can be better imagined than described. There would be some three or four trains waiting to come in, and at least two to go out, and both up and down roads were blocked by a train of empty passenger coaches, which an exasperated staff was trying to transfer from the arrival to the departure side. Added to this the tunnel was full of dense smoke, sulphur dioxide, and various compounds of tri-nitro profanity, so that it was impossible to see two yards. The shunting engine at the goods station contributed its quota by keeping up a continuous whistle in a vain endeavour to get the points set for it to make a dive into the tunnel, whilst drivers, signalmen and shunters hurled uncomplimentary epithets at one another. There were several smashes, generally and fortunately to empty coaches, and finally, after several temporary wooden structures had been added as enlargements to the station in 1882, the whole was rebuilt and the tunnel taken down and rebuilt by a deep retaining-wall cutting containing some half-a-dozen roads.'[2]

The new station was completed with ten platforms, still none too long, in 1888, each company having half, including separate approach lines.

The similarities between the joint stations at Carlisle and Perth mentioned in Chapter 5 were to some extent perpetuated when they were enlarged. Both had Blyth & Cunningham roofs and identical footbridges decorated in Gothic style to harmonise with the buildings. A broad island platform with matching offices was added to the old single through platform at Carlisle in 1880, while the enlargement of Perth followed in 1885–7, where through running to Dundee at last became possible by the replacement of the Dundee dock with new platforms with awnings on the curve, and the new entrance

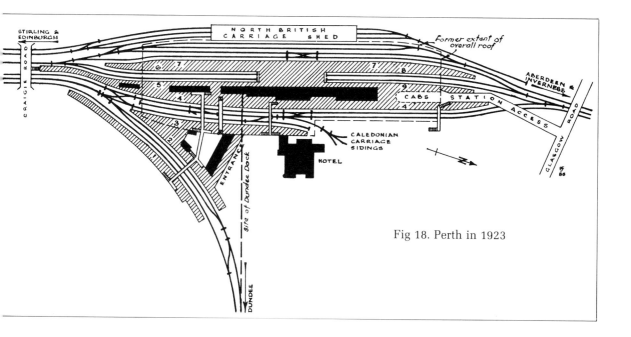

Fig 18. Perth in 1923

building linking it with the main station became known as the 'Dundee Corridor'. The original iron *porte-cochère* was dismantled and re-erected in front of it. The main station itself was converted from a single platform to an island layout by building a new platform along the original frontage, a unique development, and a third short through platform was added opposite. The island platform could take two full-length trains on each side, and additional bays were provided on the down side.

Some impression of the pressures leading to rebuilding can be gained from Hull, which before 1904 had four platforms and three short bays yet, after what amounted to virtually total reconstruction (apart from the old entrance block which was relegated to other uses) had nine full-length platforms, a short bay and four excursion platforms. Likewise, the rebuilding of Edinburgh Princes Street in 1894 increased accommodation from three short platforms to seven of twice the length. The Brighton company had a particular problem at Victoria because the South Eastern & Chatham station on one side and Buckingham Palace Road on the other completely blocked sideways expansion. In 1906 Sir Charles Morgan, the Brighton's engineer, devised the ingenious solution of rebuilding the station lengthways. He managed to increase the number of platform lines from seven to nine and made them twice the length of the old. Six of the tracks were in pairs along the inner half of the station, but then split into three, enabling two trains to use each platform independently. The old, narrow cross-platform was replaced by a large concourse at the same time.

By far the largest reconstruction work was carried out by the London & South Western at Waterloo, started in 1900 by W. Jacomb-Hood, the LSWR

The 'Brighton' side at London Bridge, seen here in 1959, was by far the more orderly and the roof was much acclaimed in its day. Significantly, it has been retained in the new station (*R. C. Riley*)

chief engineer, but not completed by his successor A. W. Szlumper until 1921. Previously it was an even more chaotic station than London Bridge, if that were possible, and by 1885 had haphazardly accumulated sixteen platforms in which state it remained for fifteen years. The original wooden-roofed station dating from 1848 still contained the main departure platforms, numbered 1 and 2, and one of the arrival platforms, numbered 3, while the other, No 4, was just outside the old roof. This part was called the Central station, and Platforms 2 and 3 had lines on either side which they shared with Nos 1 and 4 respectively. To add to the confusion, two platforms beyond the cab road along the south-east side were known as the South station and were also numbered 1 and 2. Beyond another cab road on the opposite side was the Windsor station with four platforms, and beyond that again the newest part, the North station, with six. There were four concourses, if they could be called such, the central one projecting much further towards Waterloo Road than the others, necessitating a footbridge towards the inner end. To make matters worse No 3 and 4 platform lines converged, crossed the inner end of the central concourse and went out through an arch in the wall and over a bridge across Waterloo Road to a junction with the South Eastern's London Bridge–Charing Cross line. To enable passengers to cross it, a moveable bridge was provided that could be drawn back when a train was required to pass. For a short time London & North Western trains used it on a Euston–Cannon Street service via Kensington, and it was in quite frequent use for transferring vehicles to and from the South Eastern. This was not all, for there were three other Waterloo stations as well. In 1869 the South

Eastern opened its Waterloo Junction station on the viaduct outside (now Waterloo East), and in 1898 the London & South Western opened its Waterloo & City tube line from an underground station in the basement, connected to the main line by a lift for transferring rolling stock. Finally there was the private Waterloo station of the London Necropolis Co, in York Street from 1854 and moved to Westminster Bridge Road in 1902, from which the LSWR ran funeral trains to the Necropolis Co's cemetery at Brookwood. When the new main line station was finished it was a model of what a terminal should be. The six relatively modern platforms and roofing of the North station were retained, but the rest was entirely rebuilt to give a total of twenty-one platforms in line along a broad, sweeping concourse, forming Britain's largest station.

The large-scale rebuilding of Manchester Victoria over a longer period was less successful. To the original Manchester & Leeds Railway station of 1844 a separate suburban station, known as Ducie Bridge, was added in 1855, followed ten years later by additional platforms in the old station. Disagreement between the Lancashire & Yorkshire and the London & North Western over a sharing arrangement led to the latter building its own five-platform station, called Exchange, close by in 1884–5, with an inconvenient ¼ mile-long covered way to Victoria where the LYR was left in sole possession, although the LNWR still had to run through it to reach Exchange

The wrought-iron ticket barrier and subway entrance at Manchester Victoria in the early 1920s (*National Railway Museum*)

from the east. Large-scale reconstruction in 1884 resulted in a Victoria in two parts, comprising six through platforms and a bay separated from a five-platform terminal portion by through lines for goods and LNWR trains. In 1904 five more terminal platforms were added, followed by a large new concourse and frontage block completed in 1909, involving extensive culverting of the River Irk which already ran underground beneath the company's offices opposite. While the final layout was a vast improvement on the old, there was still an inconveniently long walk from the main entrance through a subway to reach the through platforms.

The difficulties that beset the North British Railway in obtaining land for extending Waverley station in Edinburgh, referred to in Chapters 3 and 6, formed only part of the problem of capacity. The closure of Canal Street station in 1868, and subsequent opportunity to acquire the site of Waverley Market, gave the railway the chance to replan the station, instead of which it appears to have enlarged it piecemeal over the next twenty years, including narrow platforms which extended untidily beyond the North and Waverley bridges. Possibly the erection of new overall roofs and rebuilding Waverley Bridge and the approach road, finished in 1874, was all that could be afforded. As a consequence it was not long before conditions were as bad as ever. E. Foxwell's description in his *Express Trains, English and Foreign,* published in 1888, sounds almost unbelievable today:

> On the platforms of the Waverley station in Edinburgh may be witnessed every evening in summer a scene of confusion so chaotic that a sober description of it is incredible to those who have not themselves survived it. Trains of caravan length come in portentously late from Perth, so that each is mistaken for its successor; these have to be broken up and remade in insufficient sidings, while bewildered crowds of tourists sway up and down among equally bewildered porters on the narrow village platform reserved for these most important expresses; the higher officials stand lost in subtle thought, returning now and then to repeated enquiries some masterpiece of reply couched in the cautious conditional, while the hands of the clock with a humorous air survey the abandoned sight, till at length, without any obvious reason and with sudden stealth, the shame-stricken driver hurries his passengers off into the dark.

The flood of traffic on the new short route to Aberdeen, created by the opening of the Tay and Forth bridges in 1887 and 1890, proved to be the final straw, and in the peak holiday season of the latter year an express could take over an hour to cover the last 3 miles into Waverley. By this time the layout appears to have comprised a main island platform with an irregular series of narrow bays at each end and an island suburban platform outside the south wall. A large part of the trouble lay in the tunnels strangling both approaches to the station. The much-vaunted 'Bridges Route' simply could not work with such a bottleneck at its southern end, and there was no option but to bore second tunnels under Calton Hill, The Mound and at Haymarket, and completely rebuild Waverley, spurred on no doubt by the success of the

The elaborate wooden booking office and mosaic flooring at Edinburgh Waverley in 1976, before they were removed. The NBR coat of arms can be seen on the right (*Royal Commission on Ancient Monuments, Scotland*)

Caledonian's fine new Princes Street station. The entire operation took eight years and in 1900 the new station was opened. It was built as a huge island, with through platforms on each side long enough to take two trains, which could arrive and depart separately over scissors crossings in the centre, and eight full-length bays at each end. To accommodate them, North Bridge as well as Waverley Bridge had to be rebuilt, and in 1898 an island suburban platform was added outside the south wall, making Waverley the largest station in Britain until the rebuilding of Waterloo.

Birmingham Snow Hill also had to endure a second complete rebuilding between 1906 and 1912, thirty-five years after the replacement of Brunel's shed, with two broad island platforms each having two bays in the northern end. In the down side bays space was saved by releasing incoming engines on an ingenious sector table at the buffer stops. There were no bays at the south end, where broad staircases led down from the concourse, but a separate terminal station was opened at Moor Street in 1909 for local trains. Here incoming locomotives at two of the three platforms were released by a traverser.

The space-saving principle of the island platform, with rails on either side and bays in the ends, was increasingly adopted during the last thirty years of the century. It was particularly suitable for locations where the entrance

Edwardian Snow Hill, Birmingham, in 1952: the combined cab drive, concourse and booking hall, airy and well lit but swamped by random advertising (R. E. G. Read)

building was above or below rail level, and led to economy in platform buildings as only one set was required for each pair of platform faces. The London & North Western rebuilt three stations in this fashion on its main line, starting at Crewe in 1867 with two island platforms with bays. The familiar pattern of rapid outgrowth soon became apparent, made worse by using the central through lines for stabling engines and coaches. Goods trains waited hours for a path through the station, and after advantage was taken to sort them out on Sundays, when passenger traffic was light, the situation was as bad again by Wednesday. Wholesale enlargement was carried out in the decade up to 1906, during which a third large island with bays was built on the west side, while the goods lines were completely segregated and taken under the passenger lines in tunnels. To help the interchange of passengers two footbridges were provided, and there were booking-offices on the platforms. Local passengers were issued with free platform tickets at the entrance on the road bridge as was also the case at Stockport Edgeley and Rugby, (and at Hellifield on the Midland), all of which were island platform stations. All also had very meagre entrances, Rugby and Stockport being little more than holes in the wall leading to subways and stairs to the platforms.

Island platforms featured in the eventual rebuilding of Preston. After the early troubles recounted in Chapter 3, the station comprised two inadequate platforms with four tracks between them. The North Union Railway's entrance was on the northbound side, which *The Builder* in 1861 disparaged as a coke shed from which incoming passengers emerged into a street of beer shops.[3] In 1850 the East Lancashire Railway built its own entrance on the opposite side, with a long curving platform under an iron roof extending south-eastwards rather like a pan handle. Piecemeal alterations were made over the next thirty-nine years, but the station remained the subject of repeated complaints. There was no footbridge until about 1855, passengers having to walk across the lines, shepherded in groups by the staff at busy periods. The joint companies – the LNWR and the LYR – presented a Bill to Parliament in 1856 for a new station but, as was usually the case with joint ownership, were unable to agree on apportioning the cost, and the scheme was dropped. A deputation from the town's corporation in 1865 achieved nothing, and after part of the East Lancashire roof collapsed a year later a second one went to the Board of Trade but with no immediate result. At length reconstruction started in 1873, beginning with the replacement of the 80yd tunnel under Fishergate by a bridge spanning eight tracks. A large elliptical roof was planned but Euston-type sheds appeared instead. It was 1879 before a new broad island platform was opened, not with the intended promenade entrance along the top of a single-storey building but with a two-storey office block similar to that which appeared at Rugby. Further platforms were added progressively up to about 1913, to give a total of five islands, and the old East Lancashire entrance was replaced by a second high-level entrance. The 'pan handle' remained, increased to two through and three bay platforms, by which time the total length of the fifteen platform faces was only slightly less than at Crewe, making Preston the second largest station between London and Glasgow (p 174).

The old station at Preston, looking south in 1862. Its dilapidated state was notorious, although it appears some repairs are about to take place (*Harris Museum, Preston*)

An aerial view of the rebuilt Preston station at its fullest extent, with the curving East Lancashire 'pan handle' platforms on the right and the Park Hotel in the foreground, probably in the 1930s (*Author's Collection*)

Other important stations built with a single large island platform were Dundee Tay Bridge, in 1878, and Darlington Bank Top in 1887. The Midland Railway stations at Leicester (1895) and Nottingham (1904), and the Great Central station at Nottingham Victoria (1900), each had two wide island platforms; in all cases broad staircases and footbridges or subways gave easy and rapid access for crowds. The Darlington layout was almost identically copied in a proposal for a new station at Inverness in 1895. The original station, at the end of the line from Nairn and Aberdeen, dated from 1855, to which platforms diverging westwards to Dingwall and the far north were added in 1862, forming a unique terminal layout in the form of sharply curved letter V. It eventually had four platforms for southbound trains and three for the north. There was a short three-bay roof at the inner end but most of the platforms' lengths were open. A connecting curve gave through running from south to north, forming a triangle of lines (Fig 19), and it was there that the new station was planned. There were to be through lines complete with central scissors crossovers, bays at each end and an overall roof. An approach road led up to the western end of the island platform from an underbridge, just as at Darlington, and further to the west a second island platform was intended for excursion traffic. A new station hotel was to occupy the site of the Highland Railway's locomotive works in the centre of the triangle, which were to be moved to the north of the new station. Unfortunately the scheme remained on paper and Inverness station remains unaltered to this day. As normal services from both directions have always terminated at Inverness, the only serious disadvantage of the curious layout lies in the absence of means of releasing the locomotives of incoming trains. This is overcome by running a number of trains round the connecting curve and reversing them into a platform, a manoeuvre which has the added advantage of giving passengers a cross-platform interchange.

Among the larger stations surviving from the 1860s, Inverness has probably had the least alterations, although a seemingly timeless immunity to much-needed change at other centenarian stations dragged on well into the era of British Rail before closure or reconstruction put an end to them. When the three-span overall roof at Leeds Wellington was taken down for the amalgamation with Leeds New in 1938, the platform layout was little changed, while the insignificant frontage and poky interior at Central lasted, with the addition of one platform and a small extension to the low roof, from 1857 until its long overdue closure in 1967 (p 208). It was an ill-fitting terminal for prestige trains like the 'Yorkshire Pullman'; passengers in the Bradford portion of the train alighted in much more dignified surroundings.

In Glasgow the North British general manager in 1907 finally persuaded the locomotive superintendent that his engines were capable of taking trains up Cowlairs incline without the aid of a rope, provided that banking engines were available, which from 1908 cut out the time-consuming business with the descending brake-trucks, saved in manpower and was quicker into the bargain. This was the only main change at Queen Street. The station still

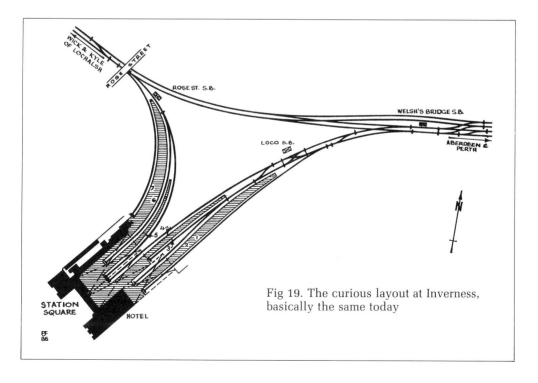

Fig 19. The curious layout at Inverness, basically the same today

suffered from short platforms, and in exchange for less delay there was a lot more smoke. Having poured so much money into its prestige station at Central, where the trains arrived from England, the Caledonian had none to spare on the shanties at Buchanan Street where trains for the north departed. The LMS rebuilt it in the 1930s (Chapter 12).

Until bomb damage dictated its removal in 1952–4, Thompson's 1840 train shed at Derby remained intact and, unlike the exterior, unchanged. By 1882 the sidings had been replaced by two island platforms, one of them on either side of the outer screen wall with an awning over the outside portion, giving a total of five through platform faces and a single bay at each end. Apart from the addition of some wooden platform buildings and a footbridge, Derby did not change and the same track layout still serves today.

In the capital that doyen of the main termini, Euston, continued to be the recipient of justified abuse, which four new departure platforms completed in 1892 did little to abate. At the head of the station a separate booking office in Drummond Street seemed, if anything, to make matters worse, and more tinkering was needed to put it right. It was 1914 before a completely new booking hall was built in front of the Great Hall, which did something to complement the Doric Arch and the Hall itself, but beyond them the operational part of the station was never worthy of a great terminus. London Bridge was worse, contending with Waterloo for the title of the most disgraceful station until the latter was rebuilt, leaving the former to bear that notoriety for another fifty years. By 1902 it had twenty-one platforms bewilderingly spread across what amounted to three separate stations: the South Eastern & Chatham's six high-level through platforms on the line to Cannon Street and Charing Cross; the same company's terminus on a lower level; and the Brighton's terminus. To confuse matters more, each company numbered its platforms separately and there was no No 3 on the South Eastern side, this number referring to a siding.

The main task at London Bridge in the 1890s was the widening of the approach viaducts eventually to take eleven tracks; the same problem in reverse, as it were, that was encountered at Euston, where the cutting from Camden required several widenings, and more so at stations approached through tunnels where the difficulties have already received some attention. Where they could not be opened out, as was done at Bradford Exchange and Liverpool Lime Street, duplicate tunnels were cut. The remodelling of the eastern approach to Birmingham New Street in 1906, to avoid confliction of the LNWR and Midland routes, required a second tunnel alongside the old, and similar expensive work took place at the south end of Huddersfield in 1886, three years after the long viaduct at the north end had been widened. The original Gas Works and Copenhagen tunnels leading out of King's Cross each had second and then third tunnels added to ease congestion of the approach lines. Work of this kind took a great deal of money before a start could be made on improving the actual station, and goes some way to explaining railway companies' reluctant attitudes to wholesale rebuilding if they thought some patching up and piecemeal extensions might defer the evil day.

The South Eastern platforms at London Bridge in their final form had individual awnings, demonstrating the railways' shift away from the overall roof concept. Waterloo and Birmingham Snow Hill had the last of the Victorian-style overall roofs; they were no longer seen as status symbols, but rather as expensive anachronisms that were difficult to maintain in anything like clean condition. Consequently many new or extended stations of the later railway period had platform canopies, not always to the satisfaction of local communities who felt their towns were being slighted. Dundee Tay Bridge, Cardiff, Sheffield Midland, Nottingham Midland and Aberdeen were rebuilt thus.

Companies also gave much more thought to controlling the flow of passengers, particularly at 'head' stations where rebuilding gave the opportunity to replace the often narrow cross-platform with a concourse or circulating area. Barriers between the buffer stops kept passengers off the platforms until a suitable time before departure, and also enabled the tickets of incoming passengers to be collected as railways gradually adopted the 'closed station' principle. This allowed them to dispense with the special ticket platforms that stood a few hundred yards outside so many stations, where all trains stopped for several minutes while a squad of ticket collectors invaded the compartments. The introduction of corridor trains also hastened the process, as travelling collectors could then be employed. Eventually 'open stations' became rare; Birmingham New Street remained 'open' by virtue of the public footbridge running across it; tickets from passengers in non-corridor trains were collected at the previous stop. Concourses at some later stations also acted as booking halls, with windows along one side as at Birmingham Snow Hill, or in a free-standing wooden office like Glasgow Central, Edinburgh Princes Street – where it was elaborately moulded – and Manchester Victoria. Although Birkenhead Woodside was built with an entrance and booking hall at the head of the station, they were never used as such. Passengers entered by a narrow doorway in the side wall and bought their tickets from a wooden office on the concourse.

In general it can be said that in making late-nineteenth-century enlargements and improvements, the railway companies' engineers and architects paid much more attention to providing for future needs than their predecessors. That it was at the expense of the visual and aesthetic aspects was perhaps a reflection of the financial pressures and a general debasement of current design standards than a conscious rejection of the heroic spirit of the pioneers.

11

Trains, Traffic and People

Despite their shortcomings, it is a tremendous tribute to the railway builders that so many of their structures have been capable of adaptation to deal with developments that, over the last thirty years, have changed what were basically Victorian methods of railway operating to a system that takes full advantage of late twentieth-century technology. Admittedly quite a lot of rebuilding may seem to have been done, until it is viewed against the total infrastructure of British Rail; in reality it is a remarkably small amount. So far we have concentrated on the static elements of stations, but they are essentially places of movement, and before moving on to survey the modern scene we should glance at how they worked up to the 1950s, which was when radical changes began.

A look at some of the numbers of daily train arrivals and departures at the height of the railways' monopoly gives an idea of the changes in activity, starting with a selection of London termini. Liverpool Street was long the country's busiest station. In 1903 there were 416 arrivals each weekday, of which 380 were suburban trains, figures that can be doubled to give the total number of train movements. As a token recognition of the need to rehouse the inhabitants of the 450 tenements that were demolished, the Act authorising the construction of the station required the Great Eastern Railway to run daily trains from Walthamstow and Edmonton at a return fare of 2d. The eastward expansion of suburbs that this policy started did not quite have the intended effect, as most of the dispossessed were too poor even to pay the low fare, much less the rents of the new terraced houses that were built, but clerks, shopworkers, the better paid artisans and craftsmen could, and by 1900 there were 30 daily cheap trains which from 1897 included a half-hourly service to Walthamstow throughout the night to cater for shift workers. By 1921 Liverpool Street was handling close on 230,000 passengers a day in 1,264 trains, some 30 per cent of whom arrived and departed in the two-hour morning and evening peaks. The station could not cope, yet enlargement was impossible.

Electrification was the real answer but was prohibitively expensive, so instead the Great Eastern embarked on a programme of track and signalling improvements aimed at using existing stock and locomotives as intensively as possible. At the peak the new system enabled an incoming train to be

Really crowded – the concourse at Waterloo during the 1938 holiday season. The train departure indicator is on the left (*National Railway Museum*)

emptied, filled and out again in 4 minutes, a remarkable achievement with steam traction and mechanical signalling. Incoming engines were used to take the next train out, and because yellow and blue stripes were painted over the first- and second-class compartment doors for quick identification, the trains were nicknamed the 'Jazz Service'. Liverpool Street had to wait until 1949 for its first electric trains, and now that the extended Underground has taken away some of the inner suburban traffic the station takes second place to Waterloo as the busiest station. In 1983 there were 985 trains in and out, carrying 150,000 passengers each weekday.

Waterloo's 1903 figure of some 600 arrivals and departures, of which over 500 were suburban, was lower than at Victoria and Broad Street but by 1983 had reached 1,129 trains, carrying close on 178,000 passengers, making it the country's busiest station as well as the largest. Stations serving the northern lines from London had much less traffic. They were smaller and had fewer suburban services. King's Cross had the most, 60 out of a total of 101 arrivals, whereas in 1903 Euston had 36 out of a total of 78. Poor little Marylebone had none at all, its grand total of arrivals – all main line – amounting to only 13. Not for nothing was it called London's quietest station. But by 1983 electrification and rationalisation had changed everything. Euston had some 400 trains entering and leaving daily while Marylebone, mainly through syphoning off some of Paddington's local and medium-distance services, had jumped to 110, despite having lost its long-distance trains. Electrification of the Great Northern lines relieved King's Cross of many of its suburban trains in favour of Moorgate, and the total increased only to 252.

Looking now at a selection of provincial stations, York in 1899 had a normal daily traffic of some 300 trains, which increased dramatically to over 420 at the height of the summer season. The station received trains from seven different companies whose kaleidoscopic selection of liveries provided a sight that disappeared after the 1923 grouping of the railways. Some measure of the growth in late nineteenth-century train services can be gained from the increase of 160 per cent in the number passing daily through York between the opening of the new station in 1877 and 1899. Further north, Newcastle was handling well over 500 daily arrivals and departures in 1901, while Manchester's Victoria station saw 750 trains a day, quite apart from over 200 goods trains that passed through. Despite closure of numerous lines in the West Midlands, the figures at Birmingham New Street have changed very little, thanks to the introduction of regular-interval inter-city trains and the concentration of all services there after the closure of Snow Hill. In 1900 there were nearly 700 trains, including around 50 during the morning and evening peak hours, increasing to about 770 in 1915 when 20 million passengers were handled. The 1985 figure is some 700 in the summer season.

The number of trains through Carlisle has reduced dramatically, as would be expected following the closure of the Waverley route from Edinburgh and drastic curtailment of trains from the former Midland and Glasgow & South Western lines. In 1900 the station received and despatched some 260 trains daily, like York from seven different railways, with a big increase during the Scottish 'season'. Many required remarshalling, an operation that today has almost been forgotten at a station which now deals with only some 130 trains. Remarshalling of coaches was a feature of many of the 220 trains handled at Shrewsbury – where in 1985 some 130 were dealt with – and, probably more than at any other station of its size, at Perth where at the height of the season whole households trekked northward in July and August, complete with servants and the enormous quantities of baggage without which the wealthier Victorians seemed incapable of moving about. Foxwell's well-known account of the 7.50am Perth–Inverness train setting out with thirty-seven vehicles from eight different railways – admittedly six – and four-wheelers – behind two engines must have been a sight worth seeing. In 1905 the 7.00pm arrival from Inverness comprised five sets of through coaches that required splitting up at Perth: three for London that had to be sent forward by different routes to Euston, St Pancras and King's Cross, and one each for Edinburgh and Glasgow, all attached to five other trains. The whole performance had to be completed in 50 minutes and involved ten shunting operations. This was normal working; when the holiday season was at its height some trains ran in two portions, and in addition the exchange of unscheduled attachments like fish vans could complicate the manoeuvres still further. In 1925 twenty-five trains were still being remarshalled at Perth each day, and there were frequent trains on the Dundee line and local branches to be handled as well. Nowadays such operations have dwindled. The Southern Region still divides trains on some of its London suburban services, which with multiple units is a quick operation, and locomotive-hauled trains from Liverpool and Manchester to Glasgow and Edinburgh combine at Preston to run as one train to Carstairs, where they divide again, and vice versa, but in general the practice is following the slip coach into the past.

Preston has always been a busy station and still remains an important junction on the West Coast main line. Until the post-war boom in road travel, followed by motorway links that made access easy, rail excursion traffic to Blackpool was a special feature of the working of the station in the summer. During the 24 hours of August Bank Holiday 1937, for instance, Preston station handled 980 trains. All Blackpool trains had to pass through the station. They came from the south, Manchester, Liverpool, the east and, worst of all, from the north which, were it not for the series of junctions south of the station (Fig 2 in Chapter 3), would have entailed reversal. As it was, trains from the north could run right through, round the curves at Preston Junction and Lostock Hall, and back through the station in the opposite direction, if necessary without stopping, thus avoiding the need to change engines at Preston.

Both North and Central stations at Blackpool were generously provided with sets of separate excursion platforms, although on the busiest days even they were stretched to cater for the traffic. Other popular seaside resorts had the same facility, notably Southport, Scarborough and Weston-super-Mare. Yet despite its daily total of some 430 arrivals and departures in the mid-1920s being more than doubled at bank holidays, Brighton had to handle them all at its main station platforms as there was no space to build special ones. Some could hold two medium-length trains, although there was no means of releasing the inner ones, and the introduction of electric multiple units in 1932 went a long way to resolving the problem.

An important part of station work involved dealing with what is called 'passenger train traffic', that is, goods carried in the guard's van or a vehicle attached to a passenger train, or in the case of large quantities, in trains of purpose-built stock running at passenger-train speeds. At large stations special facilities were provided for this traffic, which included newspapers, mail, parcels, milk, perishable foodstuffs and 'H&C', as horse and carriage traffic was known. Newspapers, mails and parcels are still prominent, but the conical milk churns that were once a familiar sight being dexterously loaded and unloaded into a van on the rear of a train are now museum pieces. It is to the railways, as much as a growing awareness of the importance of hygiene, that the reduction of disease from infected food can be attributed. Until 1865 London's milk came from a multitude of small cow-keepers who kept their frequently ill-fed animals in insanitary conditions throughout the capital. In that year an epidemic wiped them out, and a large-scale emergency operation to bring milk from the country by rail became permanent, with an immediate improvement in public health. Milk came mainly into Euston, Paddington and Vauxhall (the first station out from Waterloo). The practice spread, requiring special milk docks at most large stations, although cow-keepers were still in existence in Liverpool well into the present century. Milk trains of ventilated vans ran as passenger trains into the main centres, and in 1912, for instance, Mayfield station in Manchester was dealing with 1,000 churns a day, mostly from the dairy farming areas of Cheshire and Shropshire. The railways were also responsible for introducing fresh country-grown food into the cities, most of it carried as passenger train traffic, although very large consignments went straight to railway goods stations or cold stores. Birmingham Snow Hill handled great quantities of fruit and vegetables from Worcestershire and Herefordshire to feed the Black Country, including 10 tons of rabbits a day in 1901. Every large station had its fish dock, and the nightly express fish trains from Aberdeen and Grimsby were notable on the East Coast main line until comparatively recently. The old Aberdeen Joint station was notorious for the smell of fish until the new station was built in 1913, when separate fish docks were built away from the passenger station. Some stations were well known for their special traffics, like the large quantities of fresh-cut flowers and broccoli that came into Paddington from the West Country in spring and summer. Cardiff and Leeds Wellington, for some reason, appear to have handled unusually large quantities of commercial travellers' sample cases. Travellers were in the habit of depositing their cases in left-luggage offices while they went on their rounds with a selection of wares, and at Leeds a pen had to be erected on the platform to take the overflow. Horse and carriage docks were also an essential part of the station layout in the last century, although as it wore on the carriage business decreased. But a horse box on the rear of a passenger train was familiar until after World War II, and stations that catered for race traffic, like Doncaster, or that like Darlington Bank Top had a number of rural branch line services, were well provided with spare sidings and horse docks. Prize cattle were also carried as passenger train traffic, and were even unloaded at passenger platforms in the early years.

The working of royal trains has always been the subject of special regulations, and at stations particular care has to be taken to ensure that the door of the royal saloon stops opposite the red carpet. Royal waiting rooms at some of the London termini have already been referred to in Chapter 7, while Perth for many years had a special function in catering for Queen Victoria on her annual spring and autumn migrations to Balmoral. The royal train called at Perth for breakfast on the outward journey and for dinner on the return, and it was important that the Queen's saloon should stop opposite the door to the Station Joint Committee's boardroom and offices, which were taken over for the occasion. When the enlargements were made in 1885, a special suite was provided for the Queen's exclusive use and, at the other end of the building, a second one for the Prince and Princess of Wales and their entourage. It seems that on these occasions the Queen preferred to distance herself from Edward and his friends. The Lord Provost, other civic dignitaries, the station superintendent and railway directors would line the way across the platform, and on at least one occasion things went wrong. In 1887, when the enlargements were still incomplete, the train was routed into the new up platform, it having been forgotten that the entrance to the suites was still on the down side. The Queen had a longer walk than usual and after breakfast a path had to be cleared for her through a throng of arriving passengers. After the station hotel was enlarged in 1890, she started dining there instead, which avoided the stairs up to the royal suite which she had apparently complained about.[1]

As station carriage sidings were gradually removed to make space for more platforms, new carriage-cleaning sheds and sidings had to be provided further out. For Euston, sheds were built at Willesden, and later the cutting leading up to Camden was widened to take more, while the Midland moved its carriages from St Pancras to Cricklewood. At Paddington new sidings were initially laid a short distance from the station, augmented later at Old Oak Common. Carriage servicing was moved out of Manchester London Road quite early in its life, on the LNWR to Longsight and on the MSLR to Ardwick. They were kept as near as possible, of course, depending on the availability of land, and at some stations they remained alongside or close by. Space continued to be reserved for carriage sidings under the new overall roof when Carlisle was extended in 1880, between the new platform outer roads and the west wall, and when Newcastle Central was extended in 1893–5 five carriage sidings were provided in the same way. Perth had separate carriage sheds for each joint company. The Caledonian's was through an arch in the east wall of the station and the North British shed was built on the outside of the west wall, while the Highland's was just to the north of the station. The working of empty coaching stock added to the number of trains in and out of a station, and some very large ones have special running lines reserved for them out to the sidings.

The movement of rolling stock requires locomotives to be permanently available, and all stations of any size have one or more engines on duty called station pilots. In the days of steam they were often elderly tank engines seeing out their last days. Their functions were to attach and detach vehicles, transfer stock from one platform to another and generally be available to render any assistance that might be needed, including banking extra heavy trains out of the station if necessary. For many years the station pilot at Manchester Victoria was an old Aspinall 0-6-0 goods engine that could often be seen giving a heavy train a push up the bank to Miles Platting.

All large stations needed engine servicing facilities. One or more turntables, water tanks, ash pits and, where there was a heavy suburban service, coaling stages were installed close to the ends of the platforms so that engines could put in longer spells of duty between visits to the running shed, which might be several miles away. Liverpool Lime Street had a small engine shed for four tank engines alongside the turntable, with a water tank forming the roof, which may have been used by the station pilots and banking engines needed to assist trains up to Edge Hill.

Special regulations apply to the working of trains in and out of big stations, particularly those located at the foot of a steep gradient or tunnel, where in steam days very restricted speed limits were applied. The maximum speed permitted into Liverpool Central and through Birmingham New Street was 10mph, forcing drivers to make a cautious descent through the tunnels into both stations. The same restriction was applied to the final 200yd at the foot of the 1 in 40 into Bradford Exchange. Because tunnels leading into main stations were full of smoke for most of the time, drivers could rarely see signals at the tunnel end until they were right on top of them, so it was customary to install an automatic gong or bell operated by the train wheels passing over a treadle or electrical contact to warn drivers that they were nearing a signal. At Liverpool Central there were two gongs, one automatically operated by approaching trains and the other, having a different note, worked by the signalman to control shunting movements over the points just inside the tunnel.

Colour lights and centralised signalling from remote power boxes have largely eliminated semaphore signals and mechanical signal boxes from the station scene, although they were not as old as some of the stations themselves. In the early days points were operated by individual pointsmen, but as traffic increased and layouts became more complex the working of points and signals was gradually grouped under the control of a signal box, accompanied by the growth of the block telegraph system of regulating the passage of trains. One of the earliest boxes within a large station was the 'hole-in-the-wall' at Victoria (which it literally was), comprising a set of levers on an open platform recessed into the wall at the end of the covered way where the lines fanned out into the station. It was brought into use in 1861, and when the London, Chatham & Dover Railway opened its own station alongside in the following year a similar one was built there which lasted until 1920.

The early method of bringing trains into Waterloo was a dangerous undertaking which relied entirely on the dexterity of the pointsman. All trains stopped at the ticket platform, or later on at Vauxhall, where a removable coupling was placed between the engine and the leading coach. After restarting and the driver estimated he had reached a speed of about 10mph he slipped the coupling and accelerated his engine into a siding close to the entrance to the station. As soon as the wheels cleared the points the pointsman smartly threw over his lever and the engineless train rolled into the station by its own momentum, to be braked to a standstill by the guard. When proper signalling was introduced in 1867 a large box was built on a gantry spanning the tracks at the outer end of the station, with tall signals on the roof. Subsequent enlargements eventually made Waterloo 'A' box one of the biggest and best known in the country, and at one time eighty-one signal arms decorated its skyline. Another box existed inside the station from 1874 to 1911, known as the 'Crows Nest' from its position high up against the gable over the central section. No 3 box on the LNWR side at Manchester London Road was somewhat similar, although not as high. Large signal gantries spanning the approach tracks were prominent at many large stations, among them St Pancras, Newcastle and Glasgow Central (p186).

As lengthening platforms allowed scissors crossovers to be installed in the middle of stations, the signals and signal boxes that were necessary to control them became as much a part of the station furniture as bookstalls and benches. Before the 1867 Crewe station was enlarged the central crossover roads were controlled from No 3 box, which was slung between the two train sheds at a right angle over the through lines. After the 1906 extensions three boxes were installed in the station for this purpose, one of which, 'A' box, survived until the remodelling in 1985. Elsewhere on the London & North Western Rugby, Preston and Shrewsbury also had them, while Aberdeen Central box was built under an island platform canopy for which the supporting columns sprouted out of the signal-box roof.

Middle signal boxes on each side of Edinburgh Waverley were bracketed out from the station walls and named North and South Central boxes, and half way along the terminal portion of Bristol Temple Meads the Old Station box stood in an arch in the wall. It was a wooden one with nice herringbone pattern boarding. The Platform box at York, which served the same purpose, is a full-size specially designed specimen that stands right on the concourse, although the upper floor now serves as offices and the old interlocking room below is now the station bookstall. The lever platform perched on stilts over

Station signals 1: Manchester London Road No 3 signal box, tucked beneath the station roof, in the early 1950s before electrification (*Manchester Central Library*)

the footbridge at Birmingham New Street, with its conspicuous point rodding, is prominent on most old photographs of the station interior (page 111). Although it was open to the overall roof, it was called No 3 signal box, and worked the central crossovers and signals on the through lines between the old Platforms 1 and 2. It was a draughty place, frequently enveloped in smoke, and although a small hut was provided the signalman had little time to spend in it. Up Centre box at Perth was also smoky, located on a gantry alongside the entrance to the Caledonian carriage sidings where engines were wont to stand. Down Centre box, by contrast, was inside the station buildings on the main island platform with an overlooking bay window.

Boxes like this were located inside both sets of island platform buildings at Leicester London Road and Nottingham Victoria, where they were named Station East and West boxes, and at Nottingham Midland where they were called 'A' and 'B'. They were really long narrow rooms running across the building, virtually indistinguishable except for the nameplate fixed to the wall beneath the bay window at each end. No 4A box at Carlisle was on an upper floor of the island platform block and must have been the only signal box to have a neo-Tudor oriel window.

The signals themselves were especially prominent, as indeed they had to be, whether they were bracketed out from a wall or suspended from the station roof or a footbridge. Some companies fitted smaller arms than was otherwise normal, and the Great Western went in for its peculiar shortened varieties at locations where it felt that they improved the sighting for the train crews, although this sometimes seemed problematical. The Midland uncharacteristically did the same in the middle of Derby station, but at Nottingham Victoria the Great Central's full-size signals were very prominently slung beneath the footbridge and gantries (page 188), while the North Eastern's at York were on elaborately monogrammed brackets fitted to the roof columns. The London & North Western rarely made concessions and boldly placed its signals on full-sized posts and brackets. The arms were nearly always of standard size, which was larger than any other company's, and as a consequence they were very prominent at Rugby, Crewe, Preston and other important stations on that company's system.

Until British Rail eventually took it in hand, the numbering of station platforms was often haphazard. In the early days, when there was one arrival and one departure platform, it was all quite straightforward, but when stations stated to expand, life for the passenger could be difficult. The confusing arrangements at London Bridge and Waterloo have been referred to in Chapters 7 and 10 respectively, and when numbering of platforms became widespread the illogicality of allocating one number to an island platform with two faces seemed to escape most railways, so that when a train was standing at each side the bewildered passenger was not sure which was the one he wanted. The London & North Western, among other railways, compounded the confusion by allocating a separate series of numbers to bay platforms. It was small wonder that the song 'Oh Mr Porter' was so deservedly popular, and it was not until after the 1923 grouping that any sort of uniformity started to become established and numbers were given to platform faces. Even then the system could be somewhat random, often related to the way in which a station had expanded over the years, as was the case at Leeds New where Platform 10 was next to No 7, Nos 8 and 9 being across the footbridge on the other side of the station. Even today the practice of splitting a platform into sections lettered 'a', 'b' and 'c' for the accommodation of several trains end-to-end is not always entirely helpful,

Station signals 2: Great Central Railway signals form a prominent feature at Nottingham Victoria in 1961 (*Author*)

particularly where they are short, as at Leeds. It was 1936 before a sensible numbering system was adopted at Edinburgh Waverley, which for all its fine new layout continued to be cursed with archaic platform designations. The bays at the east end were numbered 1-8 and at the west 9-15, but the two long through platforms had no numbers at all, being named Main Up and Main Down and operated in two halves called 'east end' and 'west end'. Outside the south wall of the station the island Suburban Platform was also numberless, being known only by its name.

In order to eliminate the tiresome business of stopping trains at ticket platforms more stations were made 'closed', which meant that anyone not travelling had to buy a platform ticket. Although platform ticket machines had been in use on the Continent for a long time, it was not until the early 1900s that they were installed in Britain. One of the first was at Manchester Victoria in 1910.

Well into the present century most large stations were lit by gas, generally from the public supply but sometimes from the railway company's own gas works. Acetylene gas was tried at some stations for its better light, requiring special generating equipment, and Liverpool Street was the first London station to have electric light, in 1879, followed by Charing Cross and Cannon Street in 1881. When the MSLR introduced electric light in its portion of Manchester London Road a year later, it was such a novelty that Mancunians went to the station just to see it. The LNWR side remained gas lit for many years, like many others at which it lasted until after World War II. Gas did not give way to electricity at York, for instance, until 1957.

Passengers were given platform information by large signs like 'Over the bridge for London trains', which was all right up to a point, provided that the platforms were used in a fixed daily pattern. The signs were in the company's standard style, of course, and so had to compete with all the other information on display, not to mention the advertisements. But as stations grew in size and greater flexibility was possible, particularly at a station with an intensive suburban service, departure indicators were brought into use on which platform alterations could quickly be displayed. There were various types, usually in a large, ornate wooden frame on the concourse or at the station entrance. Some had narrow destination panels that were fitted into slots by hand, and others had times, destinations and platforms on wooden slats that were operated like a roller shutter by turning a handle. The large indicator that was recently removed from Liverpool Street was installed in 1922, supplemented by small ones just inside the platform barriers. Stations with a large concourse generally had the next departure shown at the barriers as well, while others used the clock-and-finger-board type, with lettered 'fingers' kept in a rack together with one or two blanks on which special destinations could be written in chalk. One of the most widely used types was the Benn & Cronin patent indicator which displayed removable enamelled plates carrying destinations, times and platform numbers in a wide variety of applications to suit individual requirements. It was first used at Bexhill on the London Brighton & South Coast Railway in 1915, and spread rapidly. Train arrival information is a much more recent development; formerly one had to ask or, if one knew the ropes, look for the blackboard in the telegraph office window.

At the beginning of railways and for quite a long time after, it was customary to announce the departure of a train by ringing a bell. Indeed, right up to World War II a handbell was kept for this purpose beside the clock on the main departure platform at King's Cross. Arrivals were often announced by an electric bell rung from the signal box, although this was mainly intended to advise the platform staff. At some LNWR stations the bell served the opposite purpose of warning passengers that a train was approaching that did *not* stop, and appropriate notices were placed on the platforms. Tebay, Penrith and Stafford had examples, the latter at least until 1978.

Before public address systems became commonplace, destinations were called out by the platform staff as the train entered the station, a practice still not quite extinct. At best it was always an uncertain method that depended on the diction, accent and lung-power of the caller, and has been a source of complaint from the beginning. A correspondent in *The Builder* in 1861

Next train . . . a manual train indicator and 'finger boards' still in use at Manchester Victoria in 1968 (*Author*)

recommended the practice he alleged was followed by station-masters on the Edinburgh & Glasgow Railway, of training parrots or starlings to call out the station name whenever a train stopped. One cannot be sure whether he was serious or merely trying to be sarcastic; the editor thought it would be easier to teach porters to speak more distinctly. A commentator in *The Engineer* in 1882 could well have a point today, although thankfully the occasions are now relatively few: referring to the half-dozen porters at Ludgate Hill – then a very busy station – the writer complained that 'they make the place hideous with howlings, generally supposed to consist of the names of the stations to which the trains are destined. The noise of all these undrilled porters or station-men is perhaps most hideous when it happens . . . that two up trains and a down train reach the platforms at nearly the same time . . . joining in a guerilla warfare of unintelligble words in each other's faces.' It was not always much better when loudspeakers came in.

Signs directing the public to trains, waiting rooms, lavatories and the way out (never the exit) were plentifully, though not necessarily logically, displayed and frequently were crowded out by advertisements. Some stations seemed to have more advertisements than others. At Euston and Paddington they were certainly more prominent than at St Pancras and King's Cross. Notices were usually direct and unequivocal, although the English might not always have satisfied a grammarian. 'To Cross the Line and Way Out' was a regular offender. Notices directed at the station staff were sometimes less comprehensible to the layman, like this one at the end of Platforms 6 and 7 at Leeds Central:

NOTICE TO SHUNTERS
VEHICLES LEFT on any 7 PLATFORM LINES
must STAND on at least one of the FOULING BARS

The emphasis of the heavy lettering is interesting. Or this one at Bristol:

CYLINDERS OF KING CLASS LOCOMOTIVES (60XX) ARE
NOT TO PASS THIS BOARD ON THE BAY LINE

a prohibition needing nice judgement on the part of the driver. The Great Western was particularly concerned about the protection of underline metalwork where part of a station was on a bridge, and frequently displayed notices prohibiting the discharge of water from engines. An unqualified one at Shrewsbury that caused some amusement to more than one bystander simply instructed enginemen not to discharge water. In that railwayman's bible, the Sectional Appendix to the Working Timetable, drivers entering the main up platform at Birmingham Snow Hill were instructed to draw right up to the starting signal, where the engine chimney would be clear of overhead steelwork, in order to minimise corrosion. A notice on the office gable half way down the Brunel shed at Bristol Temple Meads stated that 'Enginemen must as far as possible avoid the emission of smoke and water from their engines at this end of the station', which might have seemed rather odd in the part of the station that originally was expressly intended to accommodate engines.

The railways were on their guard against those they considered undesirable, in no uncertain terms. A notice at the foot of the Store Street stairs up to Manchester London Road, prohibiting loitering, remained there past 1965, and 'skylarking' was expressly forbidden at Charing Cross, while a board at Liverpool Central sternly warned 'workmen, cabmen, fishporters and idlers' that the adjacent closets were for the use of passengers, and not for the likes of them.

'Under the station clock' was a favourite and convenient meeting place that could not be mistaken on a crowded concourse. A few are left, like the ornate iron-framed ones at Brighton and Charing Cross, and a large pair at Liverpool Lime Street, while the old main departure platform clock at King's Cross is still there although it does not work, but it is good to see the reappearance of one at St Pancras after many years' notable absence. Most platform clocks are now electric and smaller than those they replaced, although a few of the large English Dial clocks are still ticking away, reminders of the early days of railways when lines that did not provide their engine crews with watches expected them to observe the platform clock as they swept past.

Although the Liverpool & Manchester Railway let part of its building in Liverpool Road, Manchester, as shops, it was the rapid expansion of stations from the 1860s onward that brought increased realisation of the commercial opportunities in unwanted space. Shops and kiosks appeared in growing numbers on approaches and concourses, where previously only bookstalls had been allowed. 'Conveniences' expanded, too, as hairdressing salons, bathrooms and 'wash-and-brush-up' were added to the basic facilities. At one time Newcastle Central had four bathrooms where in 1945 the charge for a bath was 6d. Frequently they were in a basement, an area not otherwise seen by the public, although many large stations have extensive cellars behind, or rather below, the scenes containing maintenance workshops, stores, boiler rooms and other essential functions. There is a maze of passages under Newcastle Central, many no longer used, while beneath Glasgow Central four levels contain such diverse activities as the lost property store for the whole of Scotland, catering stores, water pumps and a store for rubbish, taken from trains by the cleaners, that fills a complete skip each day.

As far as possible the new and enlarged stations kept parcels and other passenger train traffic separate from the passengers. Most had separate subways or bridges for trolleys, reached by hydraulic lifts or, in the case of some subways, sloping ramps such as those at Crewe and Birmingham New Street. Where postal traffic was particularly heavy, further separate bridges or subways were provided for the mails, as at Newcastle and Crewe, with a direct connection to the sorting office, if it was close by, as so many are. Before the introduction of small motor tractors that could haul a string of trolleys, now in turn superseded by the electric tractor, each trolley had to be pulled by a man. It was partly to overcome this problem that Sir John Aspinall, the Lancashire & Yorkshire Railway's chief mechanical engineer, devised an overhead electric conveyor system by which parcels and other traffic were moved around Victoria Station, Manchester, in large wicker baskets that were raised and lowered on a pulley. The conveyor was suspended from a pair of rails and the driver sat beneath it, legs astride, in a curious semi-reclining seat. His completely unprotected aerial tours of the station would make a present-day Health and Safety Inspector issue a prohibition notice on the spot. There was a luggage bridge as well, with hydraulic lifts enclosed in delicate wrought ironwork.

Station management developed into a fairly standard pattern quite early. Chief Agents at Liverpool and Manchester were responsible for goods and passenger traffic on the Liverpool & Manchester Railway, and each had a passenger station superintendent under him who in turn had an assistant, clerks and porters. At Liverpool after 1831 these included self-employed porters, probably the first example of outside porters licensed by the railway company, which issued a distinctive badge, once numerous at large stations but now long since gone. As time went on station jobs evolved into grades. In 1865, for instance, the London Brighton & South Coast Railway had seven basic grades: station-master, clerk, inspector, foreman, ticket collector, head porter and porter. Staff who were not in direct contact with the public also came under the station-master's control, such as signalmen, shunters and passenger train guards. By modern standards the numbers employed were enormous. In 1901 the staff employed from Newcastle Central totalled over 670, including 170 guards and 96 signalmen. The station had its own literary institute and reading room for the staff.

The much smaller Great Western station at Cardiff in 1907 employed 223, although it is interesting to observe that by 1923 a much larger but more modern station, Glasgow Central, dealt with far more passengers with comparatively fewer staff, thanks to centralised signalling and other less labour-intensive developments. The area coming under one man's control varied, of course, and could have been smaller; certainly the Newcastle station-master's responsibility would extend for some distance from Central station. Even so, there was still a variety of designated jobs that in today's age of the stationman seems almost bewildering. In 1923 the Glasgow Central station-master's staff of 432 comprised 2 assistants, 3 clerks, 2 yard inspectors, 7 station inspectors, 18 signalmen, 7 cabin boys, 1 phone boy, 4 excess luggage collectors, 25 ticket collectors, 4 station foremen, 8 parcel porters, 41 porters, 1 billposter, 2 searchers, 2 letter sorters (for railway letters, not GPO), 5 porter-guards, 1 underman, 7 female waiting-room attendants, 38 guards, 22 female carriage cleaners, 9 carriage lampmen, 35 yard foremen and shunters, 16 cloakroom attendants, 6 police, a parcels superintendent with 134 staff and a cashier in charge of 30 booking clerks. In 1979 the station staff numbered 360. Station-masters, or superintendents as some companies called them, were graded into classes and the supremo at a large station invariably was a Special Class station-master whose official attire was striped trousers, tail coat and silk hat, a tradition that lasted until 1968 (at Liverpool), albeit towards the end only on ceremonial occasions.

The management of a joint station was rather different, and depended to some extent on the type of station and its traffic. Where there was a clear division between the users' portions, as was the case at Manchester London Road, the employment of separate station-masters and staff was possible, and, in fact, continued there, including separate signalling, right up to nationalisation. The LNWR and later the LMS were landlords while the Great Central and its successor, the LNER, were tenants in perpetuity, a somewhat odd situation when one considers that until 1905 the Great Central had its headquarters at the station. The arrangements at Preston were more complicated and quite unique; until the amalgamation of 1921 brought the London & North Western and the Lancashire & Yorkshire railways together, the main line part of the station that had originated with the North Union Railway was joint, while the old East Lancashire side was operated solely by the LYR. Each part had its own entrance, booking office, station-master and staff.

In an endeavour to avoid some of the disastrous repercussions of divided management noted in Chapter 3, joint committees were set up at most stations, with either joint staff or separate staff under unified overall control. In some cases the agreements were ratified by legislation. The Carlisle Station Joint Committee set up by the Lancaster & Carlisle and Caledonian railways in 1857 was given statutory authority by an Act of 1861 and became a powerful body, with its own secretary and staff as well as the normal joint station superintendent and his staff. The committee was composed of equal numbers of directors from the two companies, and the other companies that came to use the station later – the Maryport & Carlisle, North Eastern, Glasgow & South Western and North British – were only tenants. When in 1876, upon the opening of its Settle & Carlisle line, the Midland sought representation on the committee in return for having agreed to pay a large proportion of the cost of extensions, the joint committee successfully kept it out until 1882. The London & North Western had by this time acquired the Lancaster & Carlisle, of course, and neither it nor the Caledonian welcomed the Midland's access to Scotland. However, when in that year the Midland promoted a parliamentary bill to gain membership of the committee, the financial terms were revised, although the two companies still retained control of the station.

Perth General station was managed by a similar joint committee, set up in 1863, that lasted until nationalisation, as did the committee at Bristol Temple Meads that was formed by the Great Western, Bristol & Exeter and Midland companies under the Bristol Joint Station Act of 1865. The GWR amalgamated with the Bristol & Exeter in 1876, and to all outward appearances, from signals to uniforms, Temple Meads looked like a GWR station, apart from the initials 'BJS' on the uniform caps and jackets of the staff. Likewise Birmingham New Street appeared to be unmistakeably London & North Western, although from 1897 it was operated jointly with the Midland. For the first thirty-four years Midland trains entered and left at the east end, mostly comprising through coaches from Derby-Bristol trains that were divided or combined at Saltley or Camp Hill, until the construction of the western tunnels to Church Road Junction, when the station was extended in 1885, allowed the Midland through running. Although the Midland was soon given what amounted to sole possession of the new platforms, it continued as a tenant until the operation of the station became joint, although the LNWR remained the legal owner and was responsible for maintenance. The joint committee comprised an equal number of members from each company, which took turns to appoint a joint superintendent.

Stations into which other railways operated under running powers, like York, often had separate booking-offices and clerks, and sometimes platform staff as well, whose duty it was to attend only to their own company's trains. Crewe, for instance, despite being a seat of power on the London & North Western, had North Staffordshire and Great Western representatives who were designated station-masters, although they really only acted as agents for their companies.

During both world wars, when civilian travel was curtailed, large stations became headquarters for military transport. The Railway Transport Officer, or RTO, became a familiar figure whose job it was to liaise with the railway in the movement of troops. Station offices were commandeered and refreshment rooms became services' canteens. Just before and after the beginning of World War II, stations in industrial cities were the scenes of the mass evacuation of children to the country, too, and later many were to suffer severe bomb damage, yet, through the efforts of the staff, were operational again in a few hours, or at the most a day or two. Memories are stirred by the memorials to employees killed on active service that the companies erected at many of their stations. The great Memorial Arch at Waterloo commemorates London & South Western men who died in 1914–18, and the smaller but no less poignant entrance arch at Stoke-on-Trent is the North Staffordshire Railway's memorial, one of its final acts before becoming part of the LMS. Other company memorials stand outside Euston, Derby and York, and commemorative tablets occupy prominent positions at stations from Liverpool Street and Paddington to Edinburgh and Inverness. Perth has one of a number of tablets recording staff lost from an individual station; and inside No 1 Neville Street at the west end of Newcastle Central brass plaques record the dead of both World Wars from the Newcastle Accounts Office.

I know only of one station that has a 'blue plaque' commemorating a notable historic feature or event, but there is one at Edinburgh Waverley to the effect that the station occupies the site of the Edinburgh Physic Garden of 1675–1763, forerunner of the Royal Botanic Garden. It was erected by the Royal College of Physicians in Edinburgh, the University and the Royal Botanic Garden authorities in 1978.

12

The Big Four and British Rail

The four large companies that came into being under the government grouping of the railways in 1923 were faced with severe problems resulting from intensive use and reduced maintenance during the 1914–18 war, coupled with a depressed economy and, above all, competition from rapidly developing road transport. In urban areas the challenge of the electric tramcar was giving way to the much greater threat of the motor bus and, a decade later, the private car. Freight and long-distance passenger traffic were less affected.

With important exceptions, most of the country's major stations were basically in quite good shape and well able to deal with the traffic of the next thirty years, thanks to the reconstruction programmes carried out by the old companies during the preceding thirty, although the same could not be said of many smaller stations, particularly south of the Thames and in industrial areas. That some were dirty, gloomy places was attributable more to economies in cleaning and painting, and the continued use of the steam locomotive, than to any inherent defects. To a certain extent the railways kept abreast of new passenger handling techniques quite well, such as the installation of electric departure indicators and public address systems for train announcements. Loudspeakers appeared at York in 1927, Euston in 1934 and Birmingham New Street a year later, although Liverpool Exchange had to do without until 1960. Waterloo had them in 1933, and in 1937 experimented with broadcasting light music between announcements. In 1940 it became a permanent feature that today has spread.

Instead of burdening busy booking clerks with passengers' enquiries, separate enquiry offices were gradually opened, some also dealing with the growing practice of reserving seats. The large wooden office that ruined the Great Hall at Euston was opened in 1930, and one was incorporated in the office extensions at Paddington in 1936. Some of the earlier ones were quite small, as it took the public time to change old habits; a small wooden office appeared on the concourse at Manchester Victoria in the 1920s, while the one in the booking hall at London Road was hardly more than a kiosk until 1931, when a ladies' waiting room was converted to make a larger office with a counter.

A greater variety of shops started to be opened on the bigger concourses. Bookstalls and tobacco kiosks had been features for a long time, but now chain shops like Boots the Chemists opened branches on stations. It was a sign of the times when the first station milk bar was opened at Hull in 1938, and the first news cinema on a station in 1933 at Victoria, followed by Waterloo the following year and Leeds City in 1938.

The adoption of new operating methods and systems was much slower. Several large stations had power-operated semaphore signalling from the beginning of the century – notably the Central stations at Newcastle and Glasgow and at Birmingham Snow Hill – but apart from the Southern Railway, which introduced colour lights at its London termini at the same time as electrification in the 1920s, mechanical signalling from a number of signal boxes continued to control trains at most stations until the 1950s and '60s. The Great Western modernised the signalling at Paddington in 1929–32 with its own version of electric colour lights, and in 1930–5 at Bristol with a more conventional system when the station was enlarged, while the LNER brought in colour lights at Darlington Bank Top in 1939 as the final part of its large-scale resignalling of the main line north of York, involving the closure of the East and West boxes on the station platform. Edinburgh Waverley was also extensively re-equipped in 1937–8 when the two boxes on the station walls became redundant, although they lingered on, disused, until 1983.

Looking at large-scale, post-war reconstruction schemes, the Great Western carried out more than the other three railways because previously it had lagged behind, a circumstance to a large degree due to its backwardness in the thirty-odd years up to the end of the 1880s, when the company stirred itself into what MacDermot called the 'Great Awakening'. Steps were then taken finally to abolish the broad gauge and, just as importantly, start projects for building over 150 miles of new main line. They were not completed until 1910, but erased the company's reputation as the Great Way Round. All these and other major improvements in services cost money at a time when other lines were undertaking important rebuilding works, although it must be said that, conversely, the new lines and widenings perhaps put the Great Western in a rather better position so far as smaller stations were concerned.

The work of enlarging Paddington that had been interrupted by the war (Chapter 10) was resumed. First the iron columns supporting Brunel's roof were replaced by steel stanchions, after several proposals to demolish the old roof had been resisted. This was finished by 1924. Then the area behind the buffers, originally occupied by turntables and sidings and later used as a parcels area, was reroofed and transformed into a spacious concourse. It was known somewhat incongruously as 'The Lawn', said to date from pre-railway days when it was a grassy plot. New offices were built on each side, and at the opposite end of the station the platforms were extended under umbrella canopies. The old Bishop's Road station was finally incorporated into the main station when two new island platforms were built. This work was all complete by 1934.

During the same decade Brunel's old wooden sheds at Swansea were replaced (in 1932) by a new station, including a Portland stone frontage block in best 1930s functional style and standardised platform awnings, while to the east Newport was given a new frontage block in 1928. It is five storeys high, in typical inter-war heavy neo-Georgian, although the 1878 stone Italianate platform buildings and some of the ridge-and-furrow awnings were retained. Newport was one of the few GWR stations to have awnings of this type. Cardiff also was completely rebuilt in 1932, again with a white stone frontage block but more ornate, including a typical 'Union Jack' balustrade, an attractive cupola and 'Great Western Railway' in large stone letters that for some years now British Rail have kept hidden behind advertisements. The booking hall has a handsome curved ceiling, and there are six platforms and a bay with the usual umbrella awnings. The two Riverside station platforms were incorporated into the main station at the same time.

The platform buildings and subway walls at Cardiff are faced with smooth off-white Carrara blocks, with the station name and direction signs in chocolate-coloured glazed ceramic lettering. The same finish was used at Bristol Temple Meads, where another big enlargement programme was completed in 1935. There the island platforms under the 1878 roof were removed to make way for two through lines, and five new ones were added outside beneath individual awnings. The 1878 platforms, one of the new island platform lines and those in the terminal part of the station were long enough for division into two by scissors crossovers so that they could take two trains apiece, and were separately numbered, thus increasing the earlier eight platforms to fifteen. Digby Wyatt's frontage was modified by removing the spire from the clock tower, and the crocketting was taken off the smaller spires. Care was taken to execute interior modernisation in keeping with the Gothic character of the original. The remodelled booking hall and main refreshment room block were given fine panelled ceilings and the booking windows had mild Gothic styling that blended well with the old. The waiting room interiors, by contrast, were undisputably 'modern'. Brunel's train shed remained virtually untouched.

Some remodelling and an external extension to the down-side building at Exeter St Davids was done in 1938–9, retaining most of the architectural features that had survived the work of 1912–14 when the overall roof had been replaced by awnings and further platforms added. A 1935 scheme to build new high-level platforms and a bridge for Southern Railway trains, avoiding crossing on the level, was however not proceeded with. The Southern itself had rebuilt Queen Street station at Exeter in 1933, removing the old two-span roof and wooden buildings and building a new neo-Georgian street-level entrance block. It was renamed Exeter Central at the same time. Plymouth North Road was the last station to be tackled by the GWR. Plans to replace the 1877 wooden sheds had been drawn up as long ago as 1898, but discarded, and when they were finally pulled down in 1938–9 the war stopped anything other than temporary wooden awnings taking their place, so that North Road became more miserable than ever until British Railways started again in 1956. Medium-sized stations rebuilt or remodelled by the Great Western included Newton Abbot, Taunton and Leamington Spa.

Finance for these schemes and those of the other railways was largely by government loans under legislation of 1929 and 1935, designed to relieve unemployment. Work on the LMS was mainly limited to refurbishment; the main project, the complete reconstruction of Euston, was stopped by the war. A grand plan for a new station was announced in 1935, for which the president of the Royal Institution of British Architects, Sir Percy Thomas, was engaged as consultant, and details released in 1937 showed a huge frontage and hotel block on Euston Road which, among other things, would have a helicopter pad on the roof, all in the best transatlantic super-cinema style. The Great Hall would have had to be demolished but it was hoped to re-erect the Doric Arch. All that actually happened was the quarrying of 100,000 tons of stone at Caldon Low in Staffordshire. Earlier Sir Edwin Lutyens, the distinguished architect, had advised on the redecoration of the Great Hall, which was completed in 1927, with electric light, but spoilt by the aforementioned enquiry office deposited in the middle.

Major LMS work outside London was confined to Manchester, Glasgow and Leeds. The walkway connecting Victoria and Exchange stations in Manchester was converted into a platform in 1928–9, making the combined length of 2,238ft the longest in Europe. At the same time the two stations were placed under unified management, and in 1934 the roof between the through and terminal portions of Victoria was partly removed and replaced by an awning. The rest disappeared in wartime bombing. Glasgow Buchanan Street was at long last reconstructed in 1932, still in timber but on a steel frame, giving the horizontally-boarded frontage with its classical wooden pilasters the appearance of a rather superior bank in one of the larger townships of the wild west. The new glass-roofed concourse was a decided improvement, but the platforms had to make do with second-hand awnings from Ardrossan North which closed in the same year, leaving Buchanan Street still the poor relation in Glasgow.

The work at Leeds was more ambitious, no less than the combination of Wellington and New stations, in conjunction with the LNER which was joint owner of New. It consisted of building a handsome new concourse across the head of Wellington station to join the existing New station concourse,

1930s architecture at its best: the new concourse at Leeds City, shortly after its opening in 1938 (*British Rail*)

complete with booking-office and other facilities. It was notable for the use of a reinforced concrete frame that anticipated present-day Portal frame construction, and for its lofty panelled ceiling with square roof lights and elegant pendant lighting. Alongside it a new Queens Hotel was designed by the LMS Chief Architect, W. H. Hamlyn, with W. Curtis Green as associate architect, and was opened with a gold key by the Earl of Harewood in the presence of the Princess Royal in 1937. There is obvious American influence in the white Portland stone façade, with Lutyens's touches as well, but on the whole it has withstood the test of time and is still a better complement to City Square than its post-World War II companions. The columns supporting the cab entrance bear arms of towns served by the LMS, while the interior rooms displayed several styles, from Italian Doric in the banqueting hall to the slightly baroque entrance to the French Restaurant which was decorated in 'Empire' taste. There were many innovations, well up to the Towle tradition (Chapter 9): the Grill Room ceiling was coffered with a large star-shaped recess in the centre containing concealed lighting; the 206 bedrooms all had baths, and the hotel was air-conditioned and double-glazed throughout. Even the Leeds Corporation tram lines in City Square were moved 30ft further away and fitted with specially insulated manganese steel points to avoid disturbing guests. The combined stations were renamed Leeds City in 1938, but otherwise the platform areas remained unchanged, apart from the removal of the remains of Wellington's overall roofing and replacement by

Midland-style awnings to match those that were already there. Leeds New, in fact, did not look any different at all.

In London, the Great Northern in its last years initiated attempts to ease congestion at King's Cross by making all but two departure platforms capable of taking arrivals, although trains waiting to depart still blocked entry. A new island platform replaced the locomotive yard between the two sets of suburban platforms, and another replaced carriage sidings on the departure side. This work was completed by the LNER in 1924, although the last carriage siding in the station did not disappear until 1938 and nothing was done about the disreputable huddle of shacks in front of the station. Passenger facilities were vastly improved during this time. At Liverpool Street the Jazz Service ceased after the General Strike of 1926 as people moved further out from London and inner suburban traffic started to decline, while Marylebone remained virtually unchanged apart from some growth in suburban traffic. After the opening of Wembley Stadium, it became the station for special trains to sporting events. Fenchurch Street witnessed the greatest change on the LNER in London, when in 1932–5 congestion was tackled by rearranging the platforms and approaches to allow more intensive use by the London Tilbury & Southend line services, which were part of the LMS. By nationalisation in 1948 the station occupied the curious position of being owned by the LNER but used almost exclusively by LMS trains. The final LNER service was withdrawn in the following year.

The company's major work in the provinces involved the extensions at York in 1938, when a new island platform was opened beyond the train shed on the west side, with umbrella awnings, and the platforms were re-numbered. In Hull, former Hull & Barnsley Railway trains started running into Paragon station upon the closure of Cannon Street in 1924, but the service was severely cut back in 1932. The Royal Station Hotel was extended and modernised in 1933–5.

Under the leadership of Sir Herbert Walker, the newly formed Southern Railway quickly set about extensive electrification on the third-rail system. It involved considerable track alterations at all the London termini during the 1920s and '30s, particularly at Victoria – where rush-hour traffic doubled in the ten years from 1927 to 1937 – and at Cannon Street. There, except for the public rooms, the hotel was closed in 1931 and became offices under the name of Southern House. The hotel at Holborn Viaduct was also used as offices, following conversion during the war. At Victoria the two stations were combined in 1924 by making openings in the dividing wall, when the concourse on the Eastern Section side (as the South Eastern & Chatham's became known) was enlarged, a new cab entrance was made from Eccleston Bridge, and platforms were lengthened and renumbered across the combined station. The same was done at London Bridge in 1928 when the platforms were renumbered sensibly, although it still remained a very confusing place.

The approach layout at Waterloo was remodelled from as far out as Wimbledon in 1936. St Paul's was renamed Blackfriars in 1937.

The South Eastern & Chatham Railway had made a start on rationalising its continental services in 1920 by deciding to concentrate them at Victoria, which the Southern subsequently publicised as 'The Gateway to the Continent'. The 'Golden Arrow' all-Pullman train was introduced in 1929, followed in 1936 by the 'Night Ferry' on which blue continental-style coaches of the International Sleeping Car Co provided a distinctively European atmosphere unique to a British station as they waited to depart for the Dover–Dunkirk train ferry. Victoria's long connection with air services began in 1939 when an Imperial Airways terminal was opened on the Buckingham Palace Road side, connected by train with the Empire flying boat base at Southampton. As a result of these changes Charing Cross lost its continental flavour, and might well have disappeared entirely had the London County Council had its way. Back in 1901 it wanted to demolish Charing Cross Bridge in order to build a new road bridge, suggesting that the railway company could build a new station on the south bank. In 1906 the South Eastern & Chatham had to place a weight restriction on the bridge when it was found to be not strong enough to carry modern locomotives; not more than two trains were allowed on it at any one time, and then not on adjacent tracks, which hampered operating work at busy periods. Despite this handicap the SECR was not over-keen, and nothing positive happened until 1925 when the Royal Commission on Cross River Traffic recommended a new double-decker road and rail bridge and a new Charing Cross station. In 1928 the 1901 scheme was revived when the LCC and the Southern agreed to an exchange of sites for a new terminus south of Waterloo Bridge, with compensation and a 75 per cent government grant. But Parliament had cold feet and rejected it. The scheme was aired again in 1936 but nothing more was done. Meanwhile the weight restriction problem had been solved in 1926 by introducing electric multiple-unit trains which still safely rumble over the bridge today.

Electrification was also the main change at Brighton station, which the new Southern electrics entered in 1932, for which platforms were lengthened and the concourse enlarged. In a way it had been foreshadowed by another of those turn-of-the-century schemes that might be called the railway promoters' last fling, like the London–Bristol scheme (Chapter 3). A London & Brighton Electric Railway was proposed, with a station in Queens Square near the sea front. A Bill reached Parliament but was rejected, as was another proposal for an underground link between Brighton station and two new stations on the promenade.

The 1923 grouping reduced the number of joint stations in cases where, like Carlisle, Nottingham Victoria and Birmingham New Street, they now came under single ownership, although changes were mainly administrative.

The old two-bay overall roof at the south end of Shrewsbury station was replaced about 1924 by individual ridge-and-furrow awnings in a style that – very properly – was neither Great Western nor London & North Western inspired. The 1901 roof at the north end remained.

In many ways the greatest changes were caused by the war. As a precaution the glass was removed from the roofs of a number of stations, most of which in London were bomb damaged, particularly severely at Paddington, St Pancras, Cannon Street and King's Cross. Paddington and King's Cross still have gaps in the offices along the departure sides, while the frontages of London Bridge and Holborn Viaduct were reduced to single storeys. The old hotels at London Bridge and Cannon Street were gutted, although the latter was repaired, and Charing Cross Hotel lost its top two storeys. The old LSWR offices and boardroom at Waterloo were destroyed, together with the Necropolis station, and Liverpool Street suffered severe damage to Hamilton House in Bishopsgate and its front office block, where the stumpy spire on the clock tower disappeared. Part of the old Chatham offices went at Victoria, and offices were also lost at Euston where the Great Hall roof was damaged. These were the major casualties; there were hundreds of instances of lesser damage. Only Fenchurch Street, Broad Street and Marylebone escaped serious incidents.

Railways in provincial cities were prime targets, of course. York, Derby and the through platforms at Manchester Victoria lost parts of their roofs, the last two permanently, and there was extensive roof damage to both sides of Birmingham New Street. Part of the offices at York was demolished, while Manchester Exchange lost the whole of its frontage block. At Plymouth, Millbay goods station was so severely damaged that the adjacent passenger station was closed in 1941 in order to use it for goods traffic, and passenger services were concentrated at North Road station.

Hard on the heels of the war came nationalisation in 1948. The railways were far more run down than after World War I, manpower was short, materials were hard to come by and most large stations were in a mess. One of the last acts of the LMS was to start the demolition of Cowper's roof over the old LNWR side at Birmingham New Street, and replace it with very utilitarian steel and asbestos awnings, including a roof over the footbridge where No 3 signal box was abolished. Working mainly at weekends, the job took two-and-a-half years between 1945 and 1948. The roof on the Midland side was repaired. The Southern decided that the skeletal roof ribs at Cannon Street were beyond repair, so the temporary awnings that had been erected underneath it remained until complete reconstruction started in 1958.

Roofs at a number of other stations were not fully re-covered after war-time removal of their glass, particularly above tracks, as at Leicester London Road and Crewe, or were clad with asbestos leaving only small parts glazed, which made them darker and gloomier than ever. Derby's roof was not repaired at all – well over 100yd were lost – but was left until 1952–4 when new pre-cast concrete awnings replaced it, giving the platforms a clean, modern look that after a few years deteriorated as the concrete weathered and became dirty. Steel and asbestos awnings replaced the roof at Bradford Forster Square about the same time. Elsewhere, overall roofs were reduced in area in the name of modernisation, usually with unhappy visual results. Carlisle and Perth, for instance, both lost their attractive end-screens in the process, in 1958 and 1969 respectively. During the 1950s the war-damaged remains of the fine Gothic roof at Middlesbrough were taken down, accompanied in 1956–7 by the arched roof that had survived the 1904 enlargement of Sheffield Midland. The roof over the north end of Shrewsbury went in the mid-1960s, and in 1960–1 the westernmost roof at Preston was replaced by awnings, although it was the newest.

Lord Beeching's Reshaping Report of 1963 introduced drastic rationalisation of services, many of which had outlived their usefulness, but which in some instances was an excuse for hasty closures that have since been regretted. Inevitably, numbers of large stations were closed in the process of eliminating duplicate services (Appendix 1). Edinburgh lost Princes Street; Glasgow lost Buchanan Street which few mourned, and St Enoch which many did. It lingered on as a car park for a few years; a few more still and efforts might have been made to find a use for it on the lines of Manchester Central. In Liverpool, Central has disappeared, the name remembered only in the underground Merseyrail station, and so has Exchange except for the hotel front which is listed and now forms part of a new office development. Manchester Central survives and, as we shall see, will shortly flourish in a new guise, but the traffic at Exchange reverted to Victoria and the station remained only for parcels and car parking, and more recently has lost its roof. Nottingham Victoria in 1967 and Sheffield Victoria in 1970 disappeared almost without trace, apart from the former's clock tower, as did Dundee West in 1965. Birmingham Snow Hill, which apart from its size was in many ways so superior to New Street, was flattened but is currently about to be resuscitated. Tracks are to be relaid as part of a second cross-city line and preliminary work has started on a new four-platform station that will enable Moor Street to be closed. Surprisingly Marylebone has lingered on, but seems set for closure within five years.

The biggest single modernisation work involving major station rebuilding was the electrification of the West Coast main line from Euston to Glasgow between 1956 and 1974. It proceeded in fits and starts according to the will of politicians and availability of finance, starting from Crewe to Manchester London Road. The frontage at London Road was replaced by a new entrance building alongside a ten-storey office block, and the main platforms were lengthened, while the MSJ platforms were rebuilt in more convenient fashion. The arched roof fortunately was refurbished, and with plentiful glazing blends well with the modern concourse. The station was officially reopened and renamed Piccadilly in 1960, when Mayfield was finally given over entirely to parcels traffic, although the whole job was not completed until 1965.

Concurrently, Euston and Birmingham New Street were completely rebuilt, so that for some years travellers to the Midlands and Manchester wandered through large-scale building operations at both ends of their journeys. Because it was averred that the new station would front on to Euston Road, the Great Hall and the Euston Arch were demolished, the latter only after the biggest protest campaign staged by conservationists before or since – including a deputation led by the President of the Royal Academy – received the personal veto of the Prime Minister, Harold Macmillan (now Lord Stockton). The Arch fell in 1961, electric main line trains started running in 1965 and the Queen opened the new station in 1968. It has twenty platforms, seventeen of which are used for regular passenger trains, beneath a flat concrete deck on which the intention was to erect an hotel, although that has still to come, if ever it does. The single-storey air-conditioned concourse is spacious, uncluttered and, after the early criticism of lack of seating had been heeded, easy to use. The front is largely of glass behind a colonnade, with flanking shops and offices, in black polished granite with white mosaic facings. It is fronted by a paved piazza on which three office blocks were built in 1979, an eight- and a fourteen-storey on the west side (one of which is now BR's headquarters called Rail House), and a ten-storey block on the east, linked by a three-storey bridge block that recalls the old Euston Hotel in that it partly hides the station entrance. Underneath the piazza and concourse are the cab rank, car park and Underground booking hall, reached by escalators. When all was finished it could be seen that Euston Square Gardens were still intact and that there would have been ample space to re-erect the Arch after all. Given imaginative treatment it would have made a perfect foil to the new station. As it is, of the old Euston only Stansby's two entrance lodges and the LNWR war memorial remain, while John Thomas's sculptured group 'Britannia' from the Great Hall adorns the waiting room, and the statue of Robert Stephenson stands on the west side of the piazza, opposite an unidentifiable three-dimensional shape entitled 'Piscator' (the nearest it gets to fishing is a faint resemblance to a whale) erected in 1981 on the east.

The rebuilding of New Street started in 1964, in which eight through platforms and six bays were converted to twelve through platforms, made possible by the elimination of Queens Drive. Trains from the east or London direction can enter any platform, but from the west Bristol and Gloucester trains are confined to the five southernmost platforms which, like the old Midland side platforms, are sharply curved. The whole station was completed in 1967 at a cost of some £4½ millions. It is covered by a low concrete deck of some 7½ acres, containing in part a long concourse called a 'passenger dispersal area' running across the platforms and housing the buffet, bookstall and other offices, the ticket office, barrier and main entrance leading to a forecourt connected to the inner ring road. Escalators lead from the concourse by the ticket office to a covered shopping centre from which there is stair and ramp access to Stephenson Place and New Street. The remainder forms the base of a multi-storey car park and a twenty-one storey block of offices and flats. There is an elevated walkway to the nearby Bull Ring shopping precinct and National bus station, and subsidiary entrances from Station Street and Stephenson Place. At the west end of the station a striking new signal box was opened in 1966, five storeys high in white ribbed concrete interspersed with black tinted windows and surrounds, aptly described by Pevsner as 'Liquorice Allsorts'.

All three stations employ extensive use of white glazed wall finishes that add light. Manchester and Euston undoubtedly have been a success, despite the long walk to the trains at Euston (a disadvantage increasingly shared by later modernised stations), but New Street is less so, particularly at platform level; on what was the LNWR side the platforms are still narrow and all rely entirely on artificial light, as do parts of those at Euston, diesel fumes are slow to disperse and narrow escalators and stairs create congestion at busy periods. Pedestrians from Station Street or from Stephenson Place – the most popular entrance – have first to ascend to the Shopping Centre deck, where they try to find their ill-signed way to the station entrance, and then go down again by two flights of stairs or escalators to reach the platforms. Furthermore, the only prominent external sign is over the so-called main entrance, there being virtually nothing but a BR flag and 'Birmingham Shopping Centre' in large illuminated letters over the most heavily used approach from New Street itself. The station was the first to be built in collaboration with property developers; perhaps this was all part of the deal.

Apart from simplification of track layouts, the West Coast main line electrification affected the other main stations, except Preston, relatively slightly. Indeed, Rugby – which lost only its roof end-screens – apart from track remodelling is virtually the same as ever it was, despite losing services to Peterborough, Leicester and Leamington. Glasgow Central and Crewe have had to wait until the present time for major alterations. Those at Glasgow are concerned with providing up-to-date passenger facilities and enlargement of the concourse at the expense of shortening some of the platforms, but Crewe in 1985 underwent more drastic treatment when the 1906 island platform on the west side was taken out of use, the track layout and junctions were remodelled to allow fast running through the station by non-stop trains, and traffic was concentrated at the two 1867 island platforms. To achieve the reconstruction at Crewe, the station was closed for seven weeks and through trains were routed through the goods line tunnels. Carlisle, of course, had already been altered.

During 1971–3 Preston's thirteen platforms were reduced to eight by restricting the two westernmost platforms to parcels traffic; by demolishing the most easterly platform and the East Lancashire 'pan handle', and at the same time closing the line out through Preston Junction, routing all East Lancashire trains over the 1908 curve between Lostock Hall and Farington Curve Junction (see Fig 2 in Chapter 3). Further changes, started in 1985, include the demolition of the long-disused LYR entrance to make way for a large shop and office development on the old Butler Street goods yard site that will include a new entrance and approach, provided money is available.

In the second rank of stations, Coventry, Wolverhampton and Stafford were completely rebuilt. Of the three Coventry, completed in 1962, is by far the most imaginative with a large, airy concourse surrounded by glass, after the fashion of the 'sixties, but impressive for all that.

Like Coventry, the new station at Plymouth, completed by BR in 1962, twenty-two years after the Great Western started it, was built to blend with the reconstruction of the war-damaged city centre. With seven through platforms it was a vast improvement on the old, its clerestorey-roofed concourse overlooked by a powerful ten-storey office block placed at right angles to the station. It is now the only station in Plymouth, Friary having closed in 1958.

After long drawn-out difficulties in gaining planning consent from the City of London Corporation, work on Cannon Street started in 1963 with the demolition of Southern House. Following the New Street example, the work was done in conjunction with property developers; British Railways had realised the value of city centre railway sites and it marked a new era in station building in which the old idea of a distinctive station frontage containing railway offices or an hotel gave way to modern lookalike office blocks in which revenue-earning potential became paramount. Consequently the exteriors of Cannon Street, Holborn Viaduct and Blackfriars need more than a second glance to realise that they actually contain an entrance to a railway station. At Cannon Street only the massive side walls and the pair of towers overlooking the river remain from the old station, gazing down on the skimpy 1960s asbestos canopies over the platforms. The final work on a new entrance, an attractive concourse and a new Underground station was not completed until 1974. Holborn Viaduct was treated similarly and completed in 1963, the old train shed behind the ten-storey frontage block being left in place until awnings replaced it in 1974. Here the entrance was given a touch of elegance by scoop-shaped arches. Blackfriars followed in 1979, where the street-level booking hall was replaced by one at rail level reached by escalators. The lines to Holborn viaduct emerge on to a new bridge literally through a hole in the wall of the front block. In the booking hall it was a pleasing touch to make a feature of the incised pilaster stones from the old frontage that spelt out the destinations that in 1886 the London Chatham & Dover hoped would be reached from its new St Pauls Station, including St Petersburg, Baden-Baden and Constantinople. The old four-span overall roof has also been retained, including the arcaded wooden screen extending out on to the river bridge.

Hull received the same treatment in 1960–2, when the old iron *porte-cochère* was replaced, although this time the offices, called Paragon House, were occupied by the railway itself until they became surplus to requirements and were let. Rationalisation, completed in 1985, has reduced the number of platforms to seven, and the two northernmost roof bays now cover a car park.

The last of the big rebuilding schemes of the 1960s was completed at Leeds where, on 17 May 1967, the Lord Mayor opened the new City station. BR did what the LMS and LNER should have done in 1932, that is to put New, Wellington and Central stations all under one roof, instead of merely joining the first two together and neglecting Central. Poor old Central. Born out of confusion and acrimony, small, dark and dingy, it finally passed into history sixteen days earlier, unsung and unloved. The new station stands on the brick-arched vaulting that supported New station, for which reason it was given an overall roof instead of the more usual individual platform awnings, the first to have been built since Birmingham Snow Hill fifty-three years before. Admittedly the roof is a far cry from the Victorian train sheds, owing its parentage to the quickly assembled lightweight industrial buildings of today. It comprises two steel Portal frames clad with patent coated steel sheeting, the larger having a single span of 150ft on a slight curve over the through platforms (page 209). The smaller span covers bay platforms set at an angle at the west end of the station to much the same plan as the old one, and daylight is admitted through translucent plastic roof lights. The rather low roof tends to trap diesel fumes from the trains. There are now five through platforms, including a new one outside the south wall, and five bays, although in general the previous track layout was not greatly altered. The platforms are connected by a footbridge, a luggage bridge and a structurally interesting subway built in a reinforced concrete frame running through the upper part of one of the cross-arches under the station. Awkward dog-leg barriers lead on to an attractive entrance hall called the North Concourse which is linked by a ticket hall to the 1938 South Concourse. Here the atmosphere changes completely; partly used for car parking it is a forlorn place, still retaining its 1930s decor and fittings and, as a listed structure, sadly waiting for someone to come up with a bright idea for a practical use. It would make an ideal crafts market on the lines of the Royal Exchange at Manchester. The new frontage is the best of the 1960s stations, the curved canopy offset by the slim twelve storeys of City House at right angles to it. A

Twentieth-century train shed: the Portal-framed roof over the rebuilt Leeds City station in 1974 (*G. W. Buck*)

five-storey block contains station offices, including a 'signal box' hidden on the top floor which took over the work of seventeen 'proper' boxes. The outer part of the former Wellington platforms retain their Midland awnings in use for parcels traffic, while the inner portion has been roofed over to form more parking space. At the same time as the station was rebuilt, the rail approaches from the west and north were completely remodelled and simplified, although from both ends they are still slow and at the west end are beset by a vast array of diamond crossings and slip points.

Two notable major schemes took place in the next decade. In the first, Bradford Exchange was replaced by a new four-platform terminus built a little further out as part of an entirely new concept: a purpose-built rail and bus interchange on the site of Bridge Street goods station. The platforms have reasonably generous awnings and the booking hall and travel centre are mostly of glass, giving something of a greenhouse effect. Compared with the old Exchange it seems insignificant alongside the large bus station, whose modern glazed ridge-and-furrow roof dominates the scene and in fact looks much more like a traditional railway station. Forster Square station still survives, despite only just escaping closure in 1968, although precariously dependent on grant-aid for its paytrains to Keighley and Ilkley, for which two platforms are more than ample; the other four and the concourse are screened off for parcels traffic and passengers now enter along a narrow passageway to a small hut ticket office. The frontage is hidden from the main

Modern perspectives: the curved glazed front of the new London Bridge station concourse reflects the angles of the forecourt canopy (*British Rail*)

square by shop and office development that makes even the Midland Hotel take a back seat.

The second was in 1979, when London commuters witnessed an event they thought would never happen: a new station was completed at London Bridge, a notable achievement on an awkward site where the difficulties were compounded by the need to stay open during the entire period of the work, as indeed applied elsewhere. Like Bradford, it is an interchange, and the frontage is strikingly formed by a large open-trussed covered forecourt for buses, with pyramidal lantern lights in the roof. One comes on it quite suddenly behind the tower block of New London Bridge House, and passes on to the light, uncluttered concourse where folding barrier doors conceal the platforms. The six high-level through platforms and the four old low-level terminal ones have attractive awnings with angled valancing, although it seems a pity that they stop well short of the stairs on both sides of the new footbridge, leaving a considerable gap that on a wet day is more than unwelcome. The arched roof over the former Brighton platforms, with its ridge-and-furrow side aisles, has been retained and refurbished together with the screen walls, where the cleaned brickwork reveals hitherto unseen original colours. There is now a total of sixteen platforms, and the entire station is clean, convenient, visually attractive and, above all, interesting; easily the best modern large-station rebuilding in Britain.

Another important development took place in Glasgow in 1979, when the low-level platforms at Central station were reopened in connection with the newly electrified Argyle line. It was the culmination of many years' work of electrification and rehabilitation of the Glasgow suburban network, in partnership with the local authority. Similar work had been done at Queen Street Low Level in 1960 when the lines north of the Clyde were electrified, and the refurbished platforms are a far cry from the smoky, dingy places of the past.

The concept of a concrete raft built over a station in order to capitalise on the site value, pioneered at Birmingham New Street and, though not so far developed, at Euston, is being pursued to its utmost at Victoria. The frontage and the Central Section (former Brighton) concourse are still as cluttered and chaotic as ever; the Southern Railway started tinkering with them before the war and it has continued ever since. Recently the old Brighton canopy has been attractively restored, complete with destinations, but the stainless steel Travel Centre beneath it and the blue Tourist Information Office on the front of the Grosvenor jar horribly, while inside a jumble of structures, advertisements and official signs continue to make life difficult at this very busy station, exemplified by the need to place a triangular erection on the concourse labelled 'Meeting Point'; the modern equivalent of 'under the station clock'. Some choice pieces of Edwardian finish have been uncovered and cleaned during the numerous alterations in the past twenty years, including a pair of LBSCR tiled wall maps which have been preserved under glass, although the green plastic telephone booths between them tend to clash. Despite enlargement of the Central Section concourse by shortening the platforms, too much extraneous matter obtrudes and there is no clear division between the rail part of the station and the air terminal part. By contrast the Eastern Section (former Chatham) concourse is still much quieter and less cluttered.

In 1962 British United Airways built a two-storey terminal on legs over the ends of the west-side platforms for a service to Gatwick Airport, and the old Imperial Airways terminal was taken over by British Overseas Airways and supplanted by an eight-storey block over the top. Now a raft has been built between the concourse and Eccleston Bridge, half way down the station, to support another glass-sided space-age office complex called Victoria Plaza. It glitters in unworldly fashion above the fine old wall in Buckingham Palace Road. Currently the raft is being extended over the outer end of the Eastern Section platforms, spoiling the vista under Hawkshaw's roof. Another raft is threatened between Eccleston Bridge and Elizabeth Bridge, when the new Brighton side will then fully resemble its progenitors. The tunnel effect that the raft gives to the platforms is only partly ameliorated by the colour scheme, ingenious though it is. A new terminal for the highly successful Gatwick Express dedicated trains is to occupy part of the existing raft, replacing the present temporary passenger reception lounge next to the reserved platforms. Perhaps when it is all finished the concourse can at last be tidied up and create among overseas visitors a more orderly impression of the first large British railway station they set foot in. Perhaps even the intention of the early 1970s to create an integrated rail, air, sea, hovercraft and Channel Tunnel terminal might one day take shape and give Victoria an ethos to replace the one it lost with the 'Brighton Belle', the 'Golden Arrow' and the 'Night Ferry', although it seems that Waterloo may be the tunnel terminus.

Two station development schemes in the City of London have recently received sanction. At the end of 1983 work started on the erection of a raft over the platforms at Fenchurch Street, designed to carry a rectangular pyramid of offices but retaining George Berkeley's listed frontage. From the confines of the narrow street it seems unlikely that one will see the receding storeys above it, and one must reserve judgement on the ultimate effect beyond hoping that it will be better than the similar attempt on the imitation oil refinery that forms the new Lloyds building nearby.

The Liverpool Street scheme has now at last started, after a prolonged interregnum that has ebbed and flowed since 1974, when a plan to demolish and rebuild aroused passionate opposition that resulted in a ministerial requirement to preserve the original western train shed. It was all bound up with the problem of what to do with Broad Street, which by that time was bereft of most of its roof and its traffic. The latest scheme is to retain both train sheds, and extend the western one with replica bays at the Liverpool Street end so that the buffer stops can be aligned and the concourse at last straightened out. This will retain the hotel but mean demolition of most of the frontage block, which in its mutilated state following war damage will not be a tragic loss, while Broad Street has already been demolished and replaced by a short temporary platform reached from the narrow Sun Street Passage, to be used until a new connection is made to bring the remnants of the service into Liverpool Street. Redevelopment of the site is under way at a cost of around £250 millions which, when completed, it is hoped will pay for the station works. If there had to be a choice between Broad Street and Liverpool Street train sheds, the former was the less important, while on railway operating grounds the decision was obvious. If they materialise as shown on the drawings, the pair of towers proposed for the new frontage will not only ably complement the train sheds and hotel but should create an elegant City landmark. Meanwhile the train sheds are undergoing attractive restoration.

The slackening of the office boom has resulted in two parallel developments from the mid-1970s into the present decade, combining wherever practicable a policy of modernisation with one of retention of existing features. Refurbished and remodelled stations are now too numerous to detail individually, beyond particularly meritorious schemes like the Travel Centre that replaced the ramshackle buildings that disgraced the front of King's Cross for so long; imaginative roof recladding and painting at King's Cross, St Pancras and York, using new materials and attractive colour schemes; clean, modernised concourses at Glasgow Queen Street and Central, and at Waterloo; refitted or restored booking halls at Edinburgh Waverley, Aberdeen, Hull and Cardiff; the delightfully restored tea-room at York. These and others like them have brought to the public eye a new appreciation of the station as an attractive prelude to modern rail travel.

Concurrently a new environmentally conscious British Rail has set about cleaning and restoring the fabric of many of its stations, generally in partnership with local authorities or private concerns. Carlisle and Sheffield were among the first in the 1960s, under the government-inspired 'Operation Springclean', and then nothing much happened until Manchester Victoria's façade was transformed in the 1970s, in conjunction with the local authority, which set a precedent for some remarkably pleasing achievements elsewhere. They included Victoria, Newcastle, Nottingham Midland, Leicester and Shrewsbury, where newly cleaned frontages have revealed detail long concealed by soot, and the stations have regained the right to be considered visual assets to the communities they serve. Many in any case are listed by the Department of the Environment as being of Special Architectural or Historic Interest, which brings its own problems, particularly with structures that are no longer required for railway use. Again some kind of partnership agreement has provided answers in certain instances of historically important buildings. The mouldering but largely intact Liverpool Road station at Manchester, 'Oldest in the World', is now the home of the Greater Manchester Museum of Science and Industry where local authorities, university and British Rail have collaborated to restore the buildings.

Likewise Brunel's train shed at Bristol Temple Meads is currently undergoing restoration by the Brunel Engineering Centre Trust with the active support of BR, the Historic Buildings Commission, the city and private sector supporters. Labour comes from the Manpower Services Commission, and the aim is to create in five years' time an exhibition centre and public hall that will give new life to Brunel's unique building in a practical manner. Another historic station, Birmingham Curzon Street, underwent a period of neglect during and after its long period of use as goods offices, but was saved from demolition by local and national conservation organisations and the city council which eventually took it over and, in 1982, gained Civic Trust and Europa Nostra awards for restoration. It is now leased as offices and craft workshops mainly concerned with setting up young unemployed people in business schemes.

One of the first fruits of local partnership was at Sheffield, where cleaning and renovation revealed Trubshaw's detail over the cab rank at the Midland station in 1966 (*Author*)

At Chester, commercial interests combined with BR to restore the West Wing and the virtually derelict Mold Wing adjacent, and it is to be hoped that work on the rest of this fine building will soon follow. Another development has been the establishment in 1985 of the independent Railway Heritage Trust, with initial funding from British Rail. The objects are twofold: to finance the restoration of listed structures still in operational railway use or, alternatively, seek external financing; and in respect of structures no longer needed by the railway, to act as a catalyst between BR and external parties. Several schemes have already started, including assistance for Bristol Temple Meads and the cleaning and restoration of the towers at Cannon Street.

British Rail went through a demolition phase that thankfully is now past, but which produced a number of battles with conservationists. A scheme to demolish Brighton station in 1973–4 caused local uproar to such an extent that it was dropped. Instead BR repaired and repainted the train shed. In 1970 there was a move by Newcastle-upon-Tyne Corporation to have all but the portico at Newcastle Central demolished in favour of a modern structure, which fortunately proved to be nothing more than a paper proposal. The great arched train hall at Manchester Central was for long a centre of controversy while it slowly rotted, but is now being superbly restored as a £14 million exhibition and leisure centre by a consortium of the local authority and a commercial organisation. One of the greatest battles since the Euston Arch raged over the future of St Pancras, and it was perhaps because of Euston that it was won. As far back as the 1930s, when the LMS converted the hotel to offices, there were suggestions that it was only fit for demolition, and then, after spending a good deal on repairing war damage, BR in 1966–7 proposed to close it and divert trains into King's Cross, but quickly retreated. In 1977 a start was made on cleaning the exterior, but when government money dried up it stopped a third of the way through, leaving a very prominent tidemark. However, the interior was thoroughly cleaned in 1980–3, bringing back the sparkle of Scott's decorative brickwork at the same time as the overhead wires for electrification were installed. Unlike King's Cross, where ugly gantries obstruct the view down the train shed, the St Pancras catenaries have been unobtrusively hung direct from the roof so that one is hardly aware that they are there. Contrarily, BR simultaneously produced a scheme to rebuild the booking hall in airline fashion, which was refused listed building consent after more campaigning by the conservation movement. Instead, British Rail then did what it should have proposed in the first place and restored the booking hall, including a tastefully matching ceiling. In 1983 it almost seemed that the interior of the Midland Grand was also secure for the future when it was leased for sympathetic conversion to commercial offices, only to be revoked when the company concerned was subjected to a successful takeover bid and the new parent saw things differently. It now seems that Scott's building may even become an hotel again, if current negotiations for restoration to the original designs continue to look encouraging. A genuine Victorian hotel with all modern conveniences sounds an expensive proposition, but could be an enormous attraction in the transatlantic tourist market.

The fight for conservation was lost at Derby, where in 1984 work started on demolishing the frontage block. Apart from the *porte-cochère* and the immediate façade it was in truth a hotchpotch that was far too wasteful of space and caused traffic problems for users arriving by car or taxi. A proposal to re-erect the *porte-cochère* at the Tramway Museum at Crich, which already has the old Derby Assembly Rooms, failed on practical grounds when the brickwork crumbled. The post-war concrete platform structures are to be reconditioned, one hopes with better results than originally.

Not all the newer work is aesthetically pleasing. The entrance building at Perth, built on the site of the 'Dundee Corridor' in 1970, has walls of pre-cast concrete panels with stone finish and plentiful glass that do anything but blend with Tite's sandstone Gothic, although the interior is clean and bright. Then one passes through a poky barrier into a narrow passageway connecting the footbridges on each side of the station. Further north, at about the same time, the colonnaded front of Inverness was replaced by an unsympathetic brick screen wall that did nothing to enhance Station Square, but allowed badly needed enlargement of the concourse. The use of brightly coloured modern finishes can also produce a discordant effect in the wrong place. The red adopted by Travellers' Fare for its buffet signing is easily identifiable but sometimes jars, as at Carlisle, while the extensive use of red external plastic surfaces for kiosks, ticket collectors' booths and circular moulded seats sometimes does rather more than add a splash of colour. On the other hand, Edinburgh demonstrates the aesthetic improvement that can be gained from the open platform policy where, in conjunction with cleaned stone, fresh paint and terrazzo flooring, removal of the barriers had created a splendid new atmosphere of spaciousness.

Unfortunately this has not happened at Liverpool Lime Street, where we have an example of the difficulties faced by designers in reconciling what is often irreconcilable. Formerly, a narrow concourse stretched in a bent line across the head of the station behind irregularly aligned buffer-stops, with a central entrance and two more in Nelson Street and Skelhorne Street on either side. The Nelson Street entrance has been sealed off and the one alongside Skelhorne Street, which was open between the roof columns, has been enclosed with glass panels as a welcome means of keeping out the wind. In the centre, superbly elegant new entrance stairs alongside the cleaned-up former hotel – now being converted to shops, offices, and flats — are enormously successful in blending with their impressive surroundings in both scale and detail. Yet the interior, by comparison, is almost anti-climactic. By pushing the buffer-stops forward, space has been made for a deeper concourse in the northern half of the station, but the other half has been made much narrower by erecting an etched glass screen bearing abstract designs that creates a passageway effect. The new concourse tends to be out of scale with the sweeping spaciousness of the curved roof, and the vista that gave Lime Street its character has been shut off by a Travel Centre and a garish 'Casey Jones' cafeteria, inducing a restless, almost claustro-phobic atmosphere which is exacerbated by the tall iron railings that turn the parcels area into a prison.

There are obvious reasons for this treatment: it has enabled the number of barriers to be reduced to two; a small, enclosed concourse is easier to keep warm than a large one open to the platforms; and these days the parcels department unfortunately requires a high level of security, although one would have thought it possible to devise something more elegant. Yet one of the great visual assets of the older type of station, that of being able to see the trains, has been lost, as has also happened at Euston, Waterloo, London Bridge and other modernised stations with solid barriers, and, in 1985, disastrously at Paddington where one passes through tunnel-like barriers between blocks of shops, completely obscuring the view along Brunel's train shed. The scheme has rightly been criticised in high places.

Developing the revenue-earning potential of station trading, providing for frequent changes in catering policy, and meeting requirements for reduced manning are but three of the widely differing demands made on the architect, while further problems arise when it is decreed that waiting rooms shall be dispensed with in favour of either limited seating in a combined waiting room and buffet, or seats on the concourse and therefore has to be as draught-proof as possible. The use of toughened glass is an imaginative step; yet if glass were also used to screen the heads of the platforms what wonderful open stations could be made at Lime Street, Paddington and others with dramatic roofs.

Looking again at contrasts, the modernised concourse at Swansea, admittedly a much smaller station, has the opposite effect, thanks to a restful colour scheme and tasteful fittings; at Crewe, too, a respect for its matureness has resulted in a most successful refurbishment. On a much vaster scale the same can be said of Waterloo, which is everything a station concourse should be – although the cut off columns in the Trips Restaurant earn a different appellation – while the recently completed work at Cardiff and York shows how an impression of space can be created.

The idea of trading on stations is now taking root more widely. In 1985 a small shopping mall was opened in Edinburgh Waverley, an admirable concept in these financially straitened times provided it is done with discrimination. Unfortunately neither the red plastic finish nor the type of some of the shops adds to the dignity of the station. At the time of writing it has been announced that 'High Street style' shopping plazas are to be introduced on some large stations, the first to be around the concourse at Paddington. Others are planned for Glasgow Central and Newcastle, designed, it is said, to complement the architecture of the stations and give an improved service and environment. One hopes the mistakes at Birmingham New Street will not be repeated and that the first priority will be to provide passenger information.

Commercial development alongside a station instead of inside it perhaps carries less environmental risk. For some time this has been going on at a number of smaller stations where old goods yards have been turned over to supermarkets or office blocks combined with a new or modernised station. It is now taking place on a larger scale at Preston and a scheme has recently been announced for Reading where the listed frontage building is to be retained, linked to a new concourse in an office complex to be built alongside.

Privatisation has so far affected the railways mainly in connection with its hotels some of which were sold in the 1950s and '60s; now the rest have gone, some renamed and doubtless all to be refurbished, although one hopes, that not too much of their rich atmosphere of solid comfort will disappear.

Appendix I

CHRONOLOGY
of principal events at selected stations

Ownership of stations is given as at date of opening, with final ownership at 1923 Grouping shown in brackets. Rebuilding dates indicate the completion or official reopening dates except where otherwise amplified. Closure dates are official dates ('as and from') unless qualified otherwise.

Abbreviations

addnl	additional	R	Railway
cl	closed; closed by	reb	rebuilt or major reconstruction; rebuilt by
c	circa		
E	east; eastern; east side (end)	reop	reopened
ext	extended	repl	replaced; replaced by
incl	including	S	south; southern; south side (end)
jc	junction	stn	station
op	opened; opened by	temp	temporary
N	north; northern; north side (end)	W	west; western; west side (end)
plat	platform		

Railway Company Abbreviations

Cal R	Caledonian Railway
CLC	Cheshire Lines Committee (GCR, MR, GNR)
GCR	Great Central Railway
GER	Great Eastern Railway
GNR	Great Northern Railway
GNSR	Great North of Scotland Railway
GSWR	Glasgow & South Western Railway
GWR	Great Western Railway
HR	Highland Railway
LBSCR	London Brighton & South Coast Railway
LCDR	London Chatham & Dover Railway
LMS	London Midland & Scottish Railway
LNER	London & North Eastern Railway
LNWR	London & North Western Railway
LSWR	London & South Western Railway
LYR	Lancashire & Yorkshire Railway
MR	Midland Railway
MSJAR	Manchester South Junction & Altrincham Railway
MSLR	Manchester Sheffield & Lincolnshire Railway
NBR	North British Railway
NER	North Eastern Railway
SECR	South Eastern & Chatham Railway
SER	South Eastern Railway
SR	Southern Railway

Aberdeen Joint stn op Cal R & GNSR 4 Nov 1867. Addnl plat 1883. Outside plat 1907. Reb Oct 1914. Completed 1920. Concourse modernised 1985.

Birmingham New Street Op LNWR 1 June 1854. Footbridge reb 1874. MR side op 8 Feb 1885. E approaches remodelled 1896. Joint Committee LNWR & MR 1897. LNWR side roof strengthened 1906; removed 1948–52. Completely reb 1967. *Queens Hotel* op 1 June 1854. Cl & demolished 1964.

Birmingham Snow Hill Op GWR 1 Oct 1852. Reb 1871. Reb 1912. Cl 6 Mar 1972. Demolished. *Great Western Hotel* op 1863. Reb 1870. Converted stn offices 1906. Cl 1972. Demolished.

Bradford Exchange Op LYR 9 May 1850. Ext & used by GNR 1 Jan 1867. Reb May 1888; complete Dec 1888. Cl 15 Jan 1973. Demolished. New stn op 15 Jan 1973. *Victoria Hotel* op 1867, purchased GNR 1893 & renamed Great Northern (Victoria). Now Victoria Hotel.

Bradford Forster Square Op Leeds & Bradford R (MR) as Market St 1 July 1846. Reb 2 Mar 1890. Renamed Forster Sq 2 June 1924. *Midland Hotel* op 1885.

Brighton Op London & Brighton R (LBSCR) 11 Apr 1840. Completed 1841. Forecourt ext over Trafalgar St 1844. Plats ext 1854. Train shed reb 1882–3. *Porte-cochère* 1882–3.

Bristol Temple Meads GWR stn (Brunel) op 31 Aug 1840. Bristol & Exeter R stn op July 1845. 'Express curve' plat op 1845. Bristol Joint Station Act 19 June 1865 (effectively GWR & MR). Extension to Brunel shed, addnl plat and train shed on curve, new frontage, all complete 1 Jan 1878. 2 addnl plats on curve 1892. Outside plats & remodelling complete Dec 1935. Brunel shed cl 6 Sep 1966; leased to Brunel Engineering Centre Trust for restoration 29 Sep 1981.

Cardiff Central Op South Wales R (GWR) 18 June 1850. Reb between 1866–80. Riverside stn op 14 Aug 1893. General stn ext 1894–6. Reb incorporating Riverside 1932. Renamed Central 7 May 1973. Concourse remodelled 1985.

Carlisle Citadel Joint stn op Lancaster & Carlisle R (LNWR) & Cal R Sep 1847. New island plat and roof 4 July 1880. Roof cut back 1958.

Chester Joint General stn op Chester & Holyhead R (LNWR), Shrewsbury & Chester R (GWR), LNWR, Birkenhead R (LNWR & GWR) 1 Aug 1848. Ext S 1890.

Crewe Op Grand Junction R (LNWR) 4 July 1837. Manchester & Birmingham R stn op 10 Aug 1842. Ext S 1847. Reb 1867. Ext W 1896–1906. W plats cl 2 June 1985. *Crewe Arms Hotel* op 1837. Purchased LNWR 1864.

Derby Joint stn op Midland Counties, North Midland & Birmingham & Derby Jc Rs (all MR) c May 1840 (op of NMR). Completed 1841. 2nd floor added over entrance c 1850. N wing 1856. New entrance on front of original op 1860s. S wing reb & Shareholders' Room added 1862. *Porte-cochère* & boardroom block 1872. New front added to 1860s entrance, & *porte-cochère* moved outwards 1892. Committee Rooms block c 1900. Train shed replaced by awnings 1952–4. Reb frontage commenced 1984. *Midland Hotel* op 1841.

Edinburgh Princes Street Op Cal R as Lothian Rd 15 Feb 1848. Cl & Princes St op 2 May 1870. Reb 1893–4. Cl 6 Sep 1965. Demolished. *Caledonian Hotel* op 21 Dec 1903.

Edinburgh Waverley Op NBR 18 June 1846. Edinburgh & Glasgow R stn op 1 Aug 1846. Edinburgh Leith & Granton R Canal St stn op 17 May 1847; cl 2 Mar 1868. Waverley ext with new roof 1869–74. Reb 1892–1900. Suburban (outside) plat op 17 Apr 1898. Booking hall remodelled; new travel centre 1970. *North British Hotel* op 15 Oct 1902.

Glasgow Buchanan Street Op Cal R 1 Nov 1849. Ext July 1862 & 1865–9. Reb LMS 1932.

Glasgow Central Op Cal R 1 Aug 1879. Booking hall & concourse completed 1882. Low Level stn op 10 Aug 1896. Addnl plat 1889. Ext 1901–6. Low Level cl 5 Oct 1964; reop 5 Nov 1979. Concourse remodelled 1985. *Central Stn Hotel* op 19 June 1885.

Glasgow Queen Street Op Edinburgh & Glasgow R (NBR) 21 Feb 1842. Ext, incl arched roof 1878–80. Low Level stn op 15 Mar 1886. Concourse, etc, remodelled 1969–73. *North British Hotel* op (as Queens Hotel) c 1780. Purchased by NBR 1880. Renamed Diplomat Hotel 1984.

Glasgow St Enoch Op GSWR & NBR 1 May 1876. Vested solely in GSWR 29 June 1883. Ext (2nd roof span) 1904. Cl 27 June 1966. Demolished. *St Enoch Hotel* op 3 July 1879. Cl 1974. Demolished.

Hull Paragon Op York & North Midland R (NER) 8 May 1848. Ext N by 1887. Reb 12 Dec 1904. New frontage offices 1962. Plats reduced N side 1984. *Royal Station Hotel* op 1851. Ext 1903–5 and 1933–5.

Leeds Central Temporary stn op LNWR 18 Sep 1848 (used also by LYR). Permanent joint stn op GNR, LNWR, Leeds & Thirsk R (NER) & LYR Aug 1857. Ext 1904. Cl 1 May 1967. Demolished. *Great Northern Hotel* Wellington Hotel acquired by GNR 1866, reb as Great Northern 1868, upper floors reb after fire 1906. Now Wellesley Hotel.

Leeds City Wellington & New stns combined by LMS & LNER 2 May 1938. Reb 13 May 1967 – former Wellington plats cl to passengers. *Queens Hotel* op MR 1863. Ext 1867 & 1898. Reb LMS 12 Nov 1937.

Leeds New Joint stn op NER & LNWR 1 Apr 1869. Ext 1878–9 (officially 5 Jan 1879). Combined Wellington as Leeds City (see above).

Leeds Wellington Op Leeds & Bradford R (MR) 1 July 1846. Ext 4 plats by 1882 & 7 plats by 1903. Combined New as Leeds city (see above).

Leicester London Road Op Midland Counties R (MR) 30 June 1840 (Campbell St). 2nd plat and new roof c 1857–8. 3rd (outside) plat 1868. Reb as London Rd 12 June 1892. Completed 1895. Plat buildings reb 1978–86.

Liverpool Central Op CLC 1 Mar 1874. Cl 17 Apr 1972. Demolished. (Note – Low Level station still open as part of Merseyrail.) *Adelphi Hotel* op 1840. Reb 1861. Purchased MR 1890. Reb 1914.

Liverpool Exchange Op LYR & East Lancashire R (LYR) as Tithebarn St (ELR) and Exchange (LYR) 13 Mar 1850. Reb LYR as Exchange 12 Dec 1886. Completed 2 July 1888. Cl 30 Apr 1977. Demolished. *Exchange Hotel* op 13 Aug 1888. Cl 3 July 1971. Façade incorporated in new office block completed 1986.

Liverpool Lime Street Op Liverpool & Manchester R (LNWR) 15 Aug 1836. Reb 1849. Reb 1865–7 (N roof span). Ext 1874–80 (S roof span). Tunnel opened out & widened 1881–5. Concourse remodelled 1955 & 1985. *North Western Hotel* op 1 Mar 1871. Cl & converted to offices 1933. Refurbished offices, shops & flats 1986.

LONDON
Broad Street Op North London R (LNWR) 1 Nov 1865. Platform level booking office and forecourt footbridges op 4 Sep 1890. Frontage screen added 1913. Roof cut back 1967–8. Demolished and temp plat op 1985.

Cannon Street Op SER (SECR) 1 Sep 1866. Layout remodelled 5-28 June 1926. Roof bombed 10-11 May 1941 & awnings erected. Roof demolished 1958–9. Completely reb 1965. New forecourt 1973. *City Terminus Hotel* op May 1867. Cl & converted to offices 1931. Demolished 1963.

Charing Cross Op SER (SECR) 11 Jan 1864. Roof collapsed 5 Dec 1905. Roof reb 1907. *Charing Cross Hotel* op 15 May 1865. Ext 1878. Bombed 16-17 Apr 1941. New top 2 floors completed 1951. *Queen Eleanor's Cross* completed 1865.

Euston op London & Birmingham R (LNWR) 20 July 1837. Doric Arch completed May 1838. Ext W 1846. Drummond St offices op 1846. Great Hall op 27 May 1849. Approach drive & lodges op 1870. Ext E 1873. New offices E & W of Arch & Drummond St 1881–7. Ext W 1 July 1892. New booking hall 1913–16. Completely reb 1961–9. Front office blocks completed 1979. *Hotel* Euston & Victoria hotels op Sep 1839. Linked & renamed Euston Hotel 1881. Cl May 1963. Demolished.

Fenchurch Street Op London & Blackwall R (GER) 2 Aug 1841. Reb Apr 1854. Layout and concourse remodelled 29 Apr 1935. Currently office block being built over stn replacing roof, commenced 1983.

King's Cross Temp stn Maiden Lane op GNR 7 Aug 1850; cl 14 Oct 1852. Present stn op 14 Oct 1852. Metropolitan R connection op 1 Oct 1863; York Rd plat op 1 Jan 1866. E roof ribs repl 1869–70; W ribs repl 1886–7. 'Main Line (Local)' stn (W) op 18 Dec 1874. 'Suburban' stn (down Met line) op 1 Feb 1878; ext July–Aug 1880; reb 7 Apr 1895. 'Local' stn ext 15 Dec 1924. New concourse & travel centre op 3 June 1973. 'Suburban' and York Rd cl 4 Mar 1977. *Great Northern Hotel* op 17 May 1854.

Liverpool Street Op GER 2 Feb 1874 (W shed). Metropolitan R connection op 1 Feb 1875; cl 1904; removed 1907. E shed op 2 Apr 1894. Redevelopment commenced May 1985. *Great Eastern Hotel* op May 1884. Ext 1901.

London Bridge London & Greenwich R (SER) stn op 14 Dec 1836. London & Croydon R (LBSCR) stn op 5 June 1839. Joint stn op July 1844; divided 1 Aug 1850 & demolished. New SER & LBSCR stns op 3 Jan 1851. LBSCR stn demolished & reb 1853; ext 1866. Original London & Greenwich plats demolished & new high-level (through) plats op 11 Jan 1864. Station unified by SR 1928. Large-scale reb 1979. *Terminus Hotel* op 1861. Purchased LBSCR for offices 1893. Demolished 1941.

Marylebone Op GCR 15 Mar 1899. *Hotel Great Central* op 1 July 1899. Purchased LNER for offices 1946.

Paddington Temp stn (Bishop's Rd) op GWR 4 June 1838; cl 29 May 1854. Bridge Stn op 16 Jan 1854. Bishop's Rd plats (for Metropolitan) op 10 Jan 1863. Outside plat added June 1878. Offices ext 1881. Addnl departure plat under main roof 1885; addnl arrival plat 1893. Further plats under 4th roof span completed 1916. Plats extended, new concourse & new E side offices 1930–4. Reb Bishop's Rd plats incorporated in main stn 11 Sep 1933. *Great Western Royal Hotel* op 8 June 1854. Remodelled 1936–8.

St Pancras Op MR 1 Oct 1868. Additional plat 1892. *Midland Grand Hotel* op 5 May 1873. Cl & converted to offices 1935.

Victoria LBSCR stn op 1 Oct 1860. LCDR (SECR) stn op 25 Aug 1862. LBSCR stn reb 10 June 1906; completed 1 July 1908. SECR new frontage block 1908. Stns unified 1924. E plats extended 1960. British United Airways Terminal op 1 May 1962. British Overseas Airways Terminal op over W side 1963. W concourse enlarged 1979. Gatwick Rail-Air Reception Centre op Sep 1980. Victoria Plaza built over W side replacing part roof 1981–4; currently expanding over E side beyond roof. *Grosvenor Hotel* Op 1861. Purchased LBSCR 1899; leased to Gordon Hotels & reop 10 Dec 1900. Ext 1907.

Waterloo Op LSWR 11 July 1848. 'North' stn op 3 Aug 1860. Necropolis stn op Oct 1854. Connection to SER op 11 Jan 1864. Waterloo Jc ('East') stn (SER) op 1 Jan 1869. 'South' stn op 16 Dec 1878. Addnl 'North' plats Nov 1885. Waterloo & City stn op 8 Aug 1898. New Necropolis stn op 16 Feb 1902. SER connection disused 26 Mar 1911. Complete reb 1900–22; official completion 21 Mar 1922. Necropolis stn bombed 16 Apr 1941 & not reb. Concourse, etc, remodelled 1978–83.

Manchester Central Temp stn op CLC 9 July 1877. Present stn op 1 July 1880. Outside plat added 1905. Cl 5 May 1969. Currently being converted to exhibition centre. *Midland Hotel* op 5 Sep 1903.

Manchester Exchange Op LNWR 30 June 1884. Plat connected to Victoria, and unified management 1929. Cl 5 May 1969. Roof demolished 1981. Through lines still in use.

Manchester Piccadilly Temp Travis St stn op Manchester & Birmingham R (LNWR) 4 July 1840. London Rd stn op jointly with Sheffield Ashton & Manchester R (MSLR-GCR) 8 May 1842. MSJAR plats op 1 Aug 1849. Reb 1866. Ext 16 May 1881. Addnl MSLR plat 15 Mar 1882. Mayfield stn op 8 Aug 1910. London Rd remodelled & renamed Piccadilly 12 Sep 1960; completed 1965. Mayfield cl 26 Aug 1960 (now parcels).

Manchester Victoria Op Manchester & Leeds R (LYR) 1 Jan 1844. LYR Head Office Hunts Bank op 1849–51; ext 1876 & 1884. Suburban stn ('Ducie Bridge') op 1855. New roof 1864. Addnl plats N Aug 1865. Five terminal plats SE op 4 Nov 1877. New through plats NW completed 1 May 1884. Terminal plats ext & 5 more added 1 Feb 1904. New frontage block Feb 1909. Hunts Bank offices demolished 1979. Three SE terminal plats filled in 1984. Concourse remodelled 1985.

Newcastle Central Op jointly by York Newcastle & Berwick R and Newcastle & Carlisle R (both NER) 29 Aug 1850. Completed 1 Jan 1851. Entrance block completed 1863. New island plat 1871. Enlarged incl 2 addnl roof spans 1893–5. W bays filled in for car park 1984. *Royal Station Hotel* op 1854. Ext 3 Oct 1892.

Perth Temp stn op Scottish Central R 22 May 1848. General stn op jointly Scottish Central R (Cal R), Scottish Midland Jc R (Cal R), Perth & Dunkeld R (HR) and Edinburgh & Northern R (NBR) c Aug 1848. 'Dundee Dock' op 1862. Ext incl new roof to part 1885–7. Original roof replaced by awnings 1911. 1885 roof cut back & N bays filled in 1969. *Royal Station Hotel* op 1865. Reb 1890.

Plymouth Friary Op LSWR 1 July 1891. Cl 15 Sep 1958.

Plymouth Millbay Op South Devon R (GWR) 4 Apr 1849. Ext 1859. Reb 1900. Cl 23 Apr 1941.

Plymouth North Road Op GWR & LSWR jointly 28 Mar 1877. Ext 1908. Reb 26 Mar 1962.

Preston North Union R (LNWR & LYR Joint) stn op 13 Oct 1838. Preston & Wyre R (LNWR & LYR Joint) Maudlands stn op 16 July 1840. Bolton & Preston R (LYR) Maxwell House stn op 1 Jan 1842. Maudlands & Maxwell House cl shortly after 1844. East Lancashire R (LYR) plats op 2 Sep 1850. Main stn reb Sep 1879. Ext E with addnl LYR bays & new LYR entrance July 1880. Ext W 1903. Outside LYR plat E, & new LYR entrance op c 1913. 1903 extension devoted to parcels traffic and LYR plats demolished 1971–3. LYR entrance demolished 1985. *Park Hotel* op LNWR & LYR 1882. Sold to Lancashire County Council for offices 6 Sep 1950.

Rugby Op London & Birmingham R (LNWR) 9 Apr 1838. Reb London & Birmingham R & Midland Counties R (MR) 1 July 1840. Ext 1849–52. Reb July 1885 – June 1886.

Sheffield Midland Op MR 1 Feb 1870. Ext 1904. Overall roof replaced by awnings 1956–7.

Sheffield Victoria Op Sheffield & Lincolnshire Junction R (MSLR–GCR) 15 Sep 1851. New roof 1867. Ext Feb 1874. New frontage 1908. Cl 5 Jan 1970. Demolished. *Royal Victoria Hotel* op 23 Sep 1862.

York Temp stn op York & North Midland R (NER) 30 May 1839. Permanent stn op YNMR & Great North of England R (NER) jointly 4 Jan 1841. Cl and present stn op 25 June 1877. Outside plat 1900. Further island plat outside 1936. *Station Hotel* (old stn) op 22 Feb 1853. New *Royal Station Hotel* op 20 May 1878 and old hotel converted offices. Renamed *Royal York Hotel* 1984.

Appendix 2

TYPES OF STATION ROOFS

The following selection is divided into sections according to type, and then arranged in date order. In some instances sources vary in quoted dimensions, in which cases those considered to be the most accurate have been selected. Certain variations can be accounted for by the width of the ribs and wherever possible widths of spans are given as the maximum distance between the internal surfaces of the cladding. Where it has not been possible to refer to printed sources or drawings, dimensions have been obtained where available by scaling from 1/1056 or 1/500 Ordnance Survey Town Plans or other drawings, indicated by 'circa' (c). Dimensions are in ft and in. 'Max Single Width' means the maximum width without intermediate supports, unless otherwise noted.

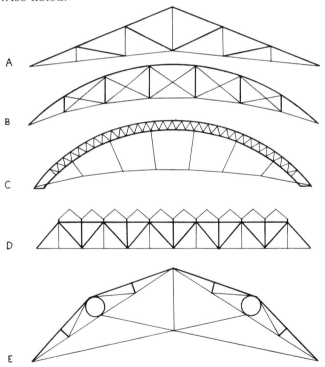

Fig 20. Some train shed roof trusses: A – the iron-trussed pitched roof at Euston, 1838, prototype of many that followed; B – crescent-trussed arch, Birmingham New Street, 1854; C – tied arch with latticed ribs, Glasgow Queen Street, 1878; D – Blyths longitudinal ridge-and-furrow roof, Glasgow Central I, 1882; E – mansard shaped roof with braced truss, Leeds New station, 1869

Year	Station	Railway	No of Spans	Max Single Width	Length	Engineer/Designer
1 Wooden & Wooden-Trussed Pitched Roofs						
1830	Liverpool Crown St	Liverpool & Manchester	1	c30	?	
1836	Liverpool Lime St I	Liverpool & Manchester	1	55	c185	Holme & Cunningham
post 1838	Preston I	North Union	2	43	c120	
1838	Nine Elms	London & Southampton	3	total 74	290	Wm Tite (?)
1839	London Bridge I	London & Croydon	1	56	212	J. Gibbs (?)
1840	Bath	GWR	1	60	c160	I. K. Brunel
1840	Bristol Temple Meads	GWR	1	74	220	I. K. Brunel
1841	Brighton I	London & Brighton	1 / 2	62 / 52	250	J. U. Rastrick
1845	Sheffield Bridgehouses	Sheffield, Ashton & Manchester	1	30	195	
1850 & 1879	Swansea High St.	South Wales	1 / 1	c55 / c60	c300	I. K. Brunel
1877	Plymouth North Road	GWR & LSWR	2 (separate)	46	c285	P. J. Margary (derived Brunel)
2 Iron-Trussed Pitched Roofs						
1837	Euston	London & Birmingham	2[1]	40	200	Charles Fox
1838	Birmingham Curzon Street	London & Birmingham	2	57	217	Charles Fox
1840	Derby Tri-junct	North Midland & others	1 / 2	56 / 42	1050	Francis Thompson (& Robt. Stephenson?)
1841	York I	York & N Mid and Gt N of England	2 (separate)	46	100	G. T. Andrews
1844	Bricklayers Arms (London)	London & Brighton and SER	3	52-6	465	Wm Cubitt
1844	Manchester Victoria I	Manchester & Leeds	1 / 1 / 1	28 / 59-6 / 26-3	700[2]	
1847	Huddersfield I	LNWR & LYR	1	c44	c514	J. P. Pritchett (?)/ A. Jee (?)
1848	Chester General	Chester & Holyhead and others	1 / 1 / 2	60 / 52 / 24	c1160	F. Thompson/ Wylde (?) (& Robt. Stephenson?)
1848	Stoke-on-Trent I & II	North Staffs	2 / 1	c30 / c25	c500	H. A. Hunt (?)
1848	Perth General I	Caledonian & others	2	55	720	Wm Tite/W. Paterson
1848	Nottingham II	MR	1 / 1 / 1	c33 / c30 / c37	c595	
1850	Liverpool Tithebarn St (Exchange I)	LYR & East Lancs	1 / 1	78 / 136	161 / 638	J. Hawkshaw

226

Year	Station	Railway	No of Spans	Max Single Width	Length	Engineer/Designer
1862	Stafford II	LNWR	2 (separate)	c33	c535	
1864	Exeter St Davids II	Bristol & Exeter	1	132	360	Francis Fox
1865	Broad Street	North London	2	95	460	Wm Baker
1867	Sheffield Victoria II	MSLR	1	84	c400	
1867	Crewe II	LNWR	1 / 1 (separate)	c70 / c80	820	Wm Baker
1874	Holborn Viaduct	LCDR	3	50-6	c325	W. Mills
1877	Manchester Victoria II – terminal platforms	LYR	1[3]	130	475	W. Hunt
1879 & later	Preston III	LNWR & LYR	1 / 1 / 1 / 1	77 / 51 / 33 / 66	992	
1886	Huddersfield II	LNWR & LYR	1	77-6	c590	
1899	Marylebone	GCR	1 / 2	40 / 50	495	Sir D. & F. Fox
1900	Nottingham Victoria	GCR & GNR	1 / 2	84-3 / 63	450	E. Parry
1907	Victoria II	LBSCR	5	50	680 & 550[4]	C. L. Morgan

3 Trussed Arch Roofs

Year	Station	Railway	No of Spans	Max Single Width	Length	Engineer/Designer
1849	Liverpool Lime St II	LNWR	1	153-6	374	R. Turner
1851	Sheffield Victoria I	MSLR	1	83	400	J. Fowler
1854	Fenchurch Street	London & Blackwall	1	105	300	G. Berkeley
1854	Birmingham New Street[5] (LNWR side)	LNWR	1	211	840	A. E. Cowper
1864	Blackfriars Bridge	LCDR	1	87-3	401-6	W. H. Thomas
1864	Charing Cross I	SER	1	164	510	J. Hawkshaw
1866	Manchester London Rd II	LNWR & MSLR	2[6]	c95	c680	W. Baker/ L. H. Moorsom
1866	Cannon Street	SER	1	190	685	J. Hawkshaw
1866	London Bridge III	LBSCR	1	88[7]	655	H. E. Wallis/ F. D. Banister
1867	Liverpool Lime Street III	LNWR	1[8]	212	645	W. Baker
1871	Birmingham Snow Hill II	GWR	1 / 1	92 / 58-3	506	T. Vernon
1878	Birkenhead Woodside	LNWR & GWR	1 / 1	98 / 91	375	R. E. Johnston
1884	Manchester Exchange	LNWR	1 / 1 / 1	62-5 / 59-5 / 71-8	c650	F. Stevenson (?)

Year	Station	Railway	No of Spans	Max Single Width	Length	Engineer/Designer
1885	Birmingham New Street (Midland side)	LNWR	1 1	58 67-6	c620 c600	F. Stevenson (?)

4 Tied Arch Roofs

Year	Station	Railway	No of Spans	Max Single Width	Length	Engineer/Designer
1862	Victoria	LCDR	1 1	127-4 129	455 385	J. Fowler
1867	Aberdeen Joint	Caledonian & GNSR	1	c110	c495	
1874	Liverpool Central	CLC	1	169	495	J. Fowler & W. M. Brydone
1878	Bristol Temple Meads	GWR & MR	1	125	500	Francis Fox
1880	Glasgow Queen Street	NBR	1	170	415	J. Carswell
1887	Darlington Bank Top	NER	3	60	1015	W. Bell
1888	Bradford Exchange	LYR	2	100	430	W. Hunt
1893	Stockton-on-Tees	NER	1 1	80 61-7	557	W. Bell
1904	Hull Paragon	NER	1 1 1 1 1	70 64-9 64-5 64-3 58-6	400	W. Bell

5 Clear Arch Roofs (no trusses or ties)

Year	Station	Railway	No of Spans	Max Single Width	Length	Engineer/Designer
1844[9]	Shoreditch	Eastern Counties	1 2	36 20-6	230	J. Braithwaite
1850	Newcastle Central	York Newcastle & Berwick and another	3[10]	60	708	J. Dobson (& Robt. Stephenson?)
1852	King's Cross	GNR	2[11]	105	800	L. Cubitt
1854	Paddington	GWR	1 1 1	69-6 102-6 68	700[12]	I. K. Brunel
1868	St Pancras	MR	1	243	689	W. Barlow/R. Ordish
1876	Glasgow St Enoch	GSWR	1[13]	198	524	J. Fowler & J. F. Blair
1877	York II	NER	1 2 2	81 55 43	795	T. Prosser
1877	Middlesbrough	NER	1 1	76 43-8	309 183	W. Cudworth/ W. Peachey
1880	Manchester Central	CLC	1	210	550	L. H. Moorsom

6 Tangentially Pitched Roofs on Arched Ribs

Year	Station	Railway	No of Spans	Max Single Width	Length	Engineer/Designer
1870	Sheffield Midland	MR	1 1 1	c62 c21 c40	c415	

Year	Station	Railway	No of Spans	Max Single Width	Length	Engineer/Designer
1870	Bath Green Park	MR	1	66	290	Wilson & Allport
			2	22		
			(one pitched roof over all)			
1879	Sunderland	NER	1	95	c465	W. Bell
1883	Brighton II	LBSCR	1	117	c650	H. E. Wallis
			1	98		
			1	46		

7 Mansard Roofs

Year	Station	Railway	No of Spans	Max Single Width	Length	Engineer/Designer
1855	Bradford Adolphus Street	GNR	1^{14}	104	c320 c460	John Fraser
1862	Dundee West I	Caledonian	1	c65	c310	
1869	Leeds New	NER & LNWR	1^{15}	92	c460	T. Prosser
			1	69		

8 Transverse Ridge-and-Furrow Roofs

Year	Station	Railway	No of Spans	Max Single Width	Length	Engineer/Designer
1860	Victoria I	LBSCR	1	124-7	800	R. Jacomb-Hood
			1	117-5		
1874	Edinburgh Waverley II	NBR	—	300^{16}	1100	James Bell
1880	Carlisle II	LNWR & Caledonian	1	128-3	c1020	Blyth & Cunningham
			1	154-6		
1887	Perth General II	Caledonian, HR & NBR	2^{17}	102	1233	Blyth & Cunningham
1889	Dundee West II	Caledonian	1	112	c700	Blyth & Cunningham
1893	Stoke-on-Trent III	North Staffordshire	1	85	485	
1894	Edinburgh Princes St	Caledonian	1	183-6	850	Cunningham, Blyth & Westland
1900	Edinburgh Waverley III	NBR	—	375^{18}	1240	Blyth & Westland
1903	Leith Central	NBR	1	220	830	Blyth & Westland
1904	Shrewsbury II	LNWR & GWR	1	150		R. E. Johnston
1907	Charing Cross II	SECR	—	164^{19}	510	
1906	Glasgow Central II	Caledonian	1	140-3	950	Blyth & Westland
			1	c208	240^{20}	
1912	Birmingham Snow Hill III	GWR	3	103^{21}	500	W. Armstrong
1922	Waterloo II	LSWR		520^{22}	540	J. W. Jacomb-Hood & A. W. Szlumper

9 Longitudinal Ridge-and-Furrow Roofs

Year	Station	Railway	No of Spans	Max Single Width	Length	Engineer/Designer
1858	Leicester Campbell Street	MR	1^{23}	68	600	
c1879	Glasgow Bridge St	Caledonian & GSWR	1	114	567	Blyth & Cunningham
			1^{24}	49		
1882	Glasgow Central I^{25}	Caledonian	1	213-6	c560	Blyth & Cunningham
1885	Bournemouth Central	LSWR	1	95	350	W. Jacomb
1890	Bradford Forster Square II	MR	2	87	550	
1895	Leicester London Road	MR	1	72	636	

Year	Station	Railway		No of Spans	Max Single Width	Length	Engineer/Designer
10 Composite Roofs							
1874	Liverpool Street – Western shed	GER	Pitched roofs	2	109	c715	E. Wilson
				1	5		
			Transept	1	90		
			Transverse ridge-and-furrow side spans	1	46-4		
				1	44-8		
1884	Manchester Victoria II – through platforms[26]	LYR Transverse ridge-and-furrow covered by longitudinal ridge-and-furrow		—	c85	c625	W. Hunt
1886	Rugby	LNWR	Central ridge-and-furrow.	2	110	1260	F. Stevenson (?)
			Two pitched sheds at each end	4	78		
1894	Liverpool Street – Eastern shed	GER	Pitched roofs	1	49-7		J. Wilson &
				2	42-3	c595	W. N. Ashbee
				1	51-7		
11 Steel Portal Frame Roof							
1967	Leeds	BR Eastern Region		1	150	490	
				1	70	210	

Notes to Appendix 2

1 Numerous extensions added up to 1892.
2 Replaced 1865 by single 87ft span pitched roof.
3 Two more spans added 1904, of 56ft and 90ft span; see Section 10, 1877 for through platforms.
4 Eccleston Bridge divided the roof longitudinally into two separate lengths.
5 See 1885 entry for Midland side.
6 Two more spans added 1881, 78ft×680ft and 110ft×500ft.
7 Also a transverse ridge-and-furrow roof on each side.
8 Second 191ft span added in 1879 by F. Stevenson and E. W. Ives.
9 Completion date; station opened 1840.
10 Two more spans added 1895.
11 Laminated timber ribs.
12 Including two 50ft wide transepts. Fourth 109ft span added and original spans strengthened with ties, 1915–16.
13 Additional tied-arch span, 140ft wide and 300ft long, added 1904 by William Melville.
14 Tangential roof on tied-arch ribs springing from platforms.
15 Trussed pitched roofs added from 1879.
16 Total width, including intermediate supports.
17 Perth I roof left *in situ*.
18 Total width, supported by five rows of columns; maximum single span 67ft 6in.
19 Total width, supported by two rows of columns.
20 Extension of Glasgow Central I roof, Section 9, 1882.
21 Width of central span including 22ft unglazed portion; side spans varied in width.
22 Total width, supported by five rows of columns; maximum single span c 118ft.
   Excluding 1885 'North Station' roof which remained *in situ*.
23 On crescent trusses.
24 Unglazed over through Caledonian lines.
25 See Section 8, 1906, Glasgow Central II, for extensions in transverse roofing.
26 See Section 2, 1877 for terminal platforms.

References

Chapter 3 The Choice of Sites (pages 21–45)
1 *The Civil Engineer & Architect's Journal*, Vol 13, Oct 1850
2 Henry-Russell Hitchcock, *Early Victorian Architecture in Britain*, 1954
3 *The Engineer*, Vol 51, 29 Apr 1881
4 George Saintsbury on *Historic Towns*, in *Notable Railway Stations, XIV: Manchester Victoria*, by T. S. Matthews, *Railway Magazine*, Vol VIII, 1901
5 *Cassell's Old and New Edinburgh*, J. Grant, Vol 1, 1884

Chapter 4 Gateways (pages 46–57)
1 R. H. G. Thomas, *The Liverpool & Manchester Railway*, Ch 7; and R. S. Fitzgerald, *Liverpool Road Station, Manchester*, Ch IV
2 G. Royde Smith, *Old Euston*, Ch III
3 Anon, *Round London*, 1896, in Carroll L. V. Meeks, *The Railway Station: an Architectural History*, 1957
4 A. E. Richardson, *Railway Stations*, in *RIBA Journal*, 8 May 1939
5 *London & Brighton Railway: Specification of Works to be done in Erecting the Brighton Terminus*, D. Mocatta, Architect, RIBA library, nd
6 J. Dobson, *The Central Railway Station, Newcastle-upon-Tyne*, in the *Civil Engineer & Architect's Journal*, Vol 11, 1848
7 In L. Wilkes, *John Dobson, Architect and Landscape Gardener*, 1980
8 Vol 12, 1849

Chapter 5 Matters of Style (pages 58–72)
1 Illustrated in R. H. G. Thomas, *London's First Railway, the London & Greenwich*, 1972
2 Information from Dr W. Fawcett of York
3 Shown on the plan in G. Dow's *Great Central*, Vol 1, and borne out by *The Builder*, Vol 19, 9 Nov 1861
4 Information from Mr David White of Carmarthen, great-grandson of Francis Thompson's sister, Betsy White
5 Samuel Sidney, *Rides on Railways*, 1851
6 J. T. Lawrence, *Notable Railway Stations, No 22: Wellington Station, Leeds*, in *The Railway Magazine*, Vol XIII, Sep 1903

Chapter 6 Early Layouts (pages 73–86)
1 Report of a meeting of directors of Lancaster & Carlisle Railway, Caledonian Railway and Maryport & Carlisle Railway, in *Carlisle Patriot*, 2 Oct 1846
2 *The London & Birmingham Railway*, 1839
3 H. Lodge, *A Short History of the L&NWR at Rugby*, in *Rugby Advertiser*, 26 Dec 1908
4 Paul Waterhouse, *London Railway Stations*, in *RIBA Journal*, 1914

Chapter 7 Taking the Train (pages 87–101)
1 H. Wade, *Notable Railway Stations: No 28 Nottingham (Midland Railway)*, in *The Railway Magazine*, Vol XV, Oct 1904
2 *The Architectural History of Euston Station*, 1959

3 *The Builder*, Vol VII, May 1849
4 *Remarks on the Accident at the Euston Square Terminus, with Hints on the Structure of Brick Columns*, anon pamphlet, RIBA Library, 1848
5 *Herapath's Railway Journal*, 8 Dec 1849
6 J. L. Lawrence, *Notable Railway Stations, No 20: Preston*, in *The Railway Magazine*, Vol XII, 1903
7 G. P. Neele, *Railway Reminiscences*, 1904

Chapter 8 The Great Iron Halls (pages 102–133)
1 Vol 27, 26 Mar 1869
2 *The Builder*, Vol XIX, 23 Feb 1861
3 William Evill, *Description of the Iron Shed at the London Terminus of the Eastern Counties Railway* in *Proc Inst Civil Engineers*, Vol III, 1844, states that it 'proceeded to the present state as funds permitted'
4 Richard Turner, *Description of the Iron Roof over the Railway Station, Lime Street, Liverpool*, in *Proc Inst Civil Engineers*, Vol 9, 19 Feb 1850
5 Joseph Phillips, *Description of the Iron Roof, in one span, over the Joint Railway Station, New Street, Birmingham*, in *Proc Inst Civil Engineers*, Vol 14, 30 Jan 1855
6 Arthur T. Walmisley, *Iron Roofs*, 2nd edn, 1888
7 Vol 49
8 *Proc Inst Civil Engineers*, Vol 197, 1914
9 Walmisley, *op cit*
10 *The Builder*, Vol VIII, 2 Aug 1850
11 *The Engineer*, Vol 21, 9 & 16 Feb 1866
12 *The Engineer*, Vol 60, 16 Oct 1885; W. B. Stocks, *Pennine Journey*, 1958
13 *The Builder*, Vol 27, 18 Dec 1869
14 *The Engineer*, Vol 12, 18 Oct 1861
15 *The Engineer*, Vol 52, 7 Oct 1881, *et seq*
16 *The Engineer*, Vol 23, 14 Sep 1866
17 *The Engineer*, Vol 24, 30 Sep 1867
18 *The Engineer*, Vol 26, 4 Sep 1868

Chapter 9 The Grand Manner (pages 134–159)
1 For a full description see *Cannon Street Station & City Terminus Hotel*, ms thesis by D. K. Kennedy, RIBA Library, 1958
2 *Suggestions respectfully submitted by Richard Turner for the Improvement of Euston Station*, (not dated, but probably 1850–60), Inst Civil Engineers Tracts, Vol 166, ICE Library.
3 Vol 27, 26 Mar 1869
4 *The Builder*, Vol 41, 13 Aug 1881
5 Vol 52, 26 Aug 1881
6 *The Engineer*, Vol 52, 16 Sep 1881

Chapter 10 Curing Chaos (pages 160–177)
1 *The Engineer*, Vol 9, 24 Feb 1860
2 *Locomotive & Train Working in the latter part of the Nineteenth Century*, Vol 2, 1952, reprinted from the *Railway Magazine*, 1917
3 Vol 19, 7 Dec 1861

Chapter 11 Trains, Traffic and People (pages 178–195)
1 Detailed in Neele, *op cit*

Bibliography

General Architecture

Curl, James Stevens. *Victorian Architecture. Its Practical Aspects* (David & Charles, 1973)

Dixon, R. & Muthesius, S. *Victorian Architecture* (Thames & Hudson, 1978)

Hitchcock, Henry-Russell. *Early Victorian Architecture in Britain* (Yale University Press, 1954)

Jordan, Robert Furneaux. *Victorian Architecture* (Penguin, 1966)

Pevsner, Nikolaus, *The Buildings of England* series (Penguin)

Railway Architecture and Engineering

Anderson, R. and Fox, G. *Midland Railway Architecture* (Oxford Publishing, 1985)

Anderson, R. and Fox, G. *A Pictorial Record of LMS Architecture*, (Oxford Publishing, 1981)

Barman, Christian. *An Introduction to Railway Architecture*, (Art & Technics, 1950)

Booth, L. G. *Timber Work*, in Pugsley, Sir Alfred (ed). *The Works of Isambard Kingdom Brunel* (Cambridge, 1976)

Buchanan, A. and Cossons, N. *Industrial Archaeology of the Bristol Region* (David & Charles, 1969)

Vaughan, A. *A Pictorial History of Great Western Architecture* (Oxford Publishing, 1977)

Walmisley, Arthur T. *Iron Roofs, Examples of Design* (1888)

Railway Stations

Betjeman, John. *London's Historic Railway Stations* (Murray, 1972)

Biddle, Gordon. *Victorian Stations* (David & Charles, 1973)

Binney, Marcus. *Save Broad Street* (Save Britain's Heritage, 1982)

Cooper, B. K. *Rail Centres: Brighton* (Ian Allan, 1981)

Dethier, Jean. *All Stations* (Science Museum, 1978)

Fitzgerald, R. S. *Liverpool Road Station, Manchester* (Manchester University Press, 1980)

Gough, John. *Leicester (London Road) Station*, in Williams, D. (ed) *The Adaptation of Change* (Leicester Museums, 1980)

Grocott, F. W. *The Story of New Street* (British Railways, 1954)

Harrison, Derek. *Salute to Snow Hill* (Barbryn Press, 1978)

Hoole, K. *Rail Centres: York* (Ian Allan, 1983)

Hoole, K. *Railway Stations of the North East* (David & Charles, 1985)

Jackson, Alan A. *London's Termini* (David & Charles 1985) 2nd edn

Johnston, C. & Hume, J. R. *Glasgow Stations* (David & Charles, 1979)

Kennedy, D. K. *Cannon Street Station and the City Terminus Hotel* (unpub thesis, 1958, RIBA library)

Makepeace, Chris (ed). *Oldest in the World, the Story of Liverpool Road Station, Manchester* (Liverpool Road Station Society, 1980)

Marsden, Colin J. *This is Waterloo* (Ian Allan, 1981)

Meeks, Carroll L. V. *The Railway Station: an Architectural History*, (Architectural Press, 1957)

Simmons, Jack. *Rugby Junction* (Dugdale Society, 1969)

Simmons, Jack. *St Pancras Station* (Allen & Unwin, 1968)

Smith, D. J. *New Street Remembered* (Barbryn Press, 1984)

Smith, G. Royde. *Old Euston* (Country Life, 1938)

Smithson, Alison & Peter. *The Euston Arch* (Thames & Hudson, 1968)

Summerson, Sir John. *The Architectural History of Euston Station* (British Transport Commission, 1959)

Thorne, R. *Liverpool Street Station* (Academy Editions, 1978)

Thrower, W. Rayner. *Kings Cross Station in the Twenties* (Oakwood Press, 1978)

Brunel, Bristol & the GWR (Ian Allan, 1985)

Paddington, 1854–1979 (British Rail & Avon-Anglia, 1979)

The New Waterloo Station (*Railway Gazette* supplement, 1927)

Waterloo Station Centenary (British Railways, 1948)

Railway Hotels

Boniface, Priscilla. *Hotels & Restaurants, 1830 to the Present Day* (Royal Commission on Historical Monuments, 1981)

D'Ormesson, Jean, & others. *Grand Hotel* (Dent, 1984)

Douglas, J. & Powell, K. *Leeds – Three Architectural Walks* (Victorian Society, 1982) (information on Great Northern Hotel)

Monkhouse, Christopher. *Railway Hotels*, in Binney, M. & Pearce, D. (ed). *Railway Architecture* (Orbis, 1979)

Queens Hotel, Leeds, commemorative brochure (LMS Railway, 1937)

Railway History

Acworth, W. M. *The Railways of England* (John Murray, 1889)

Ahrons, E. L. *Locomotive & Train Working in the Latter Part of the Nineteenth Century* (W. Heffer, 1951–4), 6 vols (Reprinted from *The Railway Magazine*, 1915–25)

Andrews, C. B. *The Railway Age* (Country Life, 1937)

Barnes, E. G. *The Rise of the Midland Railway, 1844–1874* (Allen & Unwin, 1966)

Bonavia, Michael. *The Four Great Railways* (David & Charles, 1980)

Borley, H. V. *Chronology of London Railways* (Railway & Canal Historical Society, 1982)

Christiansen, Rex, & Miller, R. W. *History of the North Staffordshire Railway* (David & Charles, 1971)

Clarke, J. M. *The Brookwood Necropolis Railway* (Oakwood Press, 1983)

Clinker, C. R. & Firth, J. M. *Register of Closed Passenger Stations & Goods Depots in England, Scotland & Wales* (1971)

Course, Edwin. *London Railways* (Batsford, 1962)

Daniels, G. & Dench, L. *Passengers No More* (Ian Allan, 1980) 3rd edn

Donaghy, Thomas J. *Liverpool & Manchester Operations* (David & Charles, 1972)

Dow, George. *The First Railway Across the Border* (LNER, 1946)

Dow, George. *Great Central* (Ian Allan, 1959)

Greville, M. D. & Holt, G. O. *The Lancaster & Preston Junction Railway* (David & Charles, 1961)

Lambert, R. S. *The Railway King* (Allen & Unwin, 1934)

MacDermot, E. T. *History of the Great Western Railway* Vols 1 & 2 (GWR, 1927); also Nock, O. S. Vol 3 (Ian Allan, 1967)

Marshall, John. *The Lancashire & Yorkshire Railway* (David & Charles, 1969)

Neele, G. P. *Railway Reminiscences* (McCorquodale, 1904; reprinted E. P. Publishing, 1974)

Pollins, Harold. *Britain's Railways, an Industrial History* (David & Charles, 1971)

Reed, Brian. *Crewe to Carlisle* (Ian Allan, 1969)

Robbins, Michael. *London Railway Stations* in *The London Journal*, Vol 1, No 2 (1975)

Robbins, Michael. *The Railway Age* (Routledge & Kegan Paul, 1962)

Simmons, Jack. *The Railway in England & Wales, 1830–1914* Vol 1 (Leicester University Press, 1978)

Simmons, Jack. *The Railways of Britain* (Routledge & Kegan Paul, 1962)

Thomas, John. *The North British Railway* (David & Charles, 1969)

Thomas, R. H. G. *The Liverpool & Manchester Railway* (Batsford, 1980)

Thomas, R. H. G. *London's First Railway, The London & Greenwich* (Batsford, 1972)

Tomlinson, W. W. *The North Eastern Railway, its Rise and Development* (1914, 2nd edn revised by K. Hoole, David & Charles, 1967)

Turner, J. Howard. *The London, Brighton & South Coast Railway* (Batsford, 1977)

Vallance, H. A. *The Great North of Scotland Railway* (David & Charles, 1965)

Vallance, H. A. *The Highland Railway*, revised edn (David & Charles, 1963)

Williams, R. A. *The London & South Western Railway* (David & Charles, 1968)

Wrottesley, John. *The Great Northern Railway* (Batsford, 1979)

LMS Centenary of the Opening of the First Main Line (Railway Gazette supplement, 1938)

Various authors, *Regional History of the Railways of Great Britain* series (David & Charles) 14 vols.

Early Railway Guides
The Midland Counties Railway Companion (E. Allen, 1840)

North Midland Railway Guide (1842, republished by Turntable Enterprises, 1973)

Nottingham & Derby Railway Companion (1839, reprinted by Derbyshire Record Society, 1979)

Parry, E. *Railway Companion from Chester to Holyhead* (T. Catterall 2nd ed, 1849)

Roscoe, T. & Lecount, P. *The London & Birmingham Railway* (1839)

Geographical & Sociological
Briggs, Asa. *Victorian Cities* (Odhams, 1963)

Edmonds, T. F. *Location of Railway Passenger Stations in British Towns* (MA thesis, Hull University, 1975)

Kellet, J. R. *The Impact of Railways on Victorian Cities* (Routledge & Kegan Paul, 1969)

Robbins, Michael. *The Railway in the British Scene*, in *Points and Signals* (Allen & Unwin, 1967)

Simmons, Jack. *The Power of the Railway*, in Dyos, H. J. & Wolff, M. (ed) *The Victorian City* Vol I, III (Leicester University Press, 1973)

Turnock, David. *Railways in the British Isles; Landscape, Land Use and Society* (A. & C. Black, 1982)

Periodicals and Magazines
The Builder
Building News
Civil Engineer & Architects' Journal
The Engineer
The Illustrated London News
The Railway Magazine
Railway World
Proceedings of the Institution of Civil Engineers
Journal of the Railway & Canal Historical Society

Acknowledgements

A number of people have helped in gathering material for this book, and I must particularly thank Anthony Lambert who read the entire text and offered valuable editorial advice, and Professor Jack Simmons who found time to read and comment on Chapter 3. To them I am most grateful, as I am to Peter Fells for drawing the diagrams and for other assistance.

I also have to thank the following for help in answering queries and giving assistance: John Glover, Rex Christiansen, the late Geoffrey Holt, Harold Forster, Leslie Porritt, John Gough, Gregory Fox, John Watling, Bill Fawcett, J. Sowerby of Brian Colquhoun & Partners, D. I. Small of Blyth & Blyth, Stephen K. Jones and John Horsley Denton.

I wish to thank the librarians and staff of the following libraries for cheerfully dealing with what were often complicated enquiries and for providing facilities for research: University of Hull, John Rylands University of Manchester, University of Bristol, Newcastle-upon-Tyne, Edinburgh, Rugby, Cardiff, Preston, Derby, Perth, the National Railway Museum at York, the Royal Institute of British Architects, the Institution of Civil Engineers, the British Library Map Library and the Royal Commission on the Ancient & Historical Monuments of Scotland.

Nor must I forget the ready help given me by the chief and regional architects of British Rail and their staffs, in particular Paul Taylor, Chris Tagholm, John Ives, Reiner Volhard, Richard Horne, Michael Edwards and Findlay McCracken. The area and station managers at the following stations kindly afforded facilities for me to go 'behind the scenes': King's Cross, St Pancras, Liverpool Street, Paddington, Waterloo, Brighton, Newcastle, Glasgow Central, Bristol, Crewe, Derby, Manchester Victoria, Perth and Stoke-on-Trent.

I must also thank those who gave me permission to use their pictures, and Paul Simons, Roy Anderson, Alison Biddle, Russell Mulford, R. C. Riley and Gordon Buck for assistance with illustrations. Finally I must thank my publisher, David St John Thomas, for his patience. He has been waiting a long time for this book.

Index

Illustrations are shown in *italic* type.